STAR WARS

A NEW HOPE

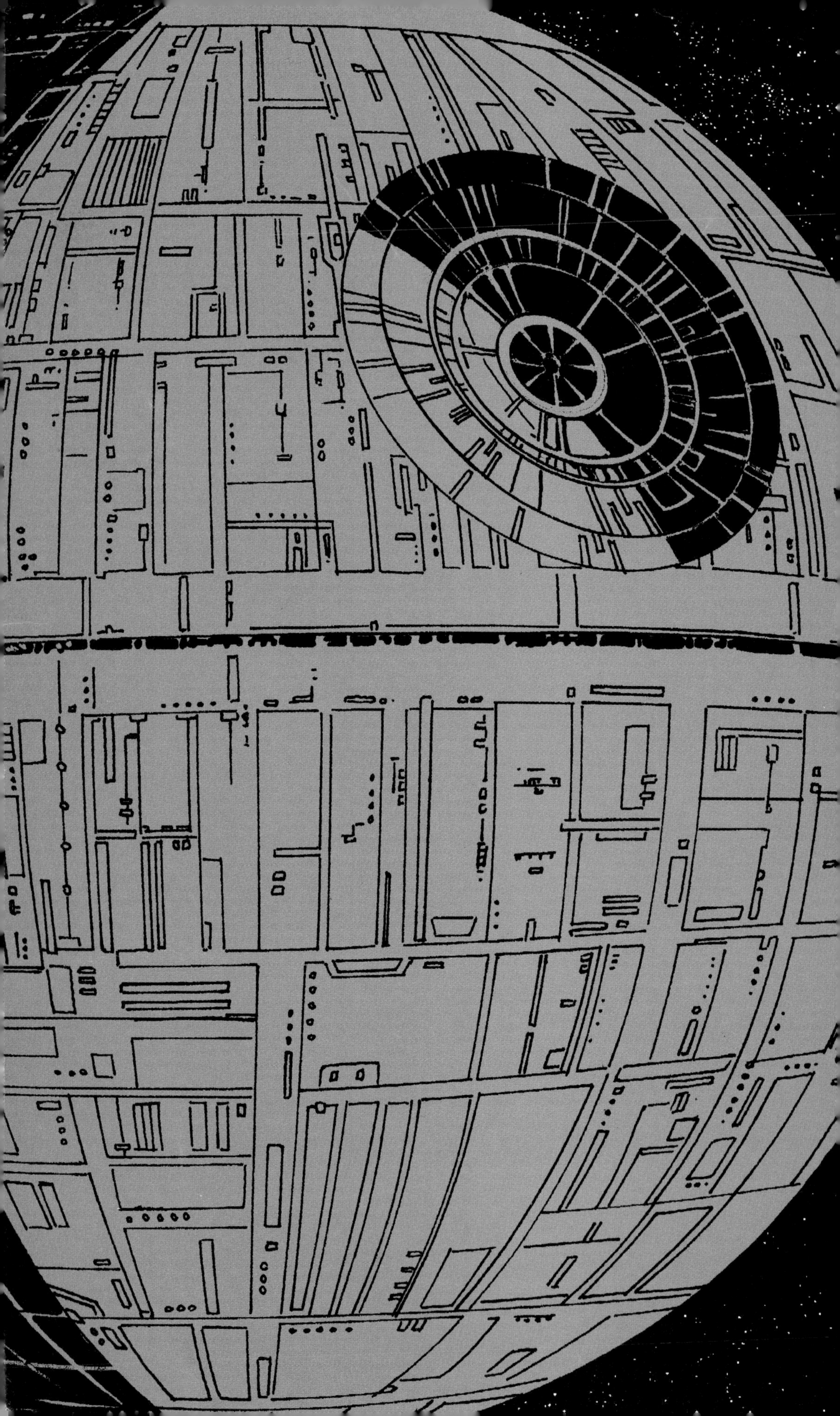

STAR WARS
A NEW HOPE

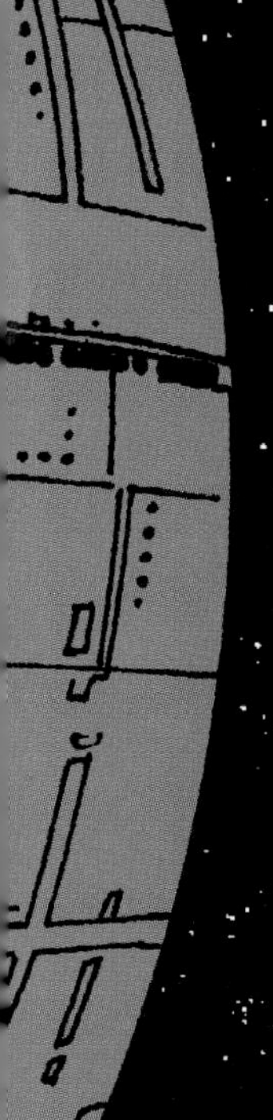

SCRIPT
BRUCE JONES

PENCILS
EDUARDO BARRETO

INKS
EDUARDO BARRETO
AL WILLIAMSON
CARLOS GARZÓN

COLORS
JAMES SINCLAIR
CARY PORTER

LETTERING
STEVE DUTRO

COVER ART
GREG & TIM HILDEBRANDT

BASED ON THE GEORGE LUCAS MOVIE, *STAR WARS*®

MIKE RICHARDSON

Series Editor
BOB COOPER

Series Assistant Editor
DAVID LAND

Collection Editor
LYNN ADAIR

Collection Design
SCOTT TICE

Collection Design Manager
BRIAN GOGOLIN

Special Thanks To
LUCY AUTREY WILSON AND ALLAN KAUSCH
At Lucasfilm

Dark Horse Comics, Inc.
Neil Hankerson executive vice president • David Scroggy vice president of publishing
Lou Bank vice president of sales & marketing • Andy Karabatsos vice president of finance
Mark Anderson general counsel • Meloney C. Chadwick director of editorial adm.
Randy Stradley creative director • Cindy Marks director of production & design
Mark Cox art director • Sean Tierney computer graphics director
Michael Martens director of sales • Tod Borleske director of licensing
Mark Ellington director of operations • Dale LaFountain director of m.i.s.

This book collects issues one through four of the Dark Horse comic-book series
Star Wars®: A New Hope Special Edition.

Published by
Dark Horse Comics, Inc.
10956 SE Main Street
Milwaukie, OR 97222

First edition: January 1997
ISBN: 1-56971-213-1

10 9 8 7 6 5 4 3

The story of Dark Horse Comics' adaptation of *A New Hope* The Special Edition actually begins nearly twenty years ago . . .

In late 1977, several months after *Star Wars* had already become a bona fide theatrical hit, comic-book artist Al Williamson was contacted by Lucasfilm to do some art samples for the already-in-production *Star Wars* newspaper strip. Thrilled that George Lucas had taken an interest in his work, Williamson contacted his good friend, writer Archie Goodwin, and asked him to help put together some sample strips. It didn't take any deliberation on Lucasfilm's part before offering the two production of the daily and Sunday *Star Wars* strip.

Unfortunately, Williamson had to decline since he was under contract to King Features drawing the "Secret Agent X-9" strip and really didn't feel like quitting. He decided to stick with something familiar and enjoyable rather than taking on something that would likely turn out to be as major a commitment as *Star Wars*. So, in the late 1970s, comics fans were introduced to *Star Wars* by Roy Thomas and Howard Chaykin's best-selling comics adaptation from Marvel Comics. This was followed by a very well-received monthly comic-book series, which included artwork by Chaykin, Carmine Infantino, Walt Simonson, Herb Trimpe, Tom Palmer, Mike Vosburg, and Michael Golden. Russ Manning's elegantly drawn *Star Wars* newspaper strip made its debut shortly thereafter.

Finally, in 1980, with the release of *The Empire Strikes Back*, events transpired to allow Williamson to draw the Marvel comics adaptation based on pal Archie Goodwin's script. Shortly thereafter, due to Russ Manning's failing health, Williamson and Goodwin took over work on the daily *Star Wars* newspaper strip in 1981, producing a memorable three-and-a-half-year run. When *Return of the Jedi* was released in 1983, there really wasn't any other choice than Goodwin and Williamson to do the comics adaptation.

By 1990, Dark Horse Comics had acquired the license to produce *Star Wars* comics. One of the first projects was reprinting, in color, the early '80s Goodwin/Williamson newspaper strips. At publisher Mike Richardson's request, Williamson took a hand reformatting the strips to fit the new comic-book format, and he contributed fourteen brand-new pieces of cover art for the twenty-issue series and three-volume collected set. Shortly thereafter, Dark Horse decided to reprint the Marvel *Star Wars* comics adaptations in a deluxe format with new interior coloring, and Williamson contributed new cover art for the *Empire Strikes Back* and *Return of the Jedi* volumes.

During summer 1995, Lucasfilm announced that in 1997 — in conjunction with the twentieth anniversary of the release of the original *Star Wars* movie — it would release expanded and updated versions of the three *Star Wars* movies. Dark Horse immediately made plans for a new comics adaptation of the first movie, incorporating the footage and new characters Lucasfilm was adding to the film. As editor of Dark Horse's *Star Wars* comics, I could think of no one other than Williamson — who had always lamented the fact that he'd missed the opportunity to draw *A New Hope* — to illustrate this new adaptation.

With a fair amount of lead time, I called Williamson and began a long process of talking him into doing the project. I knew going in that his decade-long working relationship with Marvel could preclude his involvement. The decision weighed heavily on Williamson for several months. After dozens of phone calls back and forth, he finally called in early January 1996 to decline, claiming that he'd already felt the same sort of anxiety start to build up in anticipation of doing this project as it had prior to working on the two-issue *Flash Gordon* project he'd drawn for Marvel in 1995. For this reason, rather than because of time conflicts or his existing Marvel relationship, he decided to forego working on the special edition of *A New Hope*. He just didn't feel like he'd be able to do the job as well as he would like to — and as well as the job deserved to be done.

In his heart, Williamson earnestly wanted to draw *Star Wars* again, yet he knew deep down that he wouldn't be able to do it. We tossed around the names of artists who might be up to the task. "Who worked on the *Aliens/Predator: The Deadliest of the Species* series a year or so ago?" "Eduardo Barreto, " I replied. "And, yeah, I think he'd do a great job!" So I called Barreto, who said he was finishing up work for a couple of other publishers and would love nothing more than to devote *all* of his time to drawing the new adaptation of *Star Wars* — a movie he absolutely loved!

To coincide with Lucasfilm's goal of releasing *A New Hope* The Special Edition in May 1997, Dark Horse was still planning a May 1997 release for the comics series. Barreto had started work on the series and was nearly finished with his pencils for the first of four issues when Lucasfilm announced that it was moving up the film's release date to February 1997. To keep the comics on schedule, I was going to have to hire an inker to work over Barreto's pencils, allowing the creative work to progress at a pace almost twice as fast as originally planned.

Enter Al Williamson, stage right. And this time it worked. Schedules dovetailed perfectly, and Al was absolutely committed to the opportunity to contribute inks over Barreto's pencils — to finally complete his personal cycle of work on the *Star Wars* trilogy. And when Lucasfilm moved up the release date yet again, to January, it became necessary to ask Williamson's longtime friend and collaborator Carlos Garzón to help with the inking for issues #3 and 4 of the series. It was becoming more and more like old-home week, as Garzón had worked with Williamson on the Marvel adaptations of *The Empire Strikes Back* and *Return of the Jedi*.

Hopefully, the readers will be just as happy as I am with the results: the classical artistry Al Williamson brings to the project, the sterling script adaptation by Bruce Jones, the gorgeously detailed pencilling wizardry of Eduardo Barreto, Dave Dorman's amazing set of interlocking covers for the comic-book series and Tim and Greg Hildebrandt's stunning cover for this volume, lettering by Steve Dutro — who's by far the most efficient, precise, and talented letterer with whom I've ever had the pleasure of working — and of course, the rich palettes of colorists James Sinclair and Cary Porter.

Enjoy!

Bob Cooper

A long time ago in a galaxy far, far away. . . .

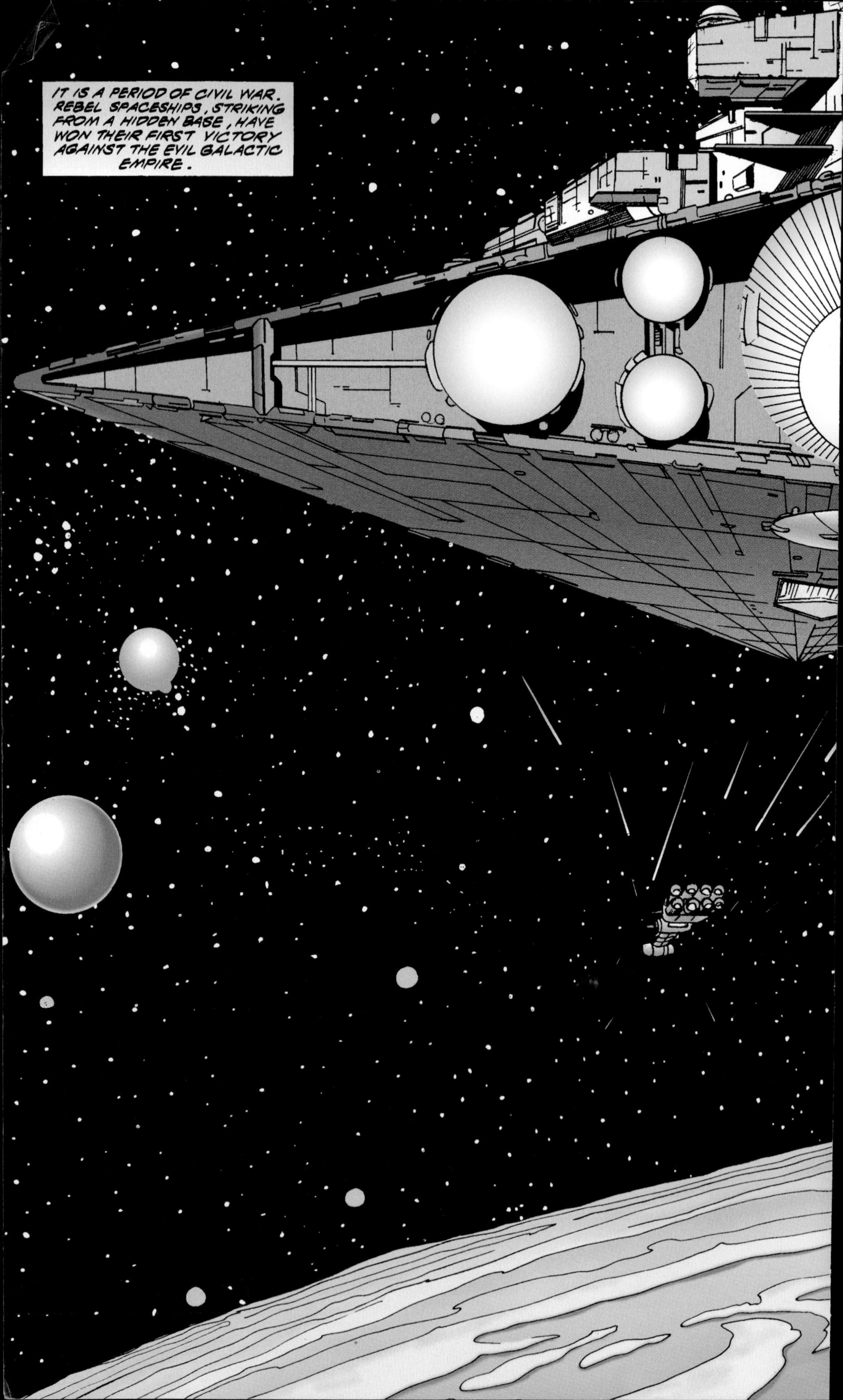
IT IS A PERIOD OF CIVIL WAR. REBEL SPACESHIPS, STRIKING FROM A HIDDEN BASE, HAVE WON THEIR FIRST VICTORY AGAINST THE EVIL GALACTIC EMPIRE.

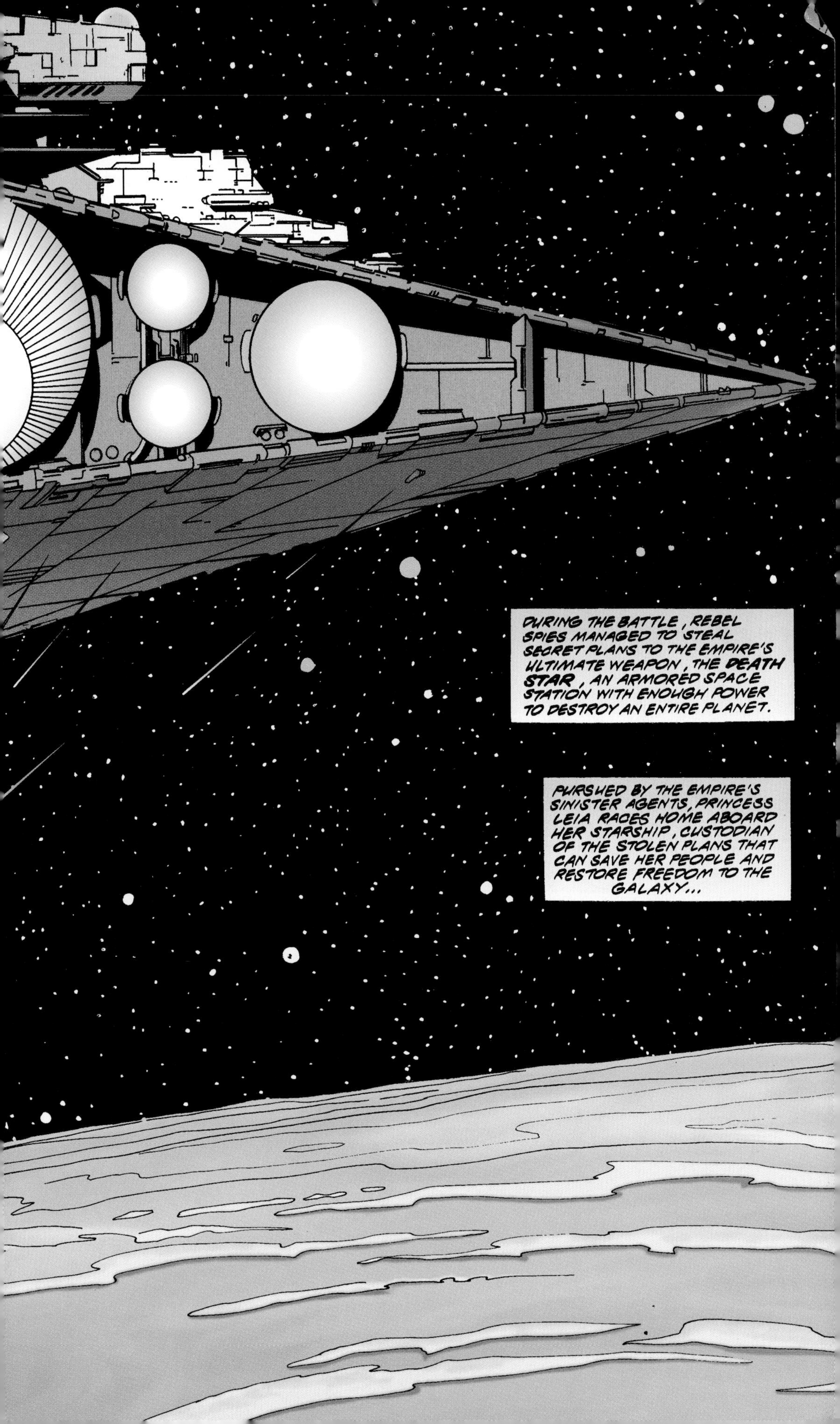
DURING THE BATTLE, REBEL SPIES MANAGED TO STEAL SECRET PLANS TO THE EMPIRE'S ULTIMATE WEAPON, THE DEATH STAR, AN ARMORED SPACE STATION WITH ENOUGH POWER TO DESTROY AN ENTIRE PLANET.
PURSUED BY THE EMPIRE'S SINISTER AGENTS, PRINCESS LEIA RACES HOME ABOARD HER STARSHIP, CUSTODIAN OF THE STOLEN PLANS THAT CAN SAVE HER PEOPLE AND RESTORE FREEDOM TO THE GALAXY...

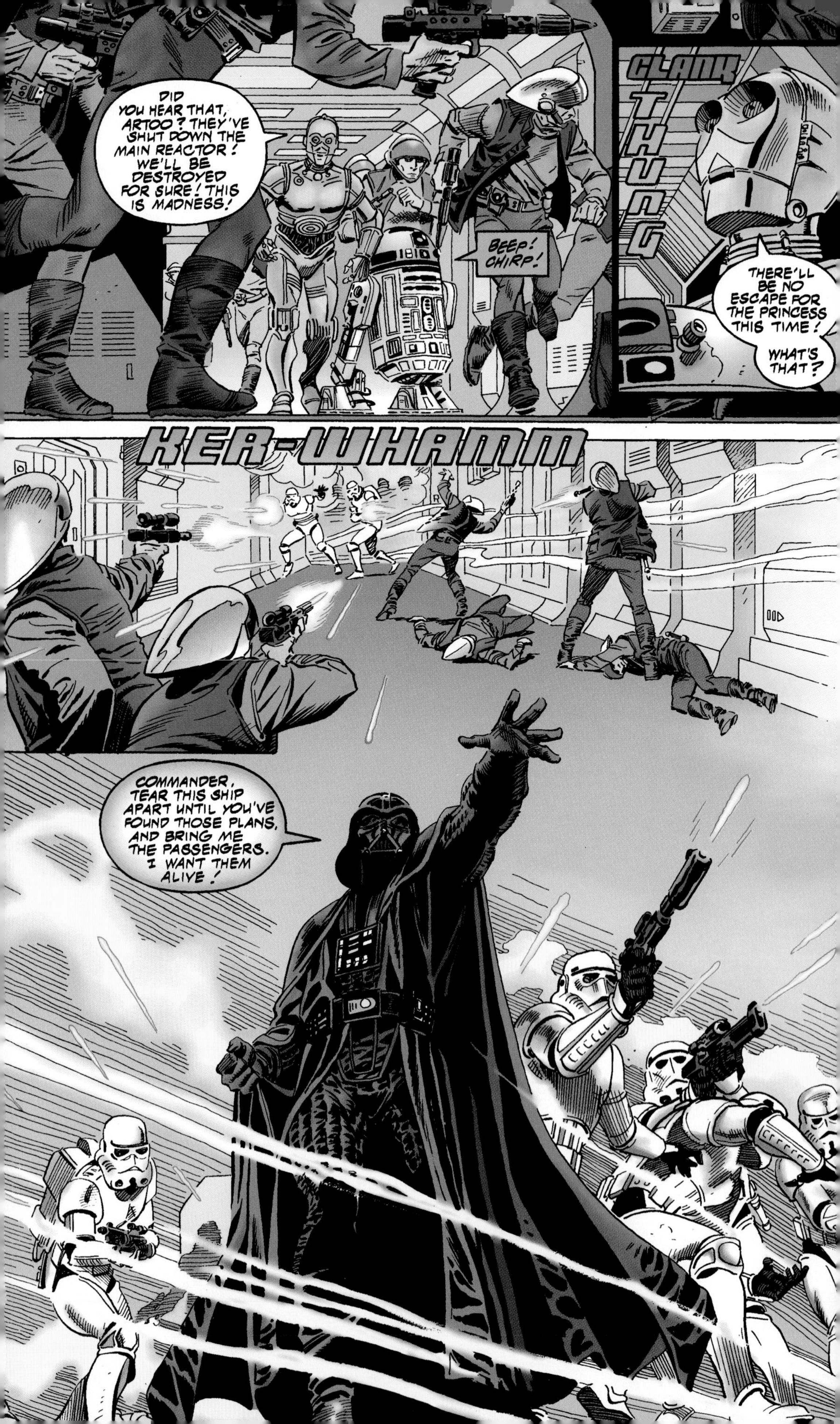
DID YOU HEAR THAT, ARTOO? THEY'VE SHUT DOWN THE MAIN REACTOR! WE'LL BE DESTROYED FOR SURE! THIS IS MADNESS!
BEEP! CHIRP!
CLANK
THUNG
THERE'LL BE NO ESCAPE FOR THE PRINCESS THIS TIME!
WHAT'S THAT?
KER-WHAMM
COMMANDER, TEAR THIS SHIP APART UNTIL YOU'VE FOUND THOSE PLANS, AND BRING ME THE PASSENGERS. I WANT THEM ALIVE!

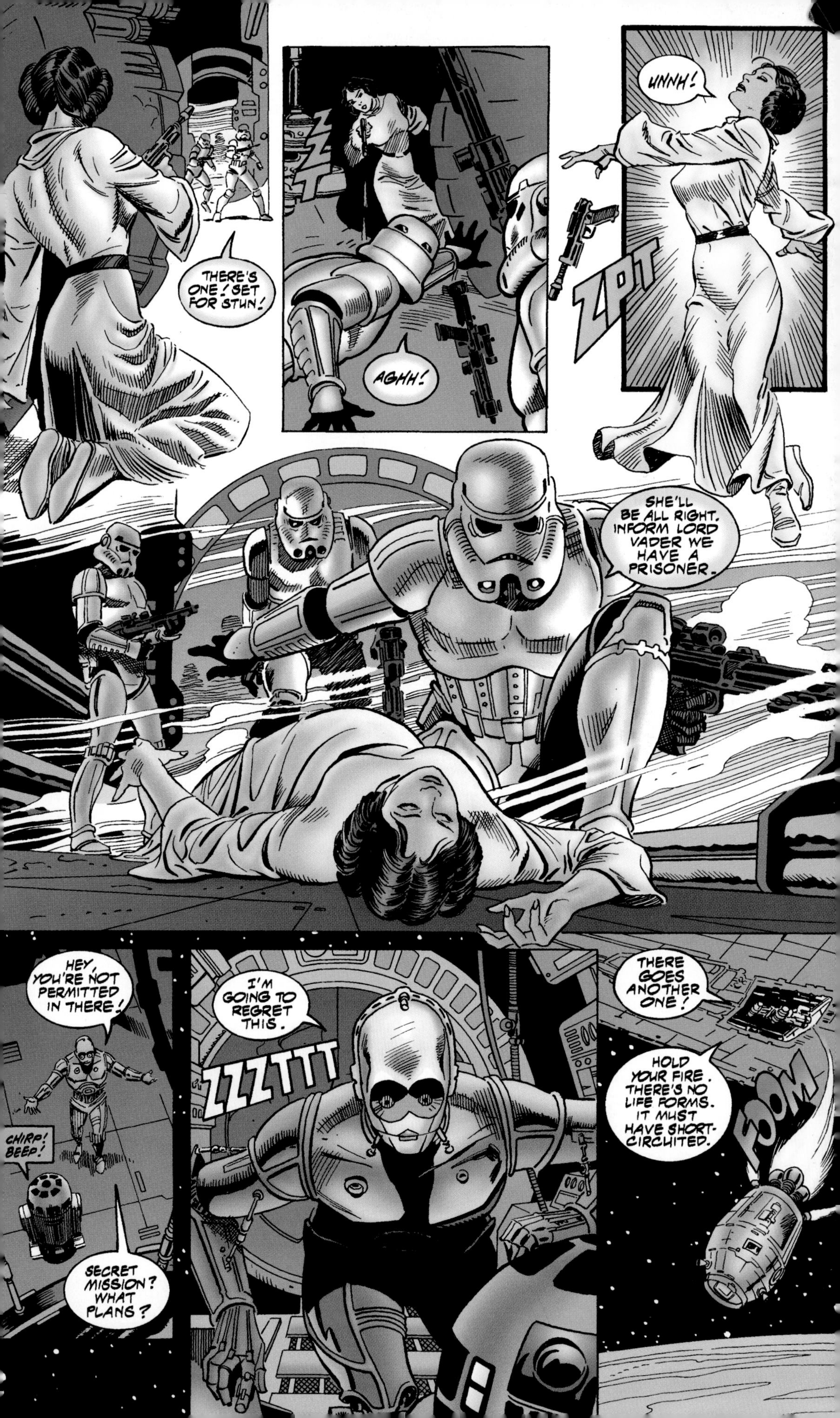
THERE'S ONE! SET FOR STUN!
ZZZ
AGHH!
UNNH!
ZPT
SHE'LL BE ALL RIGHT. INFORM LORD VADER WE HAVE A PRISONER.
HEY, YOU'RE NOT PERMITTED IN THERE!
CHIRP! BEEP!
SECRET MISSION? WHAT PLANS?
I'M GOING TO REGRET THIS.
ZZZTTT
THERE GOES ANOTHER ONE!
HOLD YOUR FIRE. THERE'S NO LIFE FORMS. IT MUST HAVE SHORT-CIRCUITED.
FOOM

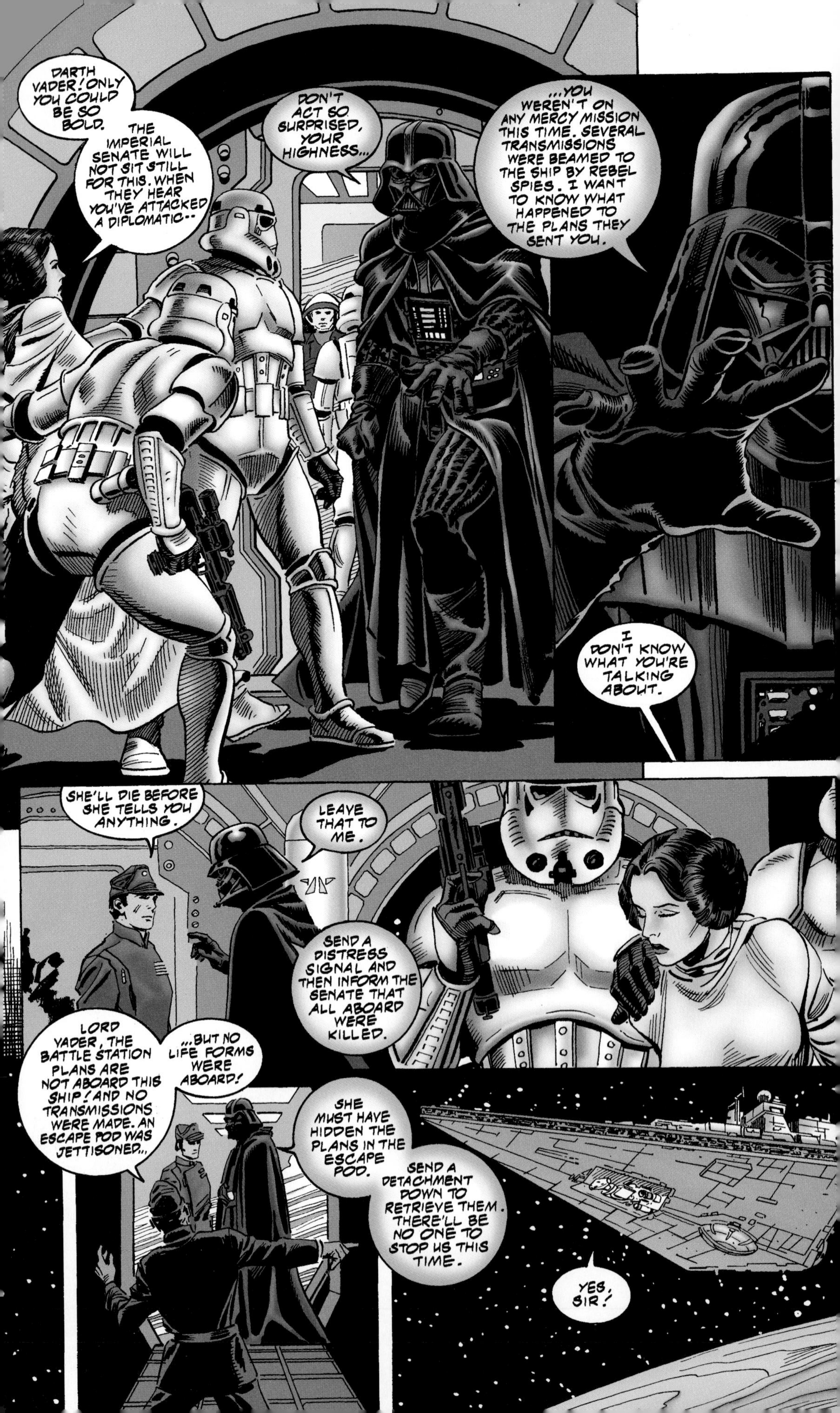
DARTH VADER! ONLY YOU COULD BE SO BOLD.
THE IMPERIAL SENATE WILL NOT SIT STILL FOR THIS. WHEN THEY HEAR YOU'VE ATTACKED A DIPLOMATIC--
DON'T ACT SO SURPRISED, YOUR HIGHNESS...
...YOU WEREN'T ON ANY MERCY MISSION THIS TIME. SEVERAL TRANSMISSIONS WERE BEAMED TO THE SHIP BY REBEL SPIES. I WANT TO KNOW WHAT HAPPENED TO THE PLANS THEY SENT YOU.
I DON'T KNOW WHAT YOU'RE TALKING ABOUT.
SHE'LL DIE BEFORE SHE TELLS YOU ANYTHING.
LEAVE THAT TO ME.
SEND A DISTRESS SIGNAL AND THEN INFORM THE SENATE THAT ALL ABOARD WERE KILLED.
LORD VADER, THE BATTLE STATION PLANS ARE NOT ABOARD THIS SHIP! AND NO TRANSMISSIONS WERE MADE. AN ESCAPE POD WAS JETTISONED...
...BUT NO LIFE FORMS WERE ABOARD!
SHE MUST HAVE HIDDEN THE PLANS IN THE ESCAPE POD.
SEND A DETACHMENT DOWN TO RETRIEVE THEM. THERE'LL BE NO ONE TO STOP US THIS TIME.
YES, SIR!

TATOOINE, IN THE JUNDLAND REGION, WHERE THE ENDLESS DESERT MEETS THE FOREBODING DUNE SEA...

WHAT A DESOLATE PLACE THIS IS! ARTOO, WHERE DO YOU THINK YOU'RE GOING?

BEEP! CHIRP! SKREEP!

WHAT MAKES YOU THINK THERE ARE SETTLEMENTS OVER THERE?

WHAT MISSION? WHAT ARE YOU TALKING ABOUT? I'VE JUST ABOUT HAD ENOUGH OF YOU! GO THAT WAY!

CHIRP! TWEEE!

YOU'LL BE MALFUNCTIONING WITHIN A DAY, YOU NEARSIGHTED SCRAP PILE!

AND DON'T LET ME CATCH YOU FOLLOWING ME BEGGING FOR HELP...

...BECAUSE YOU WON'T GET IT!

SOME TIME LATER...

THAT MALFUNCTIONING LITTLE TWERP! THIS IS ALL HIS FAULT!

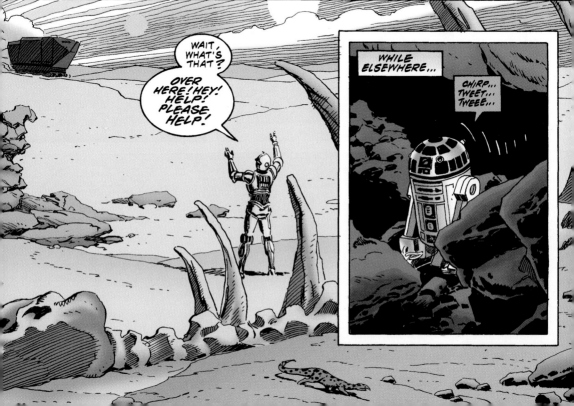

WAIT, WHAT'S THAT?

OVER HERE! HEY! HELP! PLEASE, HELP!

WHILE ELSEWHERE...

CHIRP... TWEET... TWEEE...

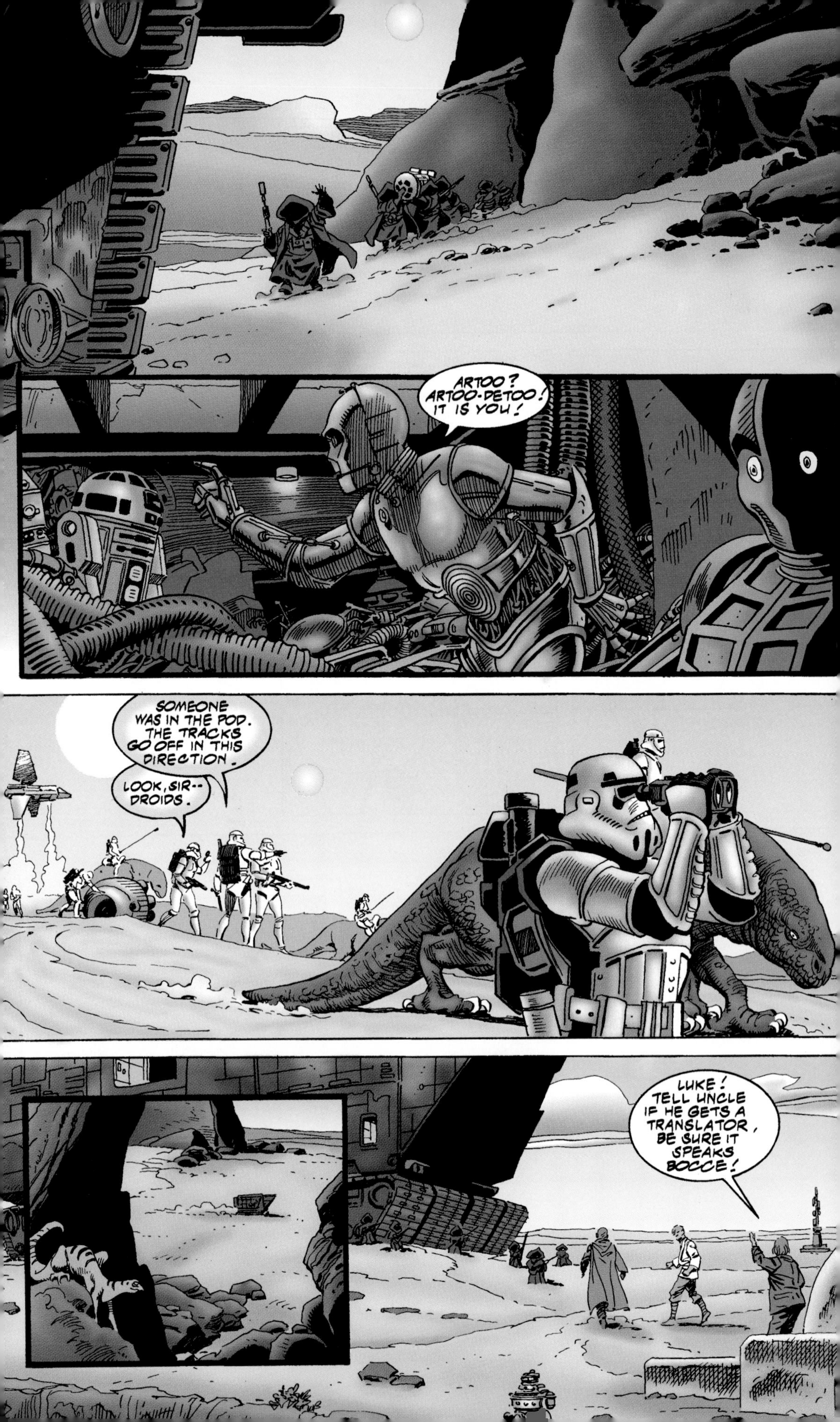
ARTOO? ARTOO-DETOO! IT IS YOU!
SOMEONE WAS IN THE POD. THE TRACKS GO OFF IN THIS DIRECTION.
LOOK, SIR-- DROIDS.
LUKE! TELL UNCLE IF HE GETS A TRANSLATOR, BE SURE IT SPEAKS BOCCE!

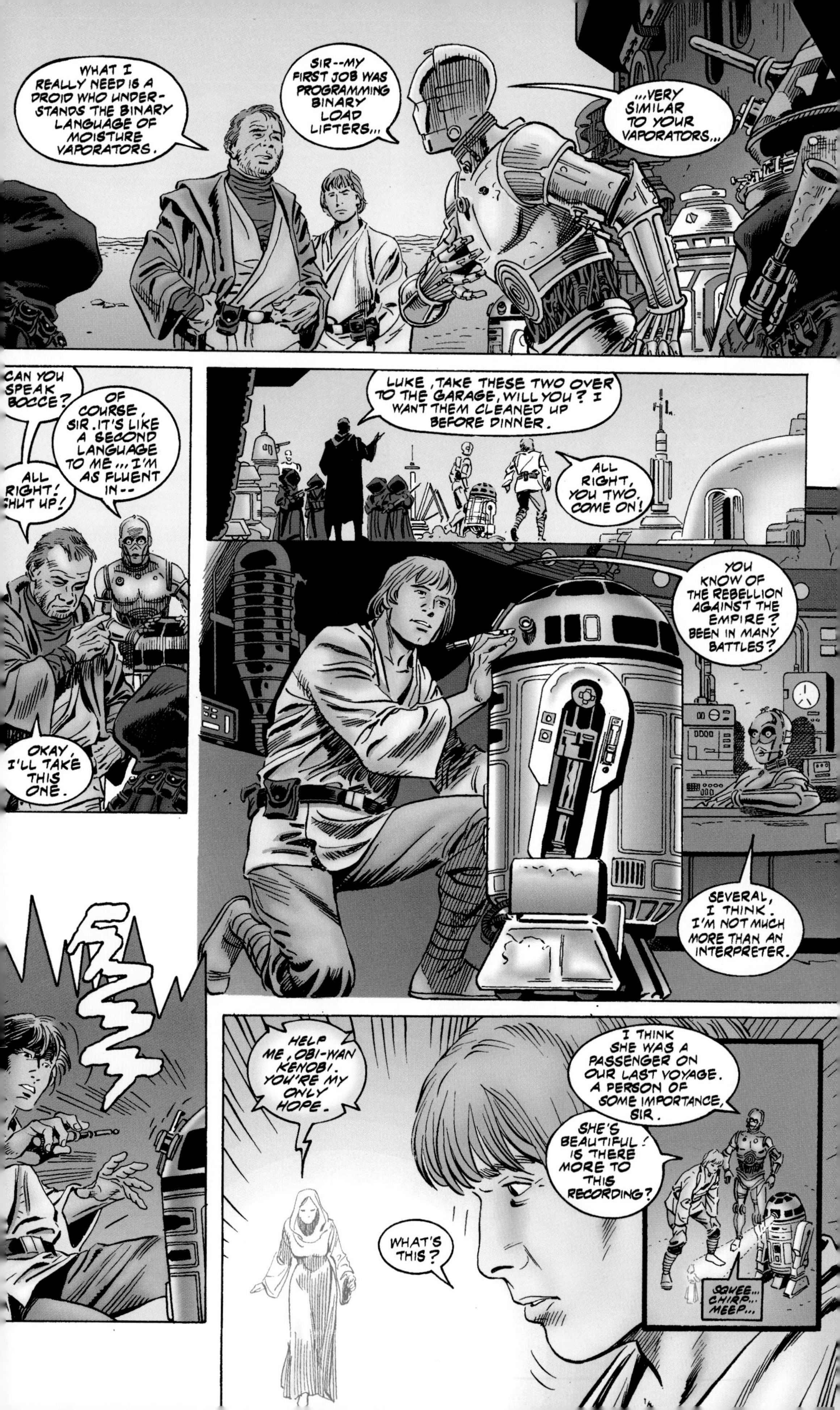
WHAT I REALLY NEED IS A DROID WHO UNDER-STANDS THE BINARY LANGUAGE OF MOISTURE VAPORATORS.
SIR--MY FIRST JOB WAS PROGRAMMING BINARY LOAD LIFTERS...
...VERY SIMILAR TO YOUR VAPORATORS...
CAN YOU SPEAK BOCCE?
OF COURSE, SIR. IT'S LIKE A SECOND LANGUAGE TO ME... I'M AS FLUENT IN--
ALL RIGHT! SHUT UP!
OKAY, I'LL TAKE THIS ONE.
LUKE, TAKE THESE TWO OVER TO THE GARAGE, WILL YOU? I WANT THEM CLEANED UP BEFORE DINNER.
ALL RIGHT, YOU TWO. COME ON!
YOU KNOW OF THE REBELLION AGAINST THE EMPIRE? BEEN IN MANY BATTLES?
SEVERAL, I THINK. I'M NOT MUCH MORE THAN AN INTERPRETER.
HELP ME, OBI-WAN KENOBI. YOU'RE MY ONLY HOPE.
WHAT'S THIS?
I THINK SHE WAS A PASSENGER ON OUR LAST VOYAGE. A PERSON OF SOME IMPORTANCE, SIR.
SHE'S BEAUTIFUL! IS THERE MORE TO THIS RECORDING?
SQUEE... CHIRP... MEEP...

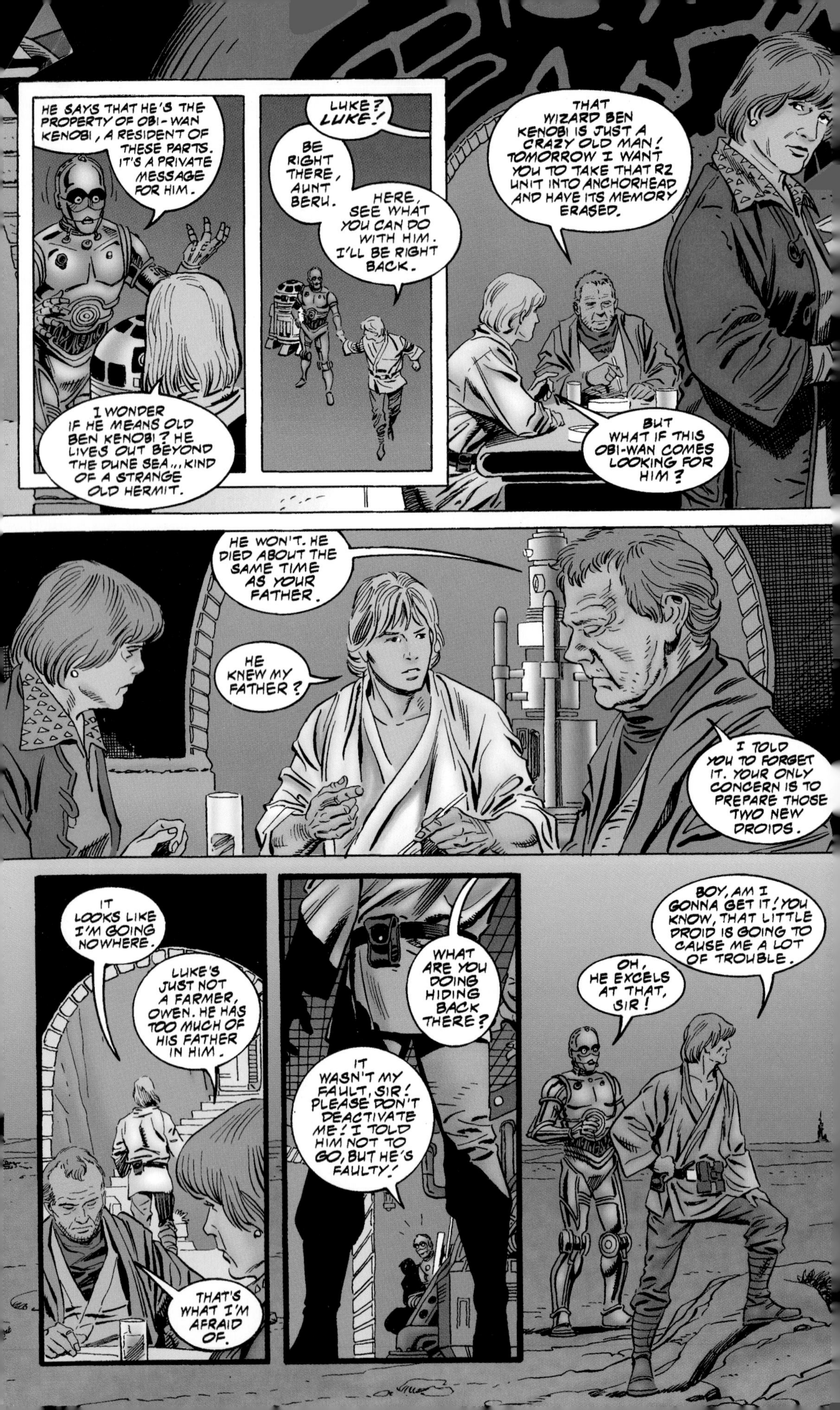
HE SAYS THAT HE'S THE PROPERTY OF OBI-WAN KENOBI, A RESIDENT OF THESE PARTS. IT'S A PRIVATE MESSAGE FOR HIM.
I WONDER IF HE MEANS OLD BEN KENOBI? HE LIVES OUT BEYOND THE DUNE SEA... KIND OF A STRANGE OLD HERMIT.
LUKE? LUKE!
BE RIGHT THERE, AUNT BERU.
HERE, SEE WHAT YOU CAN DO WITH HIM. I'LL BE RIGHT BACK.
THAT WIZARD BEN KENOBI IS JUST A CRAZY OLD MAN! TOMORROW I WANT YOU TO TAKE THAT R2 UNIT INTO ANCHORHEAD AND HAVE ITS MEMORY ERASED.
BUT WHAT IF THIS OBI-WAN COMES LOOKING FOR HIM?
HE WON'T. HE DIED ABOUT THE SAME TIME AS YOUR FATHER.
HE KNEW MY FATHER?
I TOLD YOU TO FORGET IT. YOUR ONLY CONCERN IS TO PREPARE THOSE TWO NEW DROIDS.
IT LOOKS LIKE I'M GOING NOWHERE.
LUKE'S JUST NOT A FARMER, OWEN. HE HAS TOO MUCH OF HIS FATHER IN HIM.
THAT'S WHAT I'M AFRAID OF.
WHAT ARE YOU DOING HIDING BACK THERE?
IT WASN'T MY FAULT, SIR! PLEASE DON'T DEACTIVATE ME! I TOLD HIM NOT TO GO, BUT HE'S FAULTY!
BOY, AM I GONNA GET IT! YOU KNOW, THAT LITTLE DROID IS GOING TO CAUSE ME A LOT OF TROUBLE.
OH, HE EXCELS AT THAT, SIR!

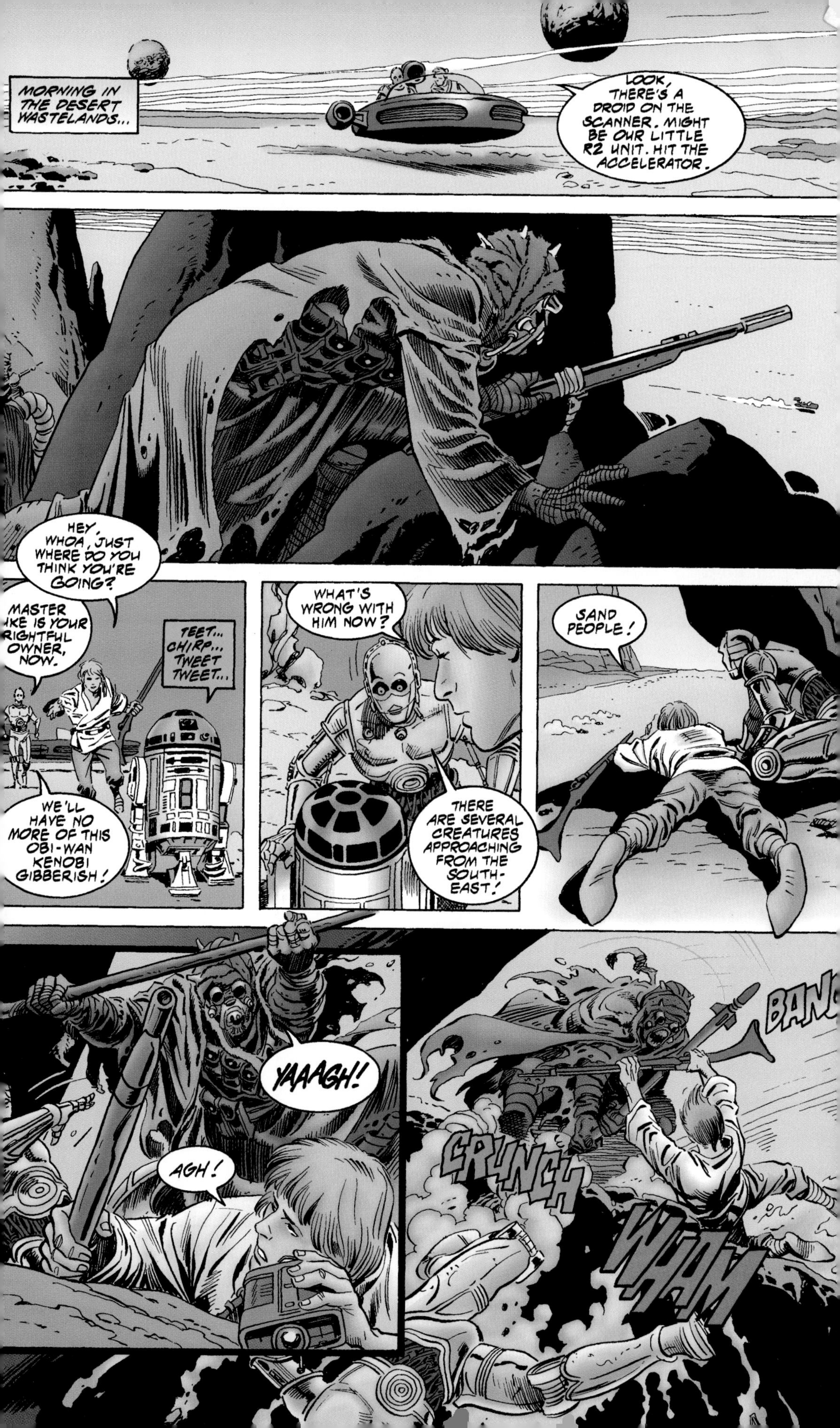
MORNING IN THE DESERT WASTELANDS...
LOOK, THERE'S A DROID ON THE SCANNER. MIGHT BE OUR LITTLE R2 UNIT. HIT THE ACCELERATOR.
HEY, WHOA, JUST WHERE DO YOU THINK YOU'RE GOING?
MASTER LUKE IS YOUR RIGHTFUL OWNER, NOW.
TEET... CHIRP... TWEET TWEET...
WE'LL HAVE NO MORE OF THIS OBI-WAN KENOBI GIBBERISH!
WHAT'S WRONG WITH HIM NOW?
THERE ARE SEVERAL CREATURES APPROACHING FROM THE SOUTH-EAST!
SAND PEOPLE!
YAAAGH!
AGH!
CRUNCH
WHAM

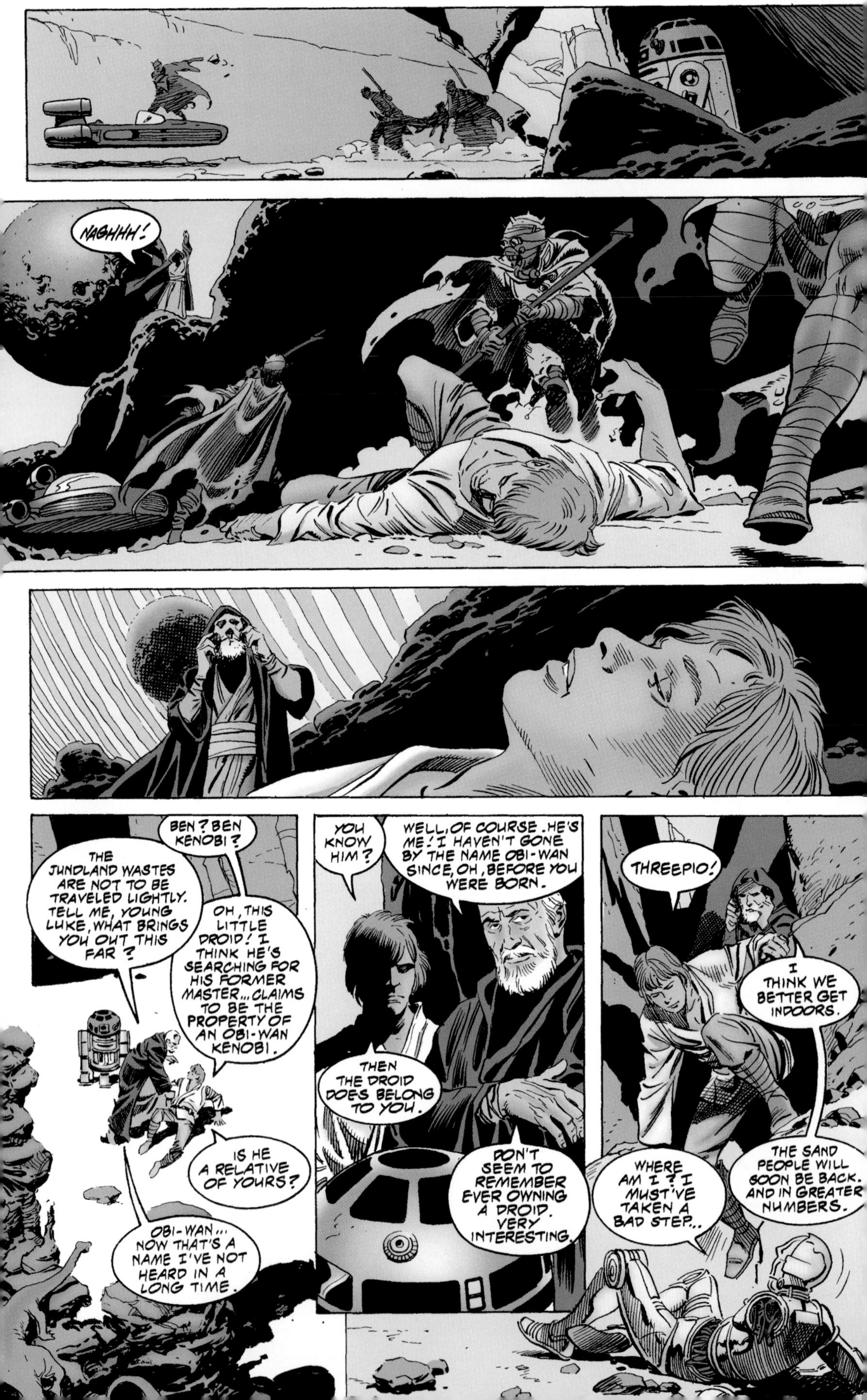
NAGHHH!
BEN? BEN KENOBI?
THE JUNDLAND WASTES ARE NOT TO BE TRAVELED LIGHTLY. TELL ME, YOUNG LUKE, WHAT BRINGS YOU OUT THIS FAR?
OH, THIS LITTLE DROID! I THINK HE'S SEARCHING FOR HIS FORMER MASTER... CLAIMS TO BE THE PROPERTY OF AN OBI-WAN KENOBI.
IS HE A RELATIVE OF YOURS?
OBI-WAN... NOW THAT'S A NAME I'VE NOT HEARD IN A LONG TIME.
YOU KNOW HIM?
WELL, OF COURSE. HE'S ME! I HAVEN'T GONE BY THE NAME OBI-WAN SINCE, OH, BEFORE YOU WERE BORN.
THEN THE DROID DOES BELONG TO YOU.
DON'T SEEM TO REMEMBER EVER OWNING A DROID. VERY INTERESTING.
THREEPIO!
I THINK WE BETTER GET INDOORS.
THE SAND PEOPLE WILL SOON BE BACK. AND IN GREATER NUMBERS.
WHERE AM I? I MUST'VE TAKEN A BAD STEP...

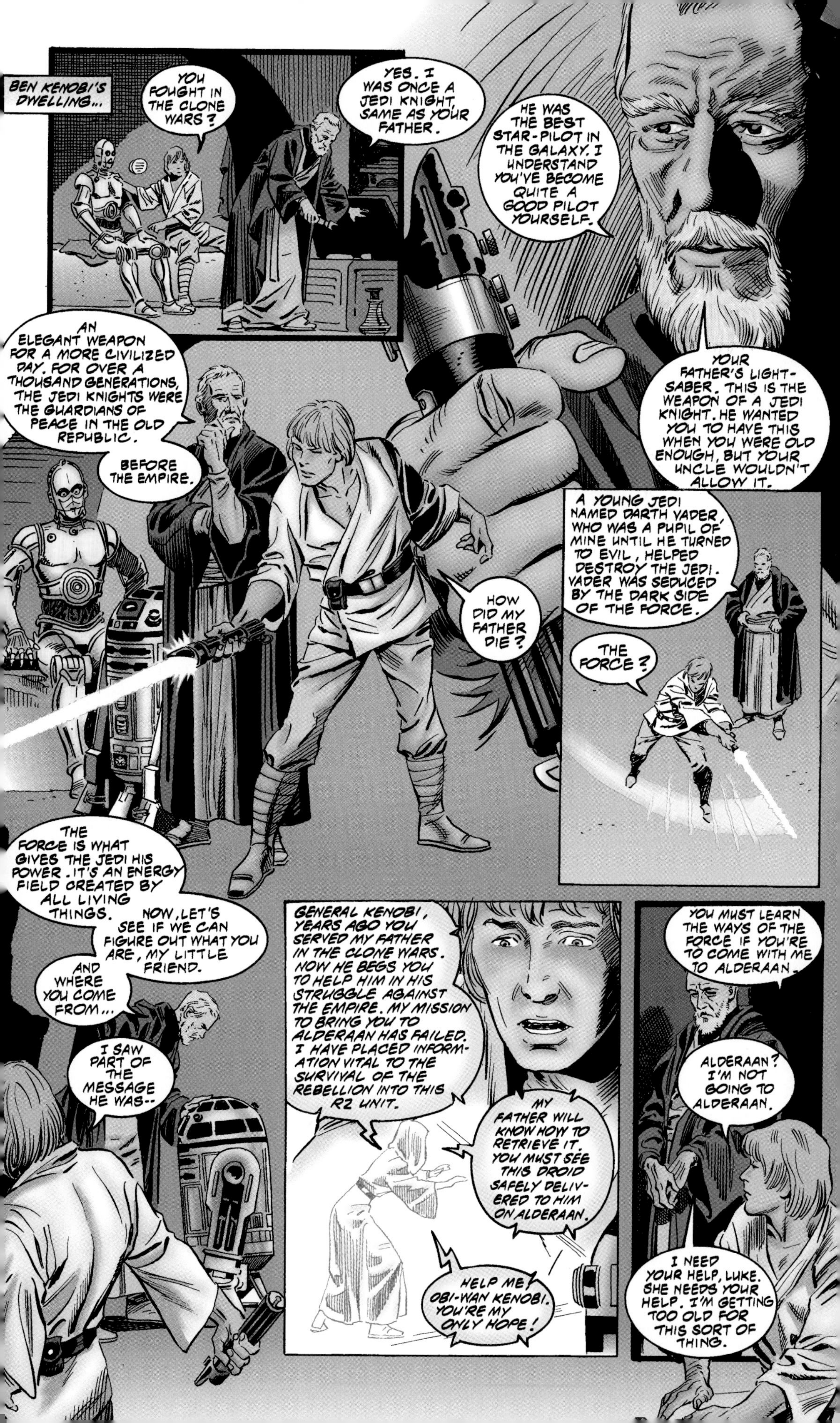
BEN KENOBI'S DWELLING...
YOU FOUGHT IN THE CLONE WARS?
YES. I WAS ONCE A JEDI KNIGHT, SAME AS YOUR FATHER.
HE WAS THE BEST STAR-PILOT IN THE GALAXY. I UNDERSTAND YOU'VE BECOME QUITE A GOOD PILOT YOURSELF.
YOUR FATHER'S LIGHT-SABER. THIS IS THE WEAPON OF A JEDI KNIGHT. HE WANTED YOU TO HAVE THIS WHEN YOU WERE OLD ENOUGH, BUT YOUR UNCLE WOULDN'T ALLOW IT.
AN ELEGANT WEAPON FOR A MORE CIVILIZED DAY. FOR OVER A THOUSAND GENERATIONS, THE JEDI KNIGHTS WERE THE GUARDIANS OF PEACE IN THE OLD REPUBLIC.
BEFORE THE EMPIRE.
HOW DID MY FATHER DIE?
A YOUNG JEDI NAMED DARTH VADER, WHO WAS A PUPIL OF MINE UNTIL HE TURNED TO EVIL, HELPED DESTROY THE JEDI. VADER WAS SEDUCED BY THE DARK SIDE OF THE FORCE.
THE FORCE?
THE FORCE IS WHAT GIVES THE JEDI HIS POWER. IT'S AN ENERGY FIELD CREATED BY ALL LIVING THINGS.
NOW, LET'S SEE IF WE CAN FIGURE OUT WHAT YOU ARE, MY LITTLE FRIEND.
AND WHERE YOU COME FROM...
I SAW PART OF THE MESSAGE HE WAS--
GENERAL KENOBI, YEARS AGO YOU SERVED MY FATHER IN THE CLONE WARS. NOW HE BEGS YOU TO HELP HIM IN HIS STRUGGLE AGAINST THE EMPIRE. MY MISSION TO BRING YOU TO ALDERAAN HAS FAILED. I HAVE PLACED INFORM-ATION VITAL TO THE SURVIVAL OF THE REBELLION INTO THIS R2 UNIT.
MY FATHER WILL KNOW HOW TO RETRIEVE IT. YOU MUST SEE THIS DROID SAFELY DELIV-ERED TO HIM ON ALDERAAN.
HELP ME! OBI-WAN KENOBI. YOU'RE MY ONLY HOPE!
YOU MUST LEARN THE WAYS OF THE FORCE IF YOU'RE TO COME WITH ME TO ALDERAAN.
ALDERAAN? I'M NOT GOING TO ALDERAAN.
I NEED YOUR HELP, LUKE. SHE NEEDS YOUR HELP. I'M GETTING TOO OLD FOR THIS SORT OF THING.

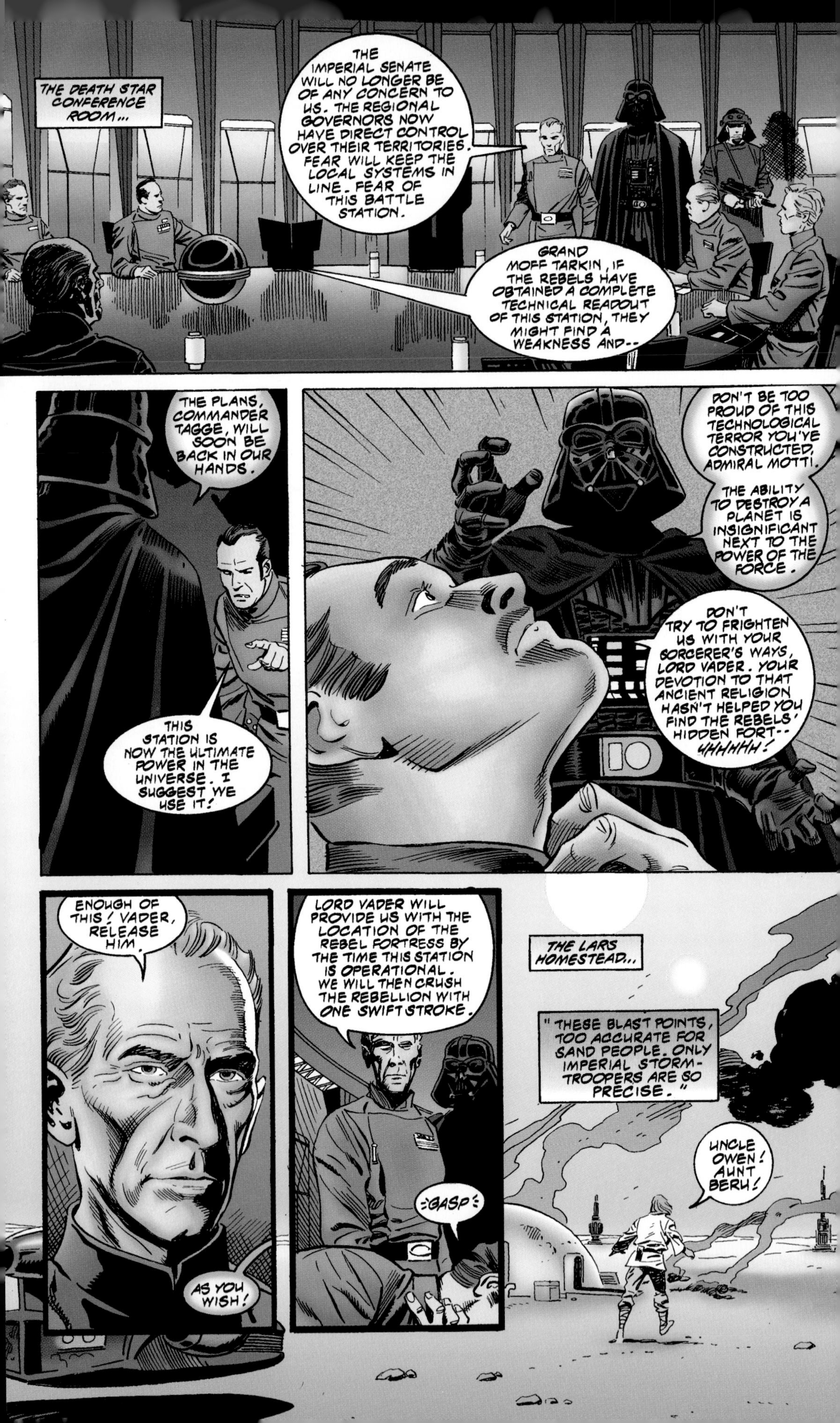
THE DEATH STAR CONFERENCE ROOM...
THE IMPERIAL SENATE WILL NO LONGER BE OF ANY CONCERN TO US. THE REGIONAL GOVERNORS NOW HAVE DIRECT CONTROL OVER THEIR TERRITORIES. FEAR WILL KEEP THE LOCAL SYSTEMS IN LINE. FEAR OF THIS BATTLE STATION.
GRAND MOFF TARKIN, IF THE REBELS HAVE OBTAINED A COMPLETE TECHNICAL READOUT OF THIS STATION, THEY MIGHT FIND A WEAKNESS AND--
THE PLANS, COMMANDER TAGGE, WILL SOON BE BACK IN OUR HANDS.
THIS STATION IS NOW THE ULTIMATE POWER IN THE UNIVERSE. I SUGGEST WE USE IT!
DON'T BE TOO PROUD OF THIS TECHNOLOGICAL TERROR YOU'VE CONSTRUCTED, ADMIRAL MOTTI.
THE ABILITY TO DESTROY A PLANET IS INSIGNIFICANT NEXT TO THE POWER OF THE FORCE.
DON'T TRY TO FRIGHTEN US WITH YOUR SORCERER'S WAYS, LORD VADER. YOUR DEVOTION TO THAT ANCIENT RELIGION HASN'T HELPED YOU FIND THE REBELS' HIDDEN FORT-- UHHHHH!
ENOUGH OF THIS! VADER, RELEASE HIM.
AS YOU WISH!
LORD VADER WILL PROVIDE US WITH THE LOCATION OF THE REBEL FORTRESS BY THE TIME THIS STATION IS OPERATIONAL. WE WILL THEN CRUSH THE REBELLION WITH ONE SWIFT STROKE.
:GASP:
THE LARS HOMESTEAD...
"THESE BLAST POINTS, TOO ACCURATE FOR SAND PEOPLE. ONLY IMPERIAL STORM-TROOPERS ARE SO PRECISE."
UNCLE OWEN! AUNT BERU!

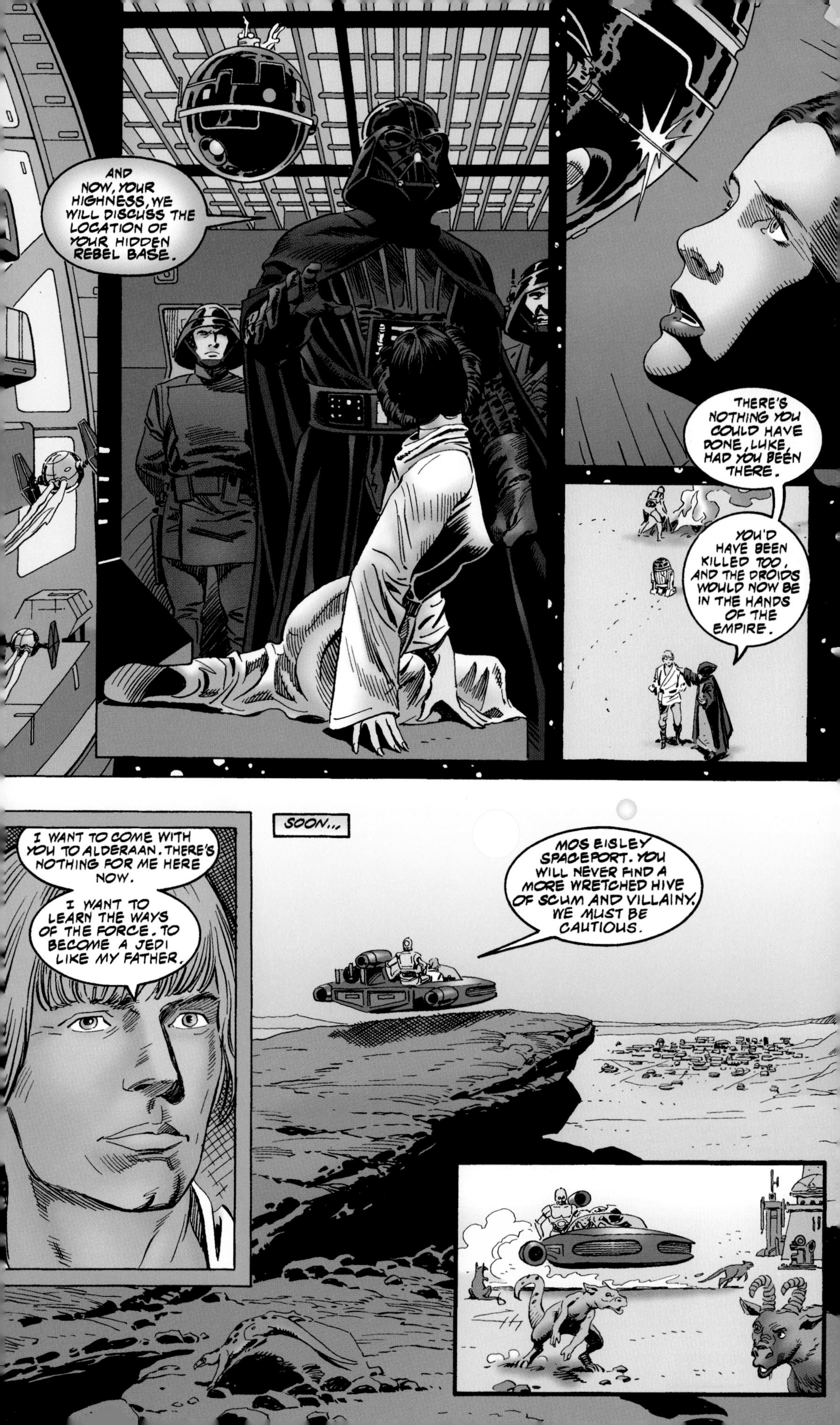
AND NOW, YOUR HIGHNESS, WE WILL DISCUSS THE LOCATION OF YOUR HIDDEN REBEL BASE.
THERE'S NOTHING YOU COULD HAVE DONE, LUKE, HAD YOU BEEN THERE.
YOU'D HAVE BEEN KILLED TOO, AND THE DROIDS WOULD NOW BE IN THE HANDS OF THE EMPIRE.
I WANT TO COME WITH YOU TO ALDERAAN. THERE'S NOTHING FOR ME HERE NOW.
I WANT TO LEARN THE WAYS OF THE FORCE. TO BECOME A JEDI LIKE MY FATHER.
SOON...
MOS EISLEY SPACEPORT. YOU WILL NEVER FIND A MORE WRETCHED HIVE OF SCUM AND VILLAINY. WE MUST BE CAUTIOUS.

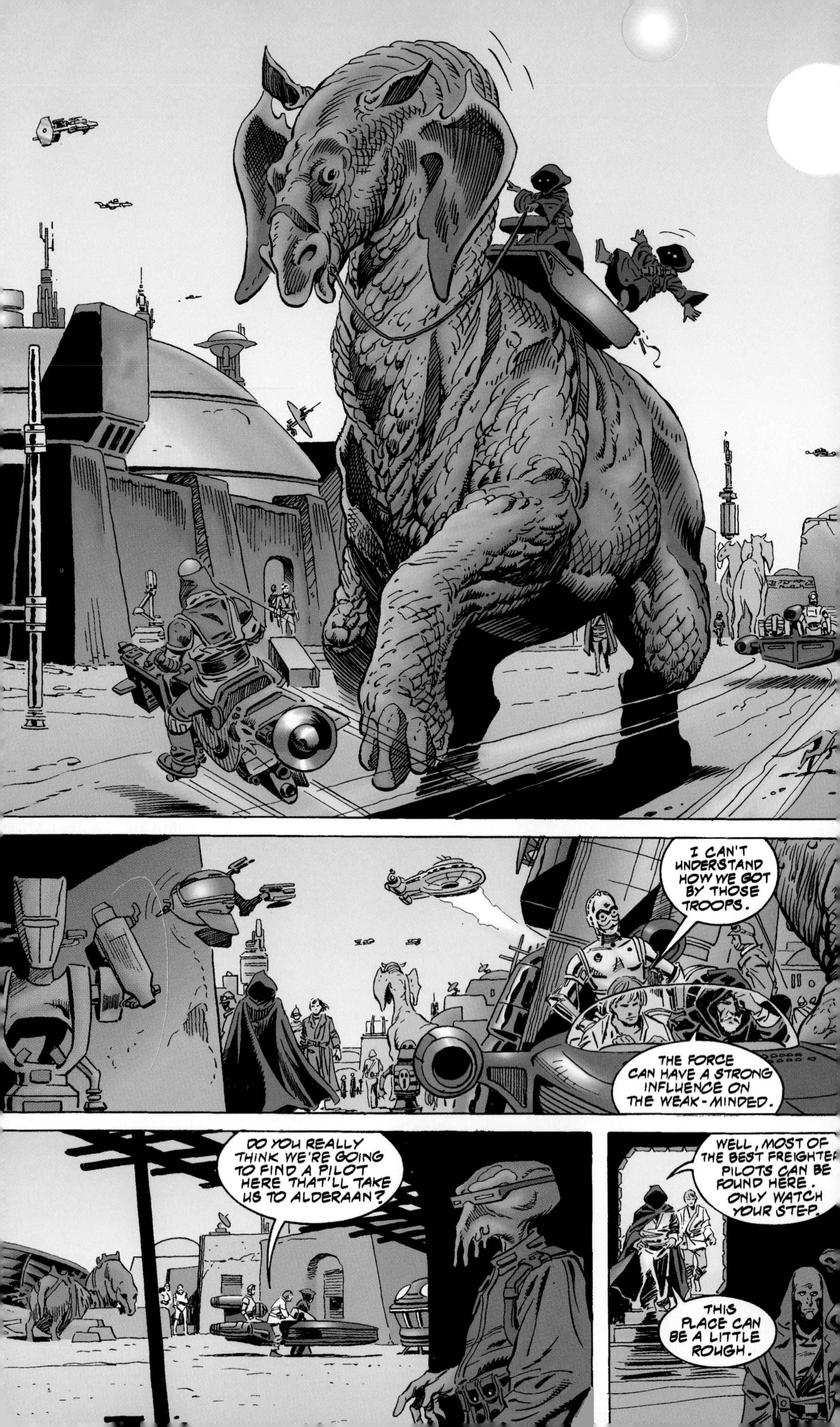
I CAN'T UNDERSTAND HOW WE GOT BY THOSE TROOPS.
THE FORCE CAN HAVE A STRONG INFLUENCE ON THE WEAK-MINDED.
DO YOU REALLY THINK WE'RE GOING TO FIND A PILOT HERE THAT'LL TAKE US TO ALDERAAN?
WELL, MOST OF THE BEST FREIGHTER PILOTS CAN BE FOUND HERE. ONLY WATCH YOUR STEP.
THIS PLACE CAN BE A LITTLE ROUGH.

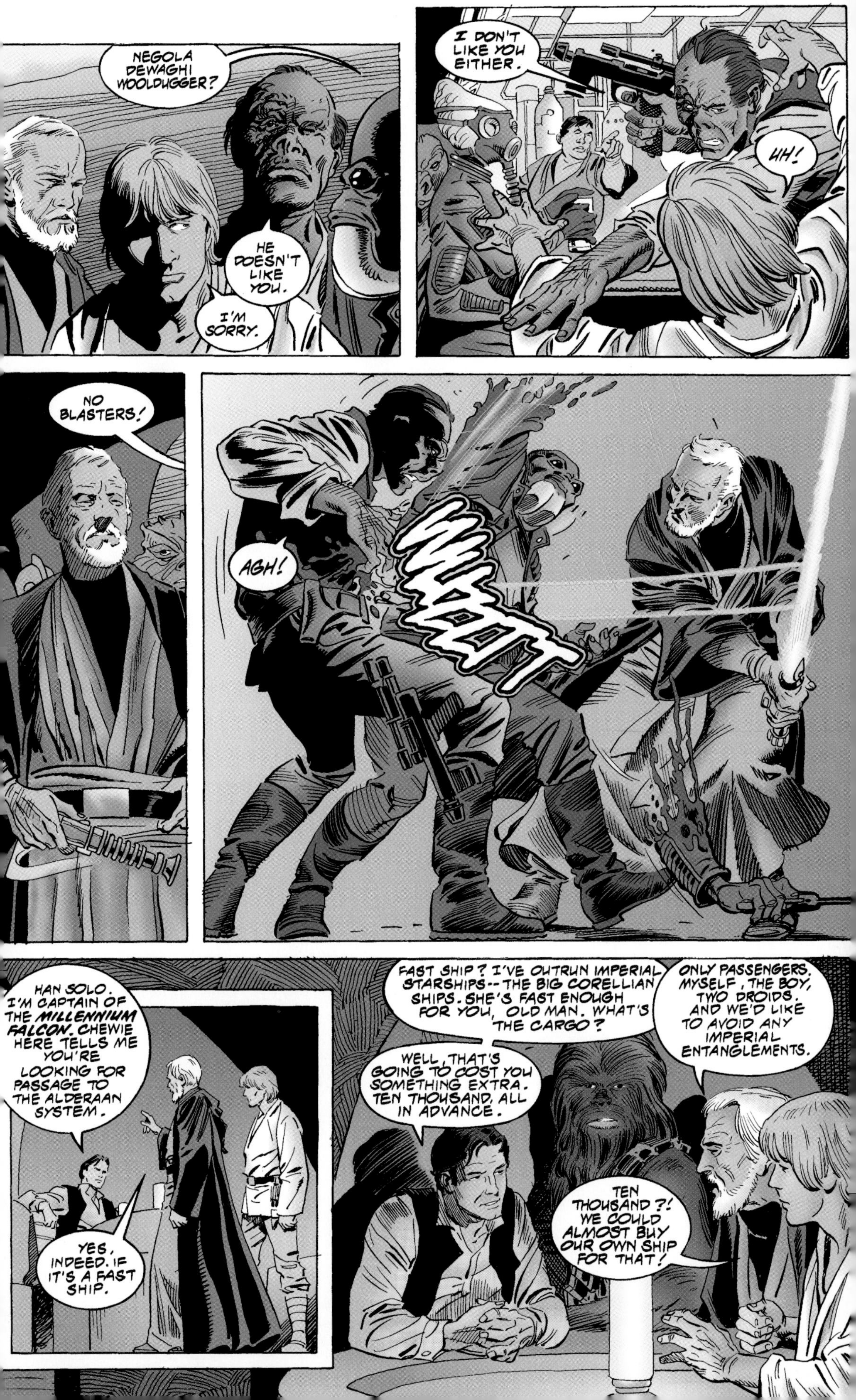
NEGOLA DEWAGHI WOOLDUGGER?
HE DOESN'T LIKE YOU.
I'M SORRY.
I DON'T LIKE YOU EITHER.
UH!
NO BLASTERS!
AGH!
HAN SOLO. I'M CAPTAIN OF THE MILLENNIUM FALCON. CHEWIE HERE TELLS ME YOU'RE LOOKING FOR PASSAGE TO THE ALDERAAN SYSTEM.
YES, INDEED. IF IT'S A FAST SHIP.
FAST SHIP? I'VE OUTRUN IMPERIAL STARSHIPS-- THE BIG CORELLIAN SHIPS. SHE'S FAST ENOUGH FOR YOU, OLD MAN. WHAT'S THE CARGO?
ONLY PASSENGERS. MYSELF, THE BOY, TWO DROIDS. AND WE'D LIKE TO AVOID ANY IMPERIAL ENTANGLEMENTS.
WELL, THAT'S GOING TO COST YOU SOMETHING EXTRA. TEN THOUSAND, ALL IN ADVANCE.
TEN THOUSAND?! WE COULD ALMOST BUY OUR OWN SHIP FOR THAT!

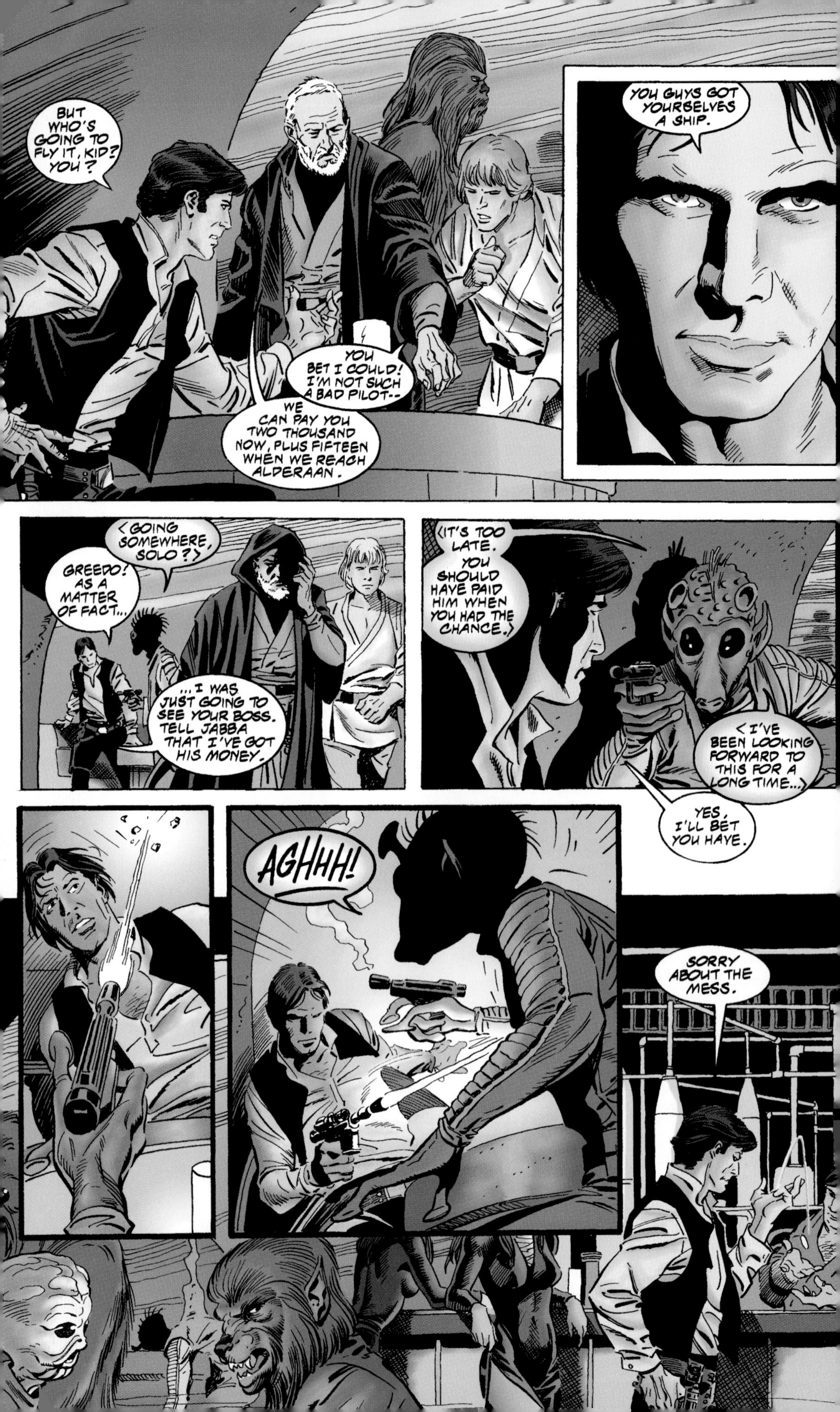
BUT WHO'S GOING TO FLY IT, KID? YOU?
YOU BET I COULD! I'M NOT SUCH A BAD PILOT--
WE CAN PAY YOU TWO THOUSAND NOW, PLUS FIFTEEN WHEN WE REACH ALDERAAN.
YOU GUYS GOT YOURSELVES A SHIP.
<GOING SOMEWHERE, SOLO?>
GREEDO! AS A MATTER OF FACT...
...I WAS JUST GOING TO SEE YOUR BOSS. TELL JABBA THAT I'VE GOT HIS MONEY.
<IT'S TOO LATE. YOU SHOULD HAVE PAID HIM WHEN YOU HAD THE CHANCE.>
<I'VE BEEN LOOKING FORWARD TO THIS FOR A LONG TIME...>
YES, I'LL BET YOU HAVE.
AGHHH!
SORRY ABOUT THE MESS.

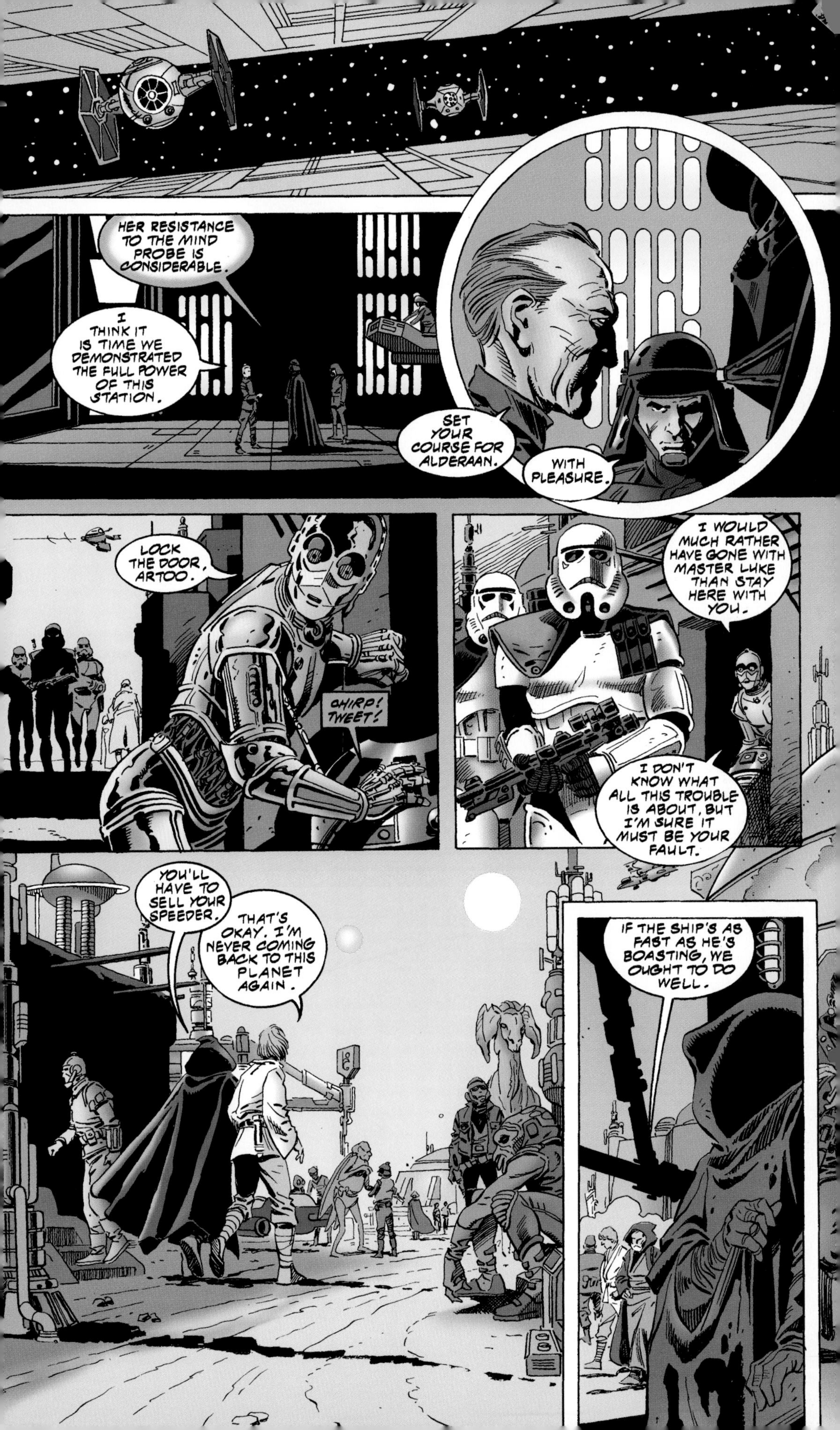

HER RESISTANCE TO THE MIND PROBE IS CONSIDERABLE.
I THINK IT IS TIME WE DEMONSTRATED THE FULL POWER OF THIS STATION.
SET YOUR COURSE FOR ALDERAAN.
WITH PLEASURE.
LOCK THE DOOR, ARTOO.
CHIRP! TWEET!
I WOULD MUCH RATHER HAVE GONE WITH MASTER LUKE THAN STAY HERE WITH YOU.
I DON'T KNOW WHAT ALL THIS TROUBLE IS ABOUT, BUT I'M SURE IT MUST BE YOUR FAULT.
YOU'LL HAVE TO SELL YOUR SPEEDER.
THAT'S OKAY. I'M NEVER COMING BACK TO THIS PLANET AGAIN.
IF THE SHIP'S AS FAST AS HE'S BOASTING, WE OUGHT TO DO WELL.

‹SOLO! COME OUT OF THERE, SOLO!›

RIGHT HERE, JABBA. I'VE BEEN WAITING FOR YOU.

‹HAVE YOU, NOW?›

YOU DIDN'T THINK I WAS GONNA RUN, DID YOU?

‹HAN, MY BOY, YOU DISAPPOINT ME. WHY HAVEN'T YOU PAID ME? WHY DID YOU FRY POOR GREEDO?›

LOOK, JABBA, NEXT TIME YOU WANT TO TALK TO ME, COME SEE ME YOURSELF. DON'T SEND ONE OF THESE TWERPS.

‹HAN, I CAN'T MAKE EXCEPTIONS. WHAT IF EVERYONE WHO SMUGGLED FOR ME DROPPED THEIR CARGO AT THE FIRST SIGN OF AN IMPERIAL STARSHIP? IT'S NOT GOOD FOR BUSINESS.›

LOOK, JABBA, EVEN I GET BOARDED SOMETIMES.

YOU THINK I HAD A CHOICE? I GOT A NICE EASY CHARTER NOW. PAY YOU BACK, PLUS A LITTLE EXTRA. I JUST NEED A LITTLE MORE TIME.

‹HAN, MY BOY, YOU'RE THE BEST. SO FOR AN EXTRA TWENTY PERCENT--›

FIFTEEN, JABBA. DON'T PUSH IT.

‹OKAY, FIFTEEN PERCENT. BUT IF YOU FAIL ME AGAIN, I'LL PUT A PRICE ON YOUR HEAD SO BIG YOU WON'T BE ABLE TO GO NEAR A CIVILIZED SYSTEM.›

JABBA, YOU'RE A WONDERFUL HUMAN BEING.

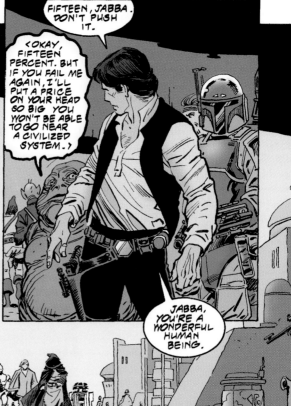

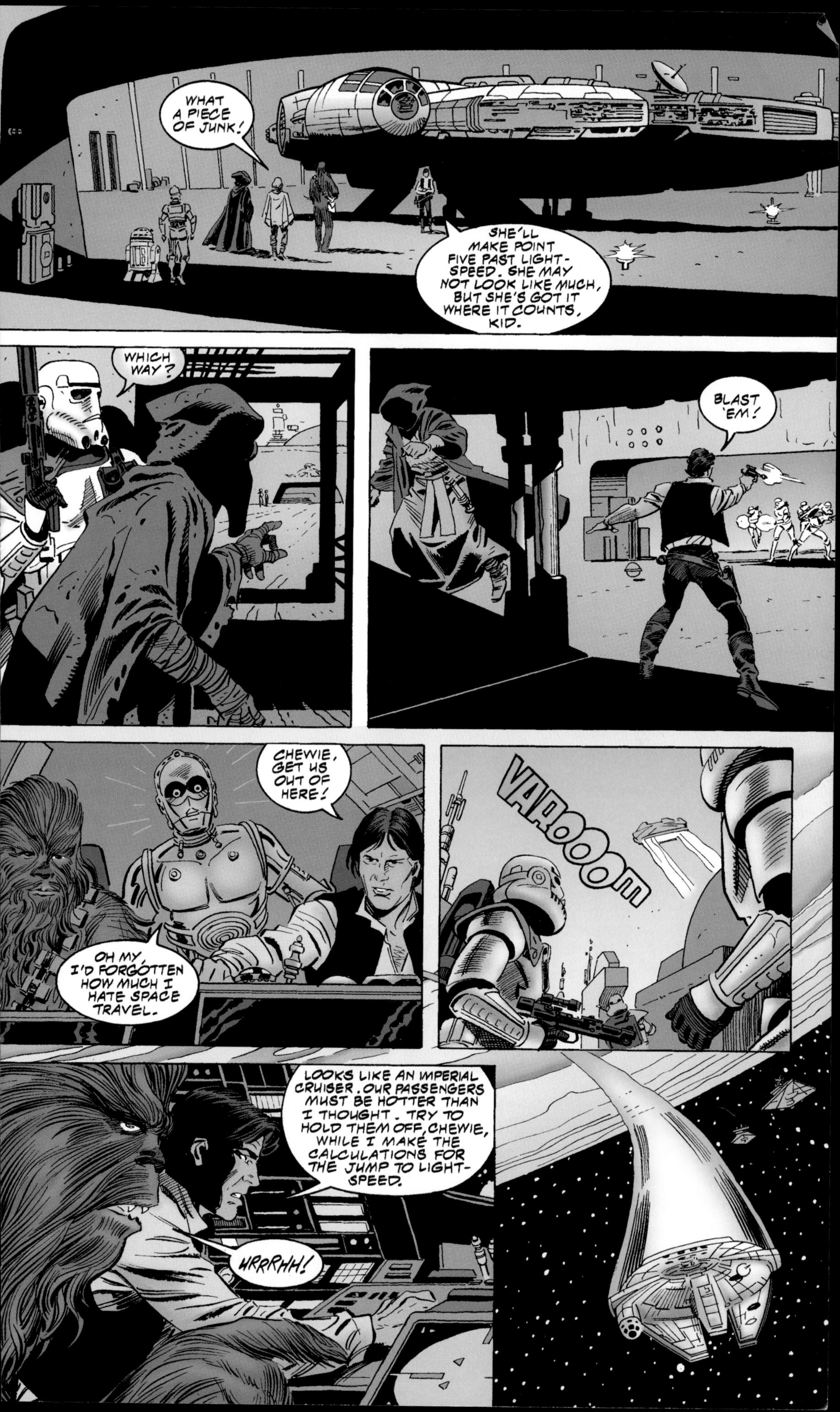
WHAT A PIECE OF JUNK!
SHE'LL MAKE POINT FIVE PAST LIGHT-SPEED. SHE MAY NOT LOOK LIKE MUCH, BUT SHE'S GOT IT WHERE IT COUNTS, KID.
WHICH WAY?
BLAST 'EM!
CHEWIE, GET US OUT OF HERE!
OH MY, I'D FORGOTTEN HOW MUCH I HATE SPACE TRAVEL.
VAROOOOM
LOOKS LIKE AN IMPERIAL CRUISER. OUR PASSENGERS MUST BE HOTTER THAN I THOUGHT. TRY TO HOLD THEM OFF, CHEWIE, WHILE I MAKE THE CALCULATIONS FOR THE JUMP TO LIGHT-SPEED.
URRRHH!

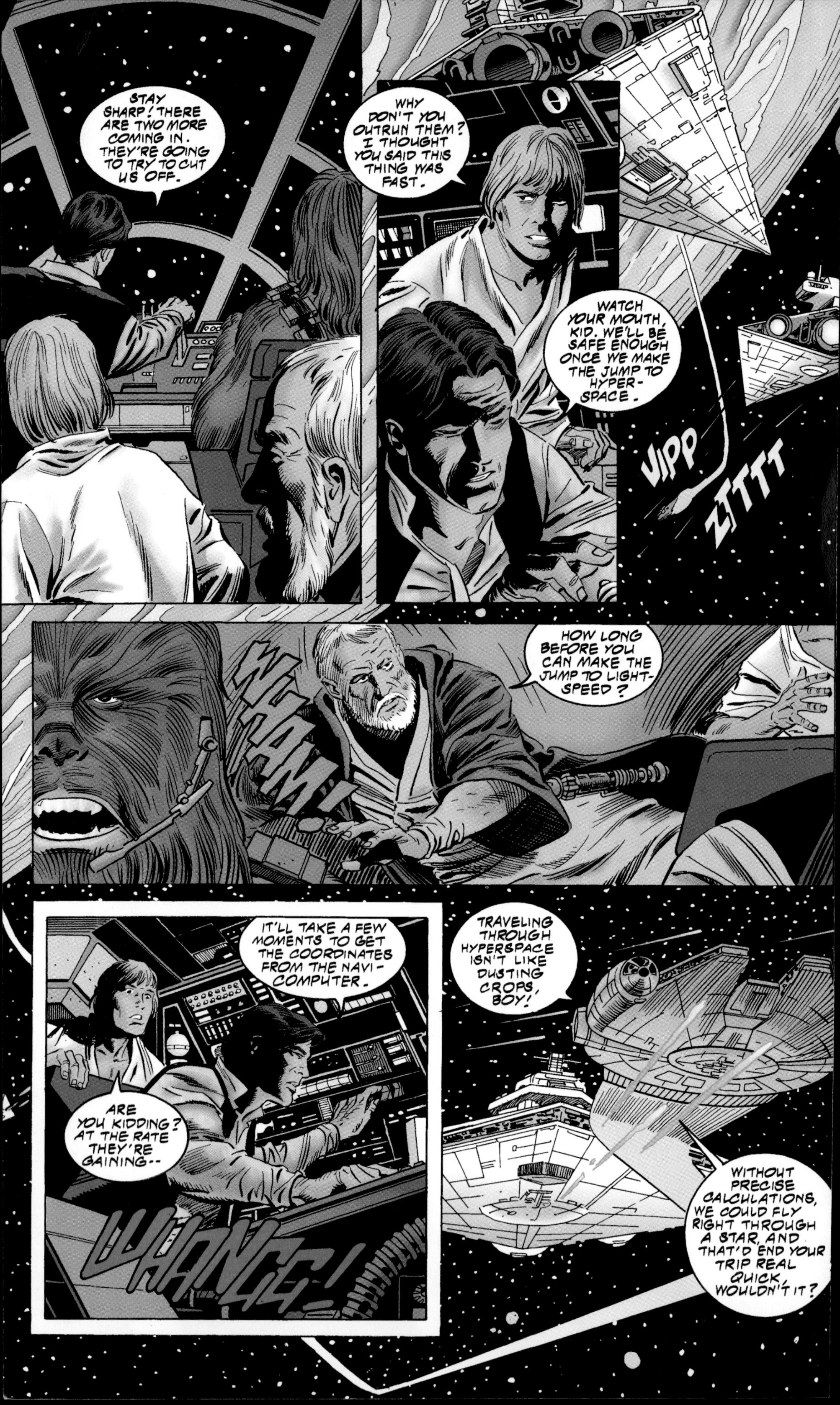
STAY SHARP! THERE ARE TWO MORE COMING IN. THEY'RE GOING TO TRY TO CUT US OFF.
WHY DON'T YOU OUTRUN THEM? I THOUGHT YOU SAID THIS THING WAS FAST.
WATCH YOUR MOUTH, KID. WE'LL BE SAFE ENOUGH ONCE WE MAKE THE JUMP TO HYPER-SPACE.
VIPP
ZZTTTT
WHAM!
HOW LONG BEFORE YOU CAN MAKE THE JUMP TO LIGHT-SPEED?
IT'LL TAKE A FEW MOMENTS TO GET THE COORDINATES FROM THE NAVI-COMPUTER.
ARE YOU KIDDING? AT THE RATE THEY'RE GAINING--
WHANGG!
TRAVELING THROUGH HYPERSPACE ISN'T LIKE DUSTING CROPS, BOY!
WITHOUT PRECISE CALCULATIONS, WE COULD FLY RIGHT THROUGH A STAR, AND THAT'D END YOUR TRIP REAL QUICK, WOULDN'T IT?

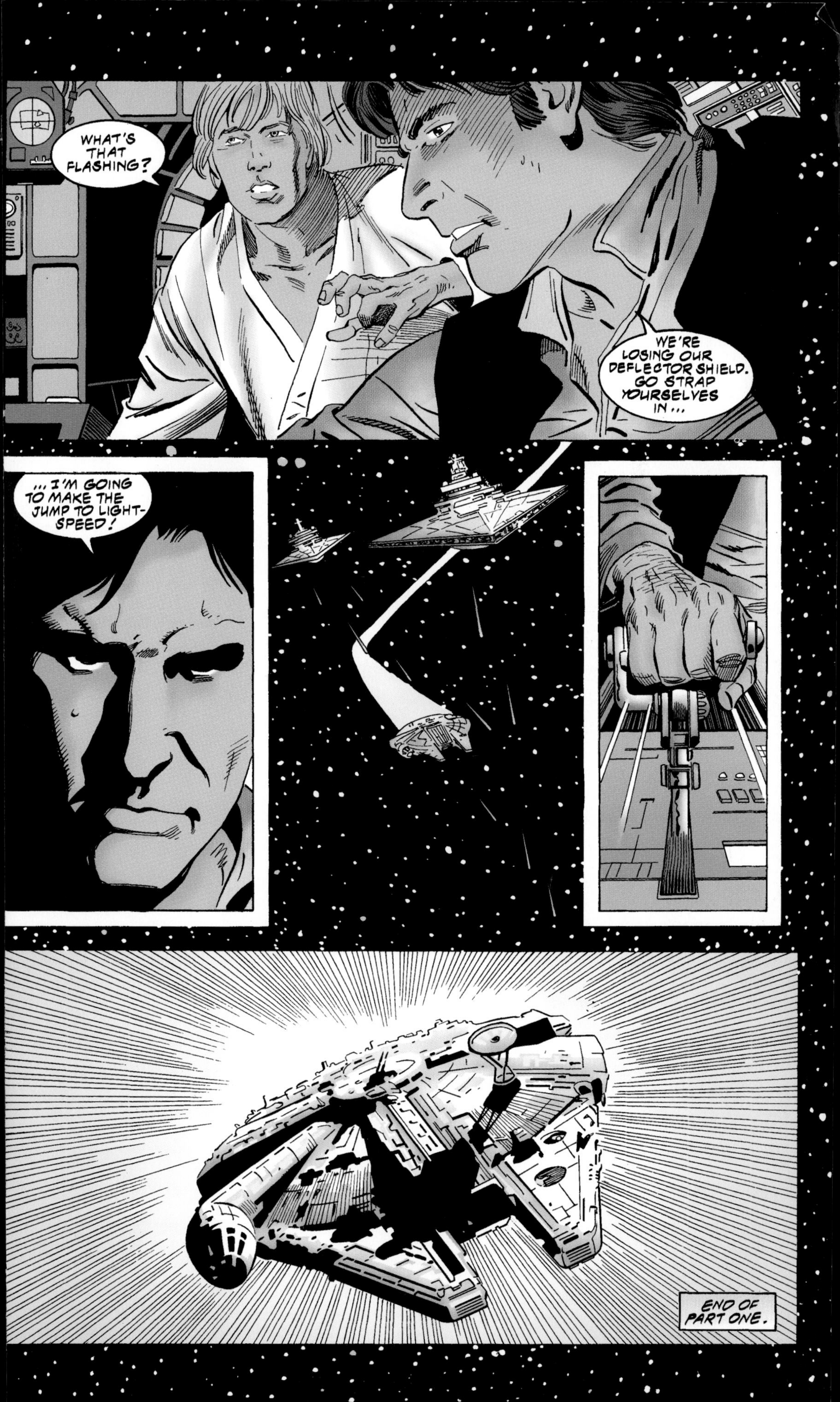
WHAT'S THAT FLASHING?
WE'RE LOSING OUR DEFLECTOR SHIELD. GO STRAP YOURSELVES IN...
...I'M GOING TO MAKE THE JUMP TO LIGHT-SPEED!
END OF PART ONE.

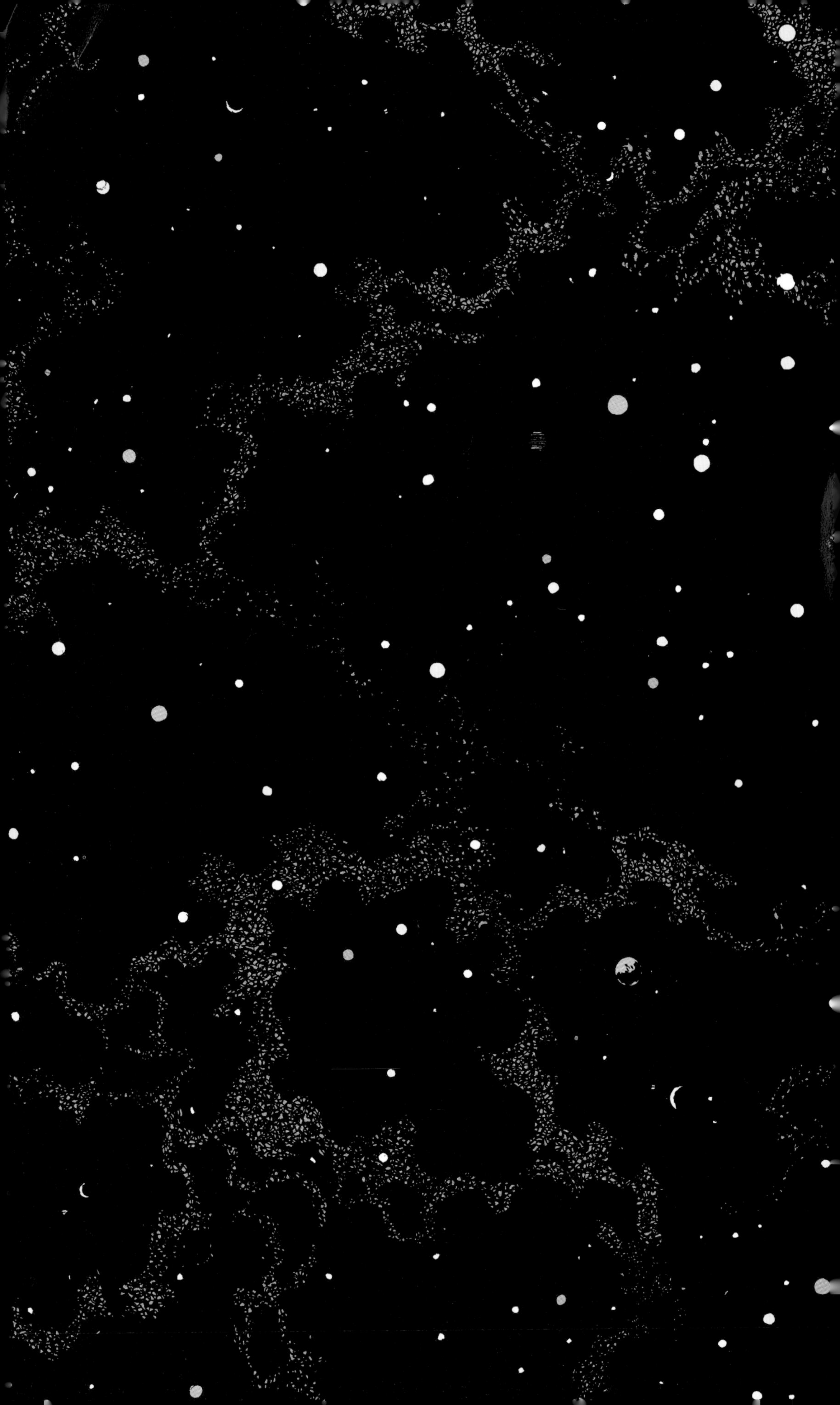

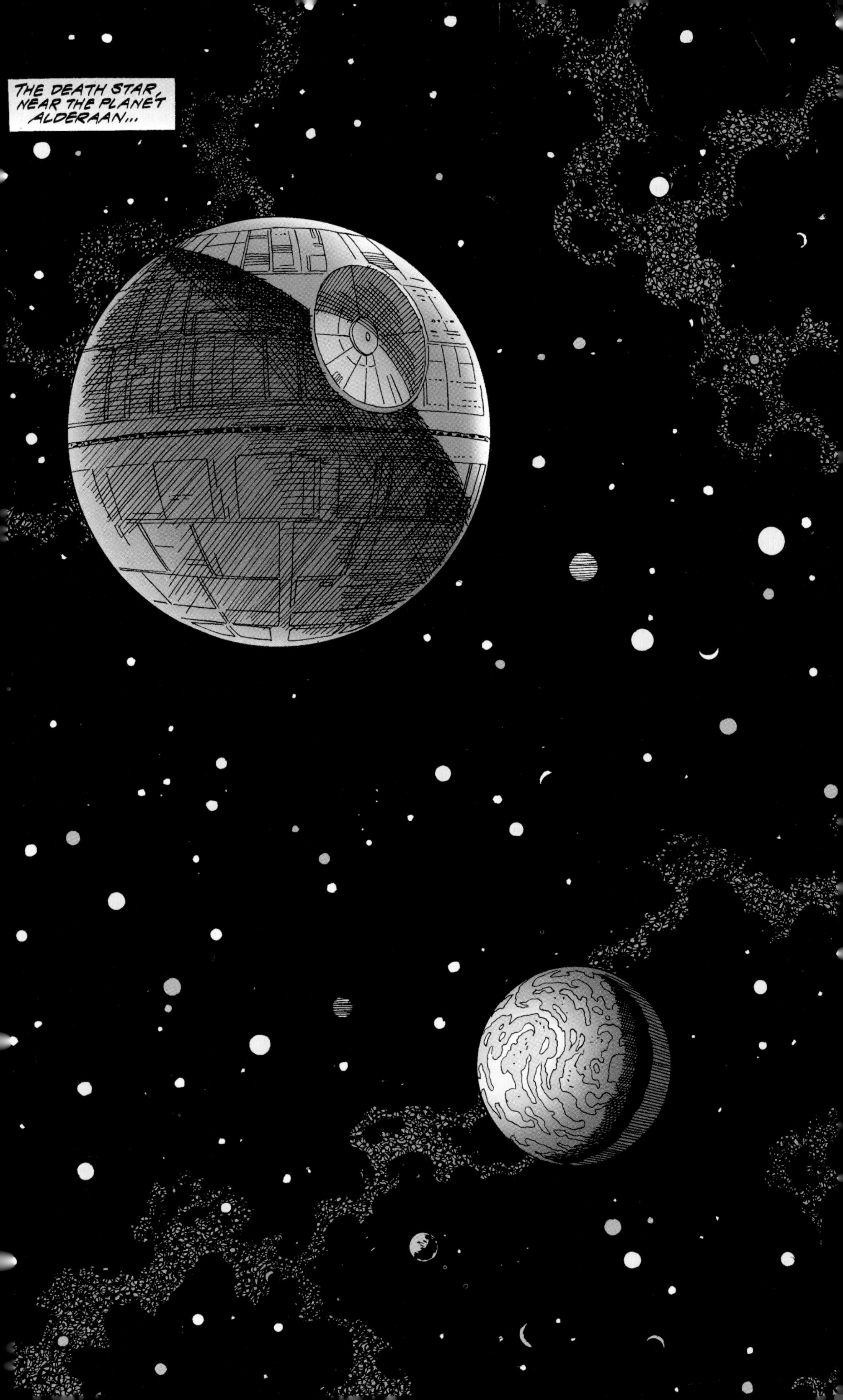
THE DEATH STAR, NEAR THE PLANET ALDERAAN...

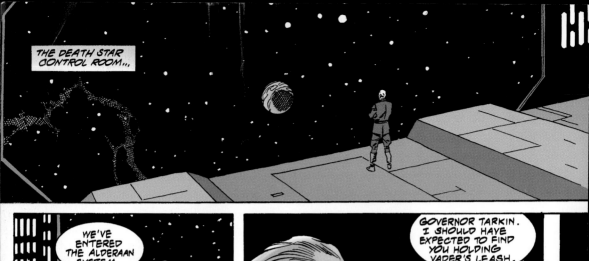

THE DEATH STAR CONTROL ROOM...

WE'VE ENTERED THE ALDERAAN SYSTEM.

GOVERNOR TARKIN. I SHOULD HAVE EXPECTED TO FIND YOU HOLDING VADER'S LEASH.

CHARMING TO THE LAST. YOU DON'T KNOW HOW HARD I FOUND IT SIGNING THE ORDER TO TERMINATE YOUR LIFE!

THE MORE YOU TIGHTEN YOUR GRIP, TARKIN, THE MORE STAR SYSTEMS WILL SLIP THROUGH YOUR FINGERS.

NOT AFTER WE DEMONSTRATE THE POWER OF THIS STATION. SINCE YOU ARE RELUCTANT TO PROVIDE US WITH THE LOCATION OF THE REBEL BASE...

...I HAVE CHOSEN TO TEST THIS STATION'S DESTRUCTIVE POWER...

...ON YOUR HOME PLANET OF ALDERAAN.

NO! ALDERAAN IS PEACEFUL! WE HAVE NO WEAPONS! YOU CAN'T POSSIBLY--

YOU WOULD PREFER ANOTHER TARGET? A MILITARY TARGET? THEN NAME THE SYSTEM! WHERE IS THE REBEL BASE?

DANTOOINE. THEY'RE ON DANTOOINE.

THERE. YOU SEE, LORD VADER, SHE CAN BE REASONABLE.

CONTINUE WITH THE OPERATION. YOU MAY FIRE WHEN READY.

WHAT?

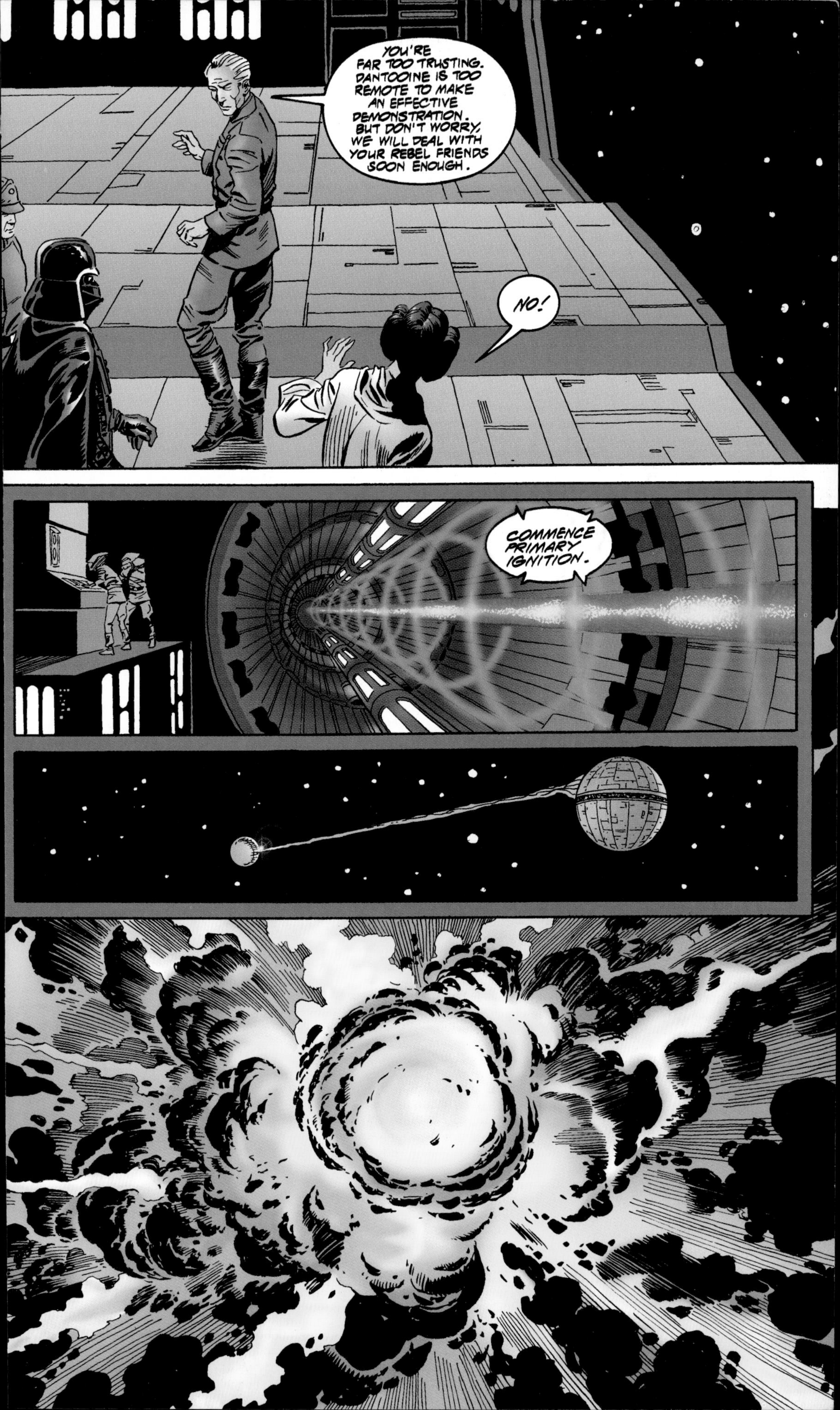
YOU'RE FAR TOO TRUSTING. DANTOOINE IS TOO REMOTE TO MAKE AN EFFECTIVE DEMONSTRATION. BUT DON'T WORRY, WE WILL DEAL WITH YOUR REBEL FRIENDS SOON ENOUGH.
NO!
COMMENCE PRIMARY IGNITION.

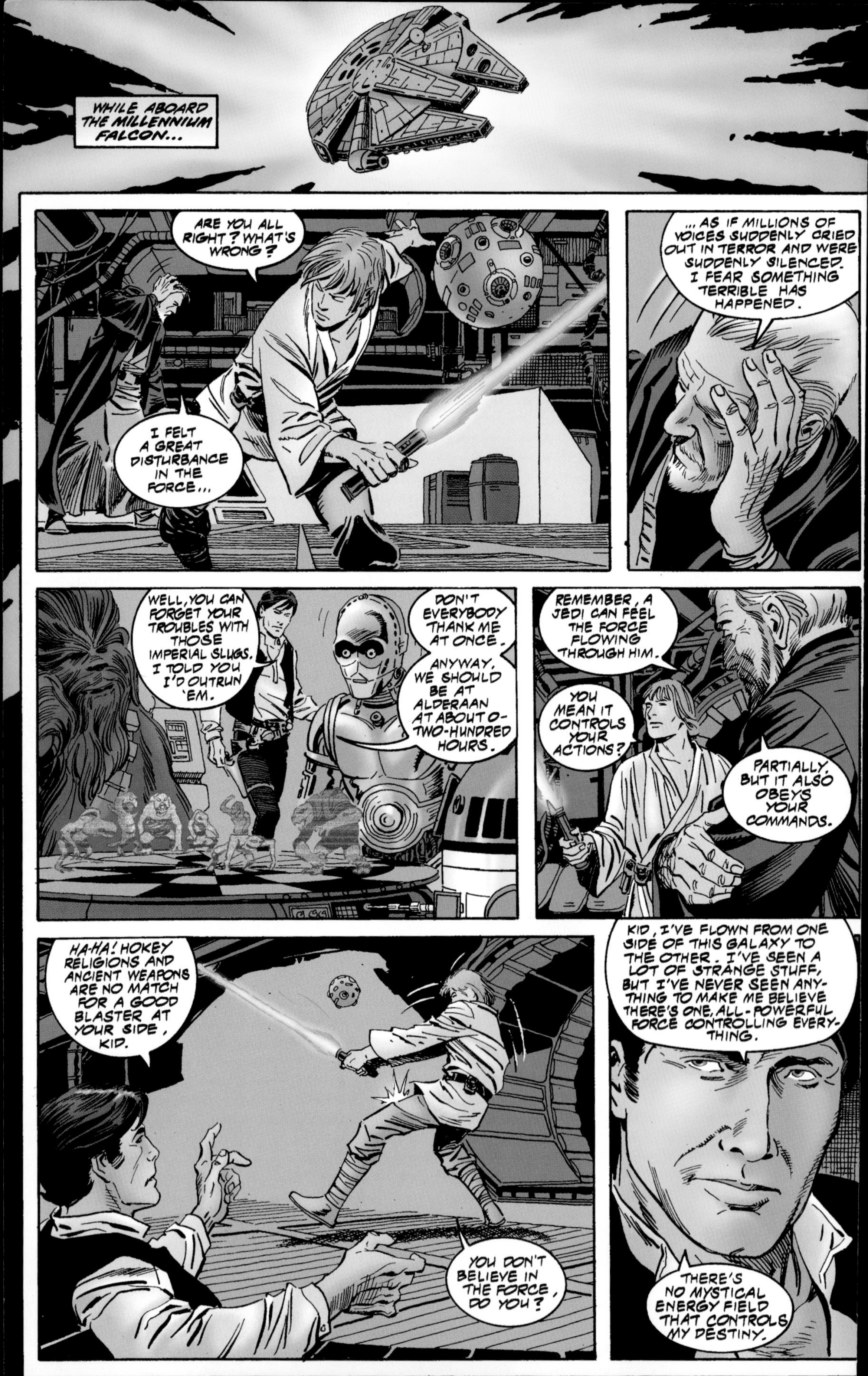

WHILE ABOARD THE MILLENNIUM FALCON...
ARE YOU ALL RIGHT? WHAT'S WRONG?
I FELT A GREAT DISTURBANCE IN THE FORCE...
...AS IF MILLIONS OF VOICES SUDDENLY CRIED OUT IN TERROR AND WERE SUDDENLY SILENCED. I FEAR SOMETHING TERRIBLE HAS HAPPENED.
WELL, YOU CAN FORGET YOUR TROUBLES WITH THOSE IMPERIAL SLUGS. I TOLD YOU I'D OUTRUN 'EM.
DON'T EVERYBODY THANK ME AT ONCE.
ANYWAY, WE SHOULD BE AT ALDERAAN AT ABOUT O-TWO-HUNDRED HOURS.
REMEMBER, A JEDI CAN FEEL THE FORCE FLOWING THROUGH HIM.
YOU MEAN IT CONTROLS YOUR ACTIONS?
PARTIALLY. BUT IT ALSO OBEYS YOUR COMMANDS.
HA-HA! HOKEY RELIGIONS AND ANCIENT WEAPONS ARE NO MATCH FOR A GOOD BLASTER AT YOUR SIDE, KID.
YOU DON'T BELIEVE IN THE FORCE, DO YOU?
KID, I'VE FLOWN FROM ONE SIDE OF THIS GALAXY TO THE OTHER. I'VE SEEN A LOT OF STRANGE STUFF, BUT I'VE NEVER SEEN ANYTHING TO MAKE ME BELIEVE THERE'S ONE, ALL-POWERFUL FORCE CONTROLLING EVERYTHING.
THERE'S NO MYSTICAL ENERGY FIELD THAT CONTROLS MY DESTINY.

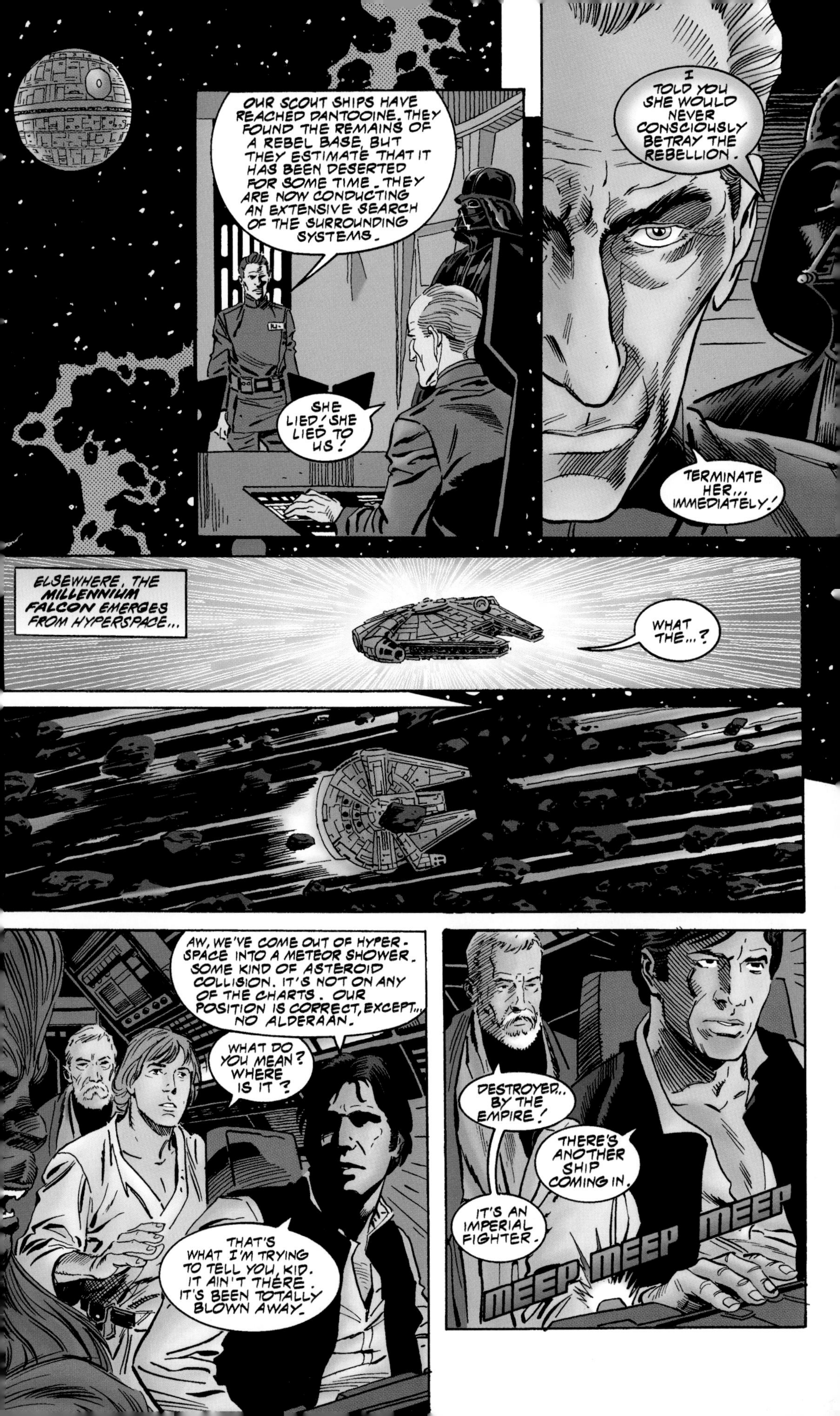
OUR SCOUT SHIPS HAVE REACHED DANTOOINE. THEY FOUND THE REMAINS OF A REBEL BASE, BUT THEY ESTIMATE THAT IT HAS BEEN DESERTED FOR SOME TIME. THEY ARE NOW CONDUCTING AN EXTENSIVE SEARCH OF THE SURROUNDING SYSTEMS.
SHE LIED! SHE LIED TO US!
I TOLD YOU SHE WOULD NEVER CONSCIOUSLY BETRAY THE REBELLION.
TERMINATE HER... IMMEDIATELY!
ELSEWHERE, THE MILLENNIUM FALCON EMERGES FROM HYPERSPACE...
WHAT THE...?
AW, WE'VE COME OUT OF HYPER-SPACE INTO A METEOR SHOWER. SOME KIND OF ASTEROID COLLISION. IT'S NOT ON ANY OF THE CHARTS. OUR POSITION IS CORRECT, EXCEPT... NO ALDERAAN.
WHAT DO YOU MEAN? WHERE IS IT?
THAT'S WHAT I'M TRYING TO TELL YOU, KID. IT AIN'T THERE. IT'S BEEN TOTALLY BLOWN AWAY.
DESTROYED... BY THE EMPIRE!
THERE'S ANOTHER SHIP COMING IN.
IT'S AN IMPERIAL FIGHTER.
MEEP MEEP MEEP

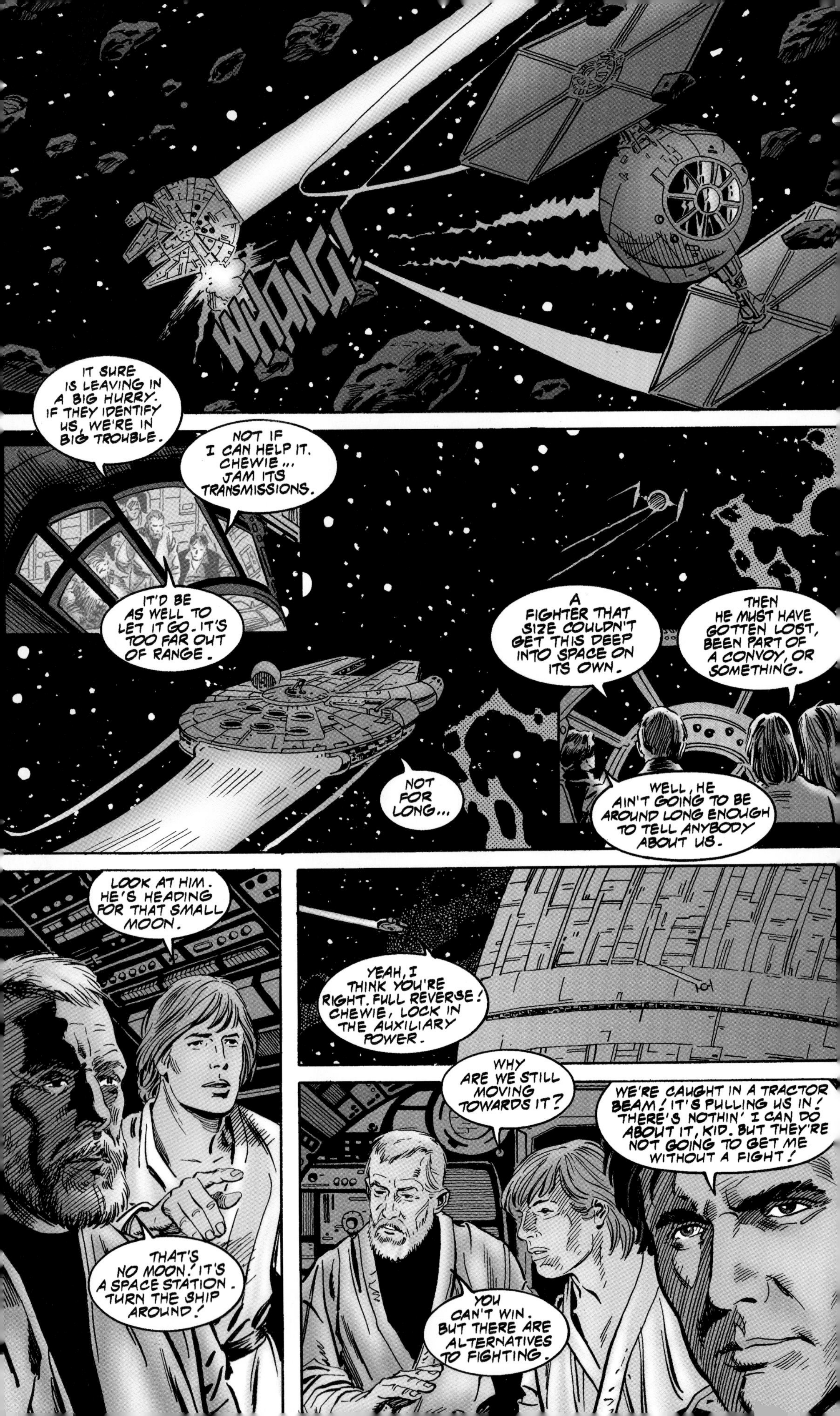
WHANG!
IT SURE IS LEAVING IN A BIG HURRY. IF THEY IDENTIFY US, WE'RE IN BIG TROUBLE.
NOT IF I CAN HELP IT. CHEWIE... JAM ITS TRANSMISSIONS.
IT'D BE AS WELL TO LET IT GO. IT'S TOO FAR OUT OF RANGE.
NOT FOR LONG...
A FIGHTER THAT SIZE COULDN'T GET THIS DEEP INTO SPACE ON ITS OWN.
THEN HE MUST HAVE GOTTEN LOST, BEEN PART OF A CONVOY, OR SOMETHING.
WELL, HE AIN'T GOING TO BE AROUND LONG ENOUGH TO TELL ANYBODY ABOUT US.
LOOK AT HIM. HE'S HEADING FOR THAT SMALL MOON.
THAT'S NO MOON! IT'S A SPACE STATION. TURN THE SHIP AROUND!
YEAH, I THINK YOU'RE RIGHT. FULL REVERSE! CHEWIE, LOCK IN THE AUXILIARY POWER.
WHY ARE WE STILL MOVING TOWARDS IT?
WE'RE CAUGHT IN A TRACTOR BEAM! IT'S PULLING US IN! THERE'S NOTHIN' I CAN DO ABOUT IT, KID. BUT THEY'RE NOT GOING TO GET ME WITHOUT A FIGHT!
YOU CAN'T WIN. BUT THERE ARE ALTERNATIVES TO FIGHTING.

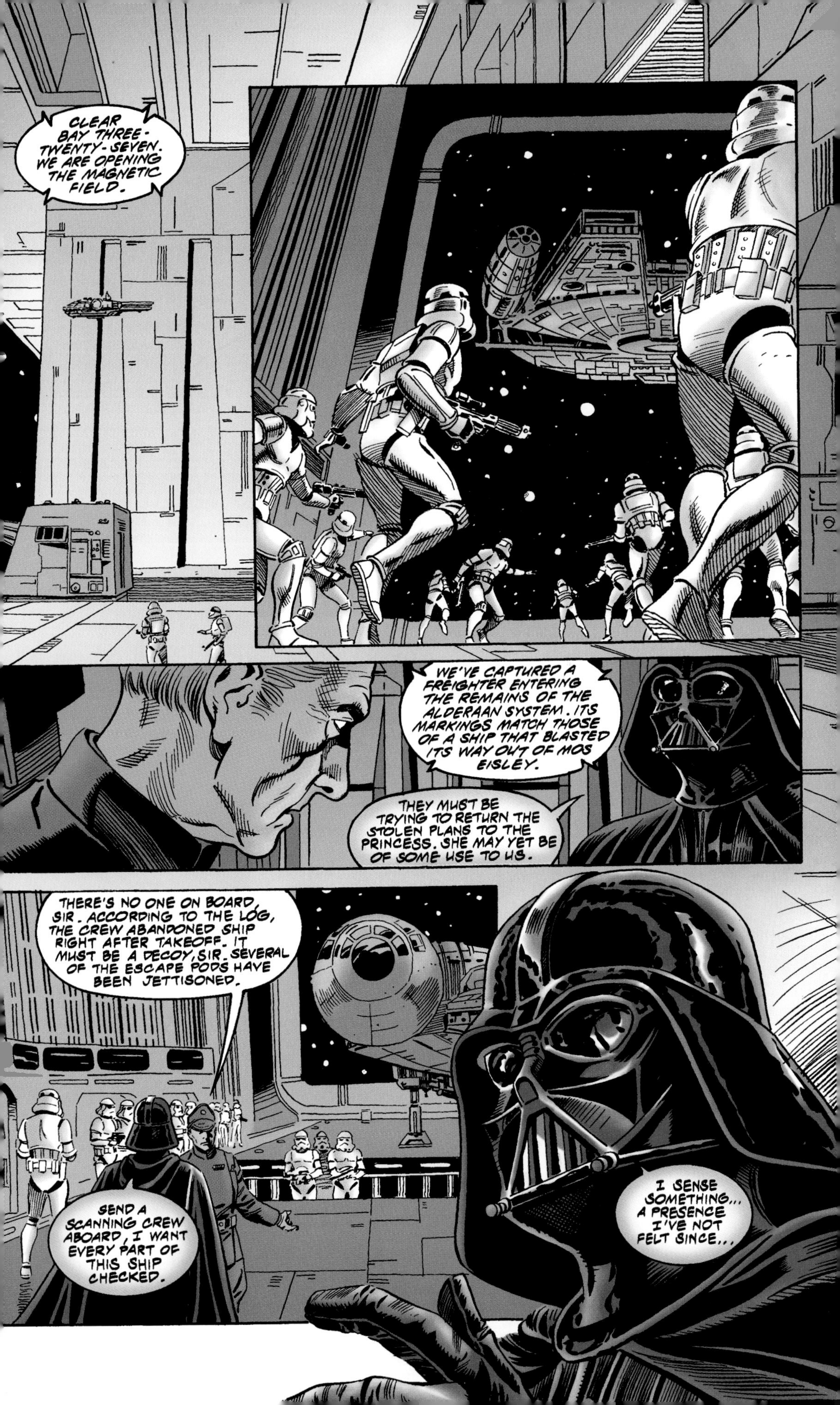
CLEAR BAY THREE-TWENTY-SEVEN. WE ARE OPENING THE MAGNETIC FIELD.
WE'VE CAPTURED A FREIGHTER ENTERING THE REMAINS OF THE ALDERAAN SYSTEM. ITS MARKINGS MATCH THOSE OF A SHIP THAT BLASTED ITS WAY OUT OF MOS EISLEY.
THEY MUST BE TRYING TO RETURN THE STOLEN PLANS TO THE PRINCESS. SHE MAY YET BE OF SOME USE TO US.
THERE'S NO ONE ON BOARD, SIR. ACCORDING TO THE LOG, THE CREW ABANDONED SHIP RIGHT AFTER TAKEOFF. IT MUST BE A DECOY, SIR. SEVERAL OF THE ESCAPE PODS HAVE BEEN JETTISONED.
SEND A SCANNING CREW ABOARD, I WANT EVERY PART OF THIS SHIP CHECKED.
I SENSE SOMETHING... A PRESENCE I'VE NOT FELT SINCE...

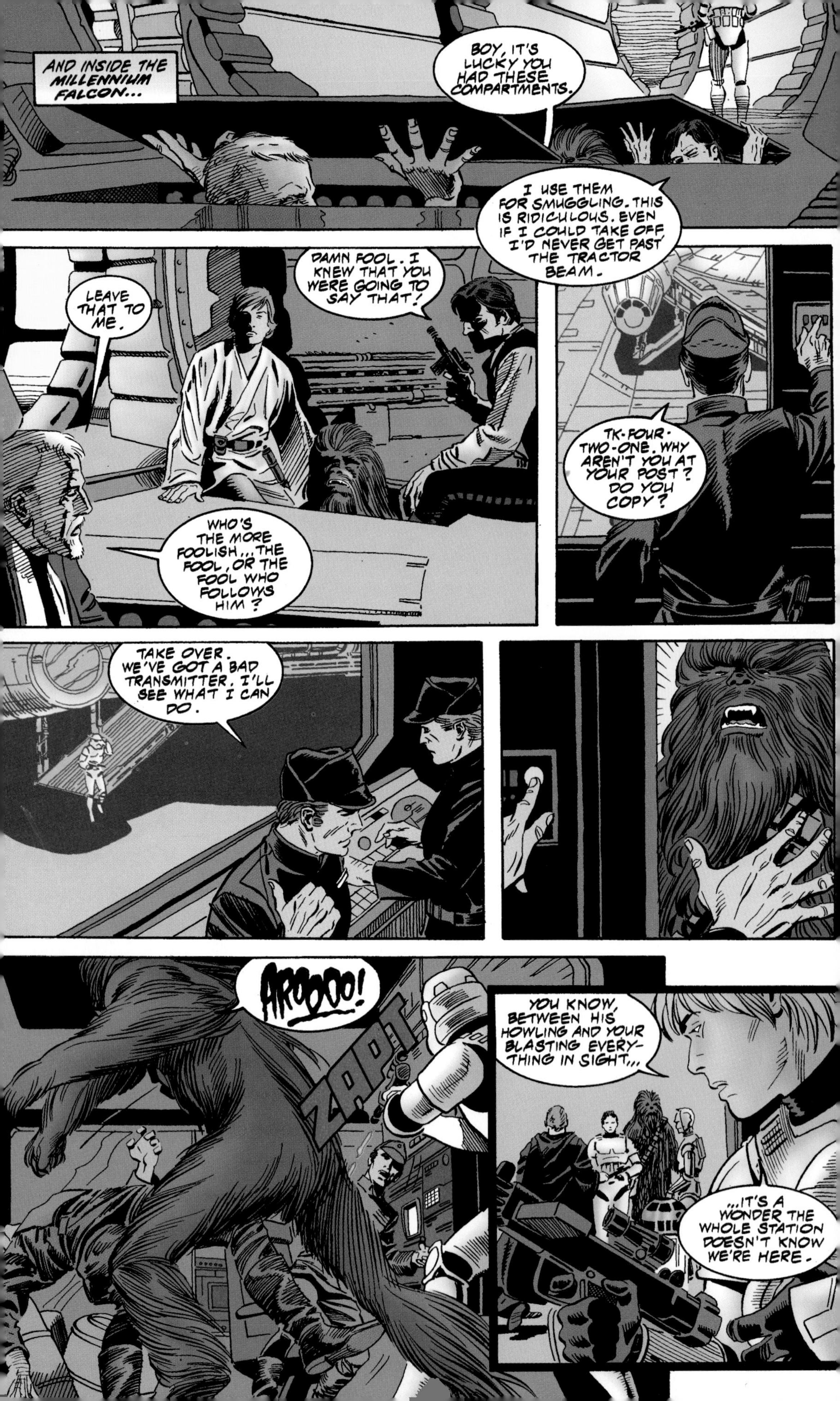
AND INSIDE THE MILLENNIUM FALCON...
BOY, IT'S LUCKY YOU HAD THESE COMPARTMENTS.
I USE THEM FOR SMUGGLING. THIS IS RIDICULOUS. EVEN IF I COULD TAKE OFF I'D NEVER GET PAST THE TRACTOR BEAM.
LEAVE THAT TO ME.
DAMN FOOL. I KNEW THAT YOU WERE GOING TO SAY THAT!
WHO'S THE MORE FOOLISH... THE FOOL, OR THE FOOL WHO FOLLOWS HIM?
TK-FOUR-TWO-ONE. WHY AREN'T YOU AT YOUR POST? DO YOU COPY?
TAKE OVER. WE'VE GOT A BAD TRANSMITTER. I'LL SEE WHAT I CAN DO.
AROOOO!
ZAPT
YOU KNOW, BETWEEN HIS HOWLING AND YOUR BLASTING EVERY-THING IN SIGHT...
...IT'S A WONDER THE WHOLE STATION DOESN'T KNOW WE'RE HERE.

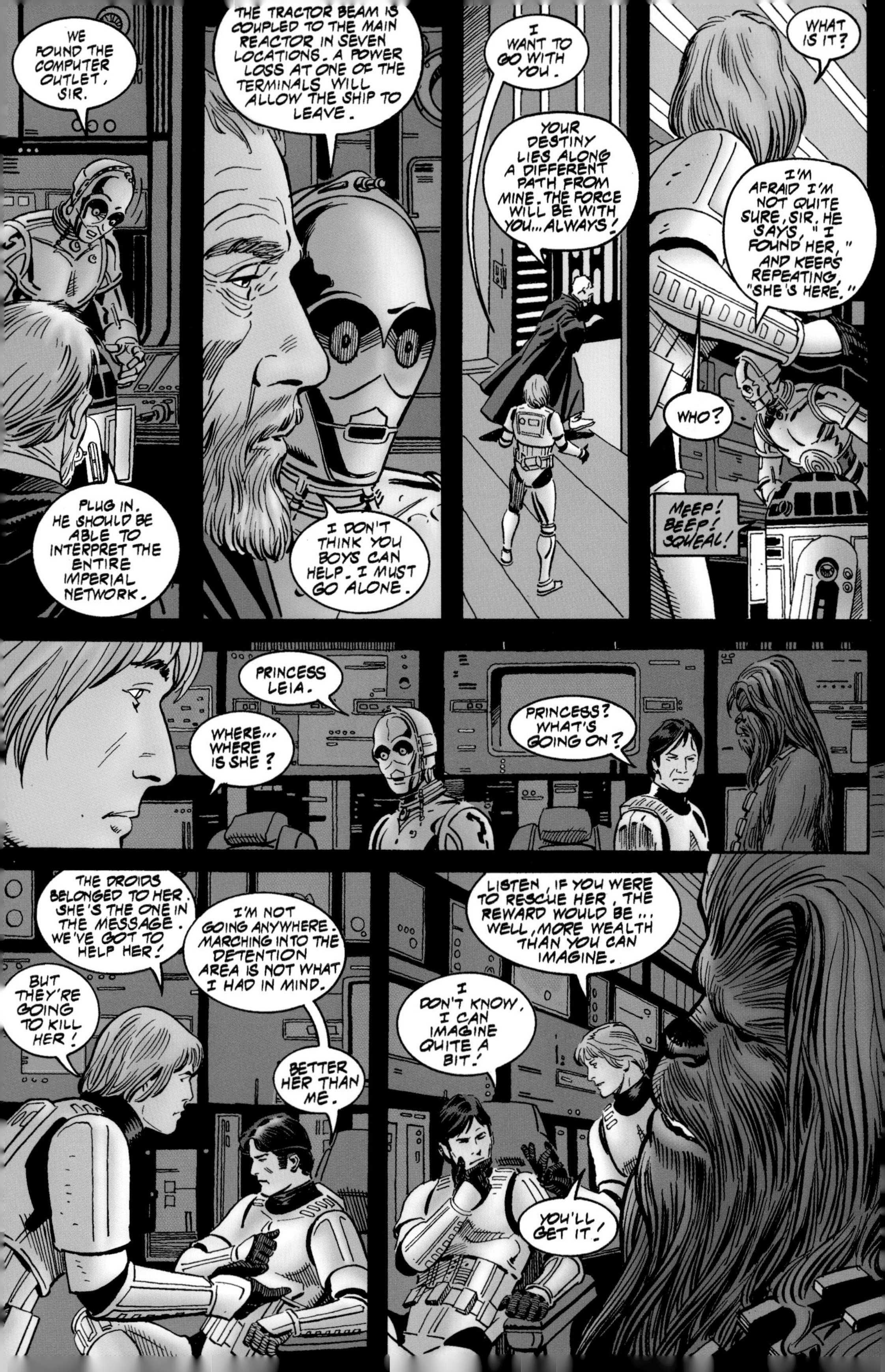

WE FOUND THE COMPUTER OUTLET, SIR.
PLUG IN. HE SHOULD BE ABLE TO INTERPRET THE ENTIRE IMPERIAL NETWORK.
THE TRACTOR BEAM IS COUPLED TO THE MAIN REACTOR IN SEVEN LOCATIONS. A POWER LOSS AT ONE OF THE TERMINALS WILL ALLOW THE SHIP TO LEAVE.
I DON'T THINK YOU BOYS CAN HELP. I MUST GO ALONE.
I WANT TO GO WITH YOU.
YOUR DESTINY LIES ALONG A DIFFERENT PATH FROM MINE. THE FORCE WILL BE WITH YOU...ALWAYS!
WHAT IS IT?
I'M AFRAID I'M NOT QUITE SURE, SIR. HE SAYS, "I FOUND HER," AND KEEPS REPEATING, "SHE'S HERE."
WHO?
MEEP! BEEP! SQUEAL!
PRINCESS LEIA.
WHERE... WHERE IS SHE?
PRINCESS? WHAT'S GOING ON?
THE DROIDS BELONGED TO HER. SHE'S THE ONE IN THE MESSAGE. WE'VE GOT TO HELP HER!
I'M NOT GOING ANYWHERE. MARCHING INTO THE DETENTION AREA IS NOT WHAT I HAD IN MIND.
BUT THEY'RE GOING TO KILL HER!
BETTER HER THAN ME.
LISTEN, IF YOU WERE TO RESCUE HER, THE REWARD WOULD BE... WELL, MORE WEALTH THAN YOU CAN IMAGINE.
I DON'T KNOW, I CAN IMAGINE QUITE A BIT!
YOU'LL GET IT!

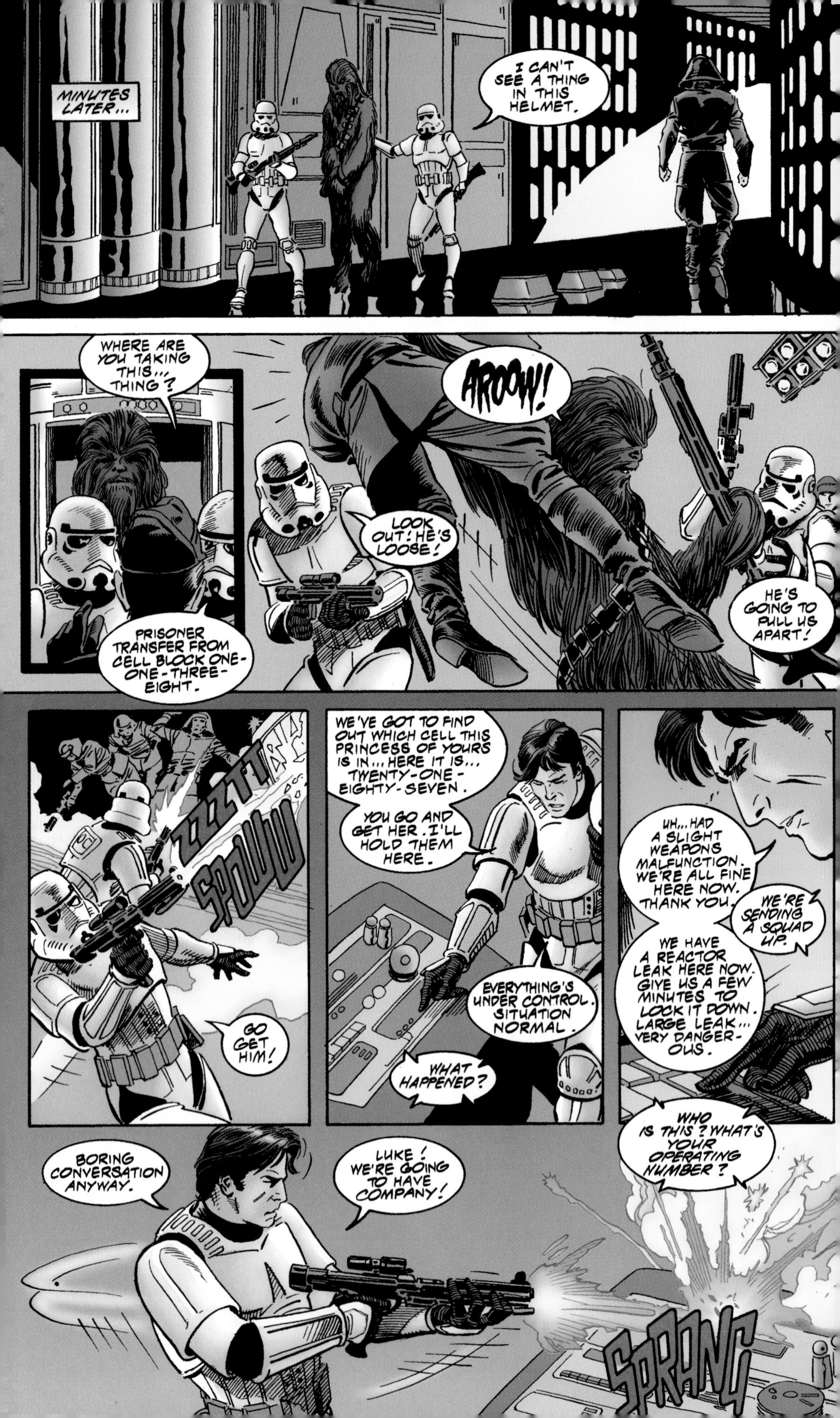
MINUTES LATER...
I CAN'T SEE A THING IN THIS HELMET.
WHERE ARE YOU TAKING THIS... THING?
PRISONER TRANSFER FROM CELL BLOCK ONE-ONE-THREE-EIGHT.
AROOW!
LOOK OUT! HE'S LOOSE!
HE'S GOING TO PULL US APART!
ZZZTT
SPOWW
GO GET HIM!
WE'VE GOT TO FIND OUT WHICH CELL THIS PRINCESS OF YOURS IS IN... HERE IT IS... TWENTY-ONE-EIGHTY-SEVEN.
YOU GO AND GET HER. I'LL HOLD THEM HERE.
EVERYTHING'S UNDER CONTROL. SITUATION NORMAL.
WHAT HAPPENED?
UH... HAD A SLIGHT WEAPONS MALFUNCTION. WE'RE ALL FINE HERE NOW. THANK YOU.
WE'RE SENDING A SQUAD UP.
WE HAVE A REACTOR LEAK HERE NOW. GIVE US A FEW MINUTES TO LOCK IT DOWN. LARGE LEAK... VERY DANGER-OUS.
WHO IS THIS? WHAT'S YOUR OPERATING NUMBER?
BORING CONVERSATION ANYWAY.
LUKE! WE'RE GOING TO HAVE COMPANY!
SPRANG

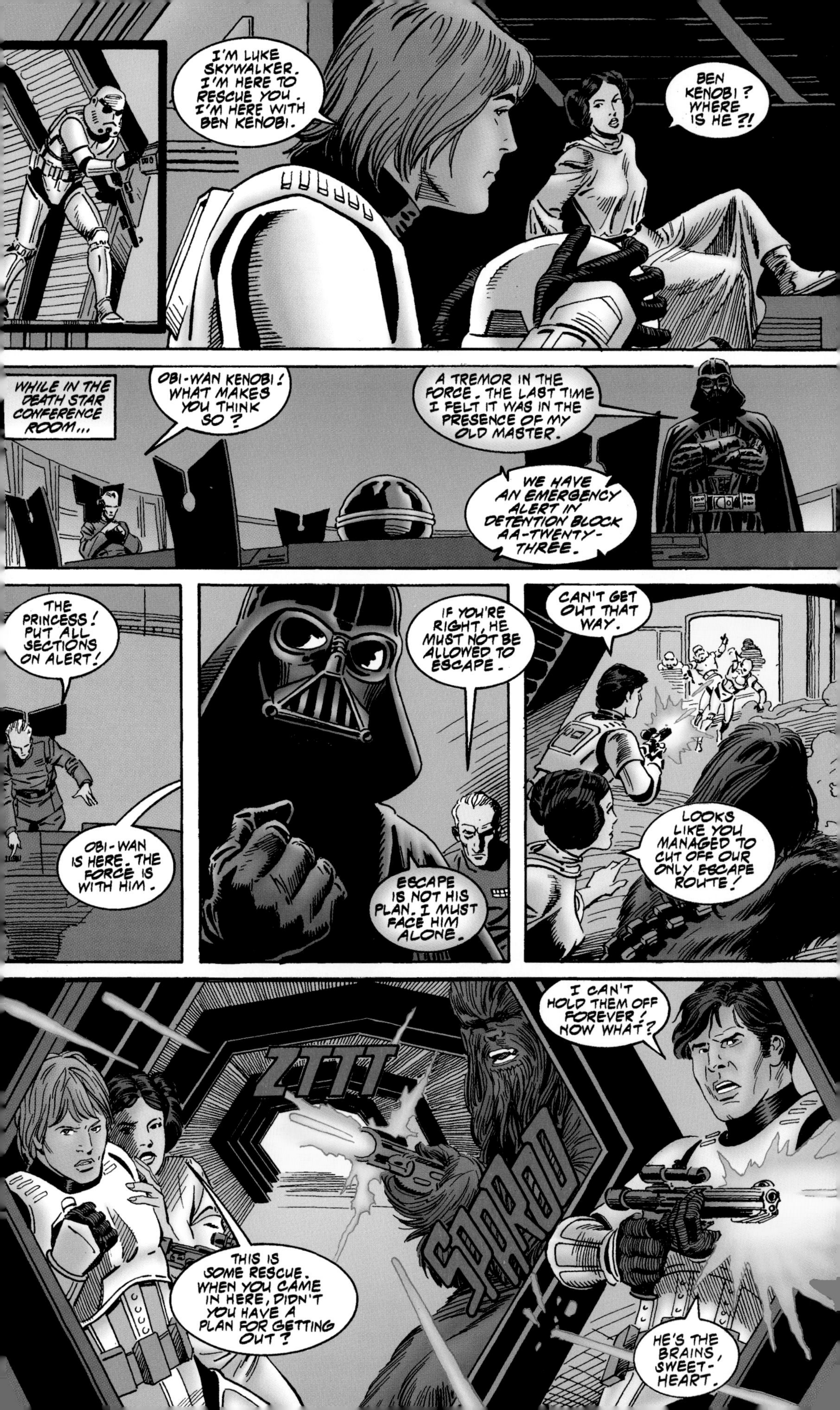
I'M LUKE SKYWALKER. I'M HERE TO RESCUE YOU. I'M HERE WITH BEN KENOBI.
BEN KENOBI? WHERE IS HE?!
WHILE IN THE DEATH STAR CONFERENCE ROOM...
OBI-WAN KENOBI! WHAT MAKES YOU THINK SO?
A TREMOR IN THE FORCE. THE LAST TIME I FELT IT WAS IN THE PRESENCE OF MY OLD MASTER.
WE HAVE AN EMERGENCY ALERT IN DETENTION BLOCK AA-TWENTY-THREE.
THE PRINCESS! PUT ALL SECTIONS ON ALERT!
OBI-WAN IS HERE. THE FORCE IS WITH HIM.
IF YOU'RE RIGHT, HE MUST NOT BE ALLOWED TO ESCAPE.
ESCAPE IS NOT HIS PLAN. I MUST FACE HIM ALONE.
CAN'T GET OUT THAT WAY.
LOOKS LIKE YOU MANAGED TO CUT OFF OUR ONLY ESCAPE ROUTE!
ZTTT
I CAN'T HOLD THEM OFF FOREVER! NOW WHAT?
THIS IS SOME RESCUE. WHEN YOU CAME IN HERE, DIDN'T YOU HAVE A PLAN FOR GETTING OUT?
HE'S THE BRAINS, SWEET-HEART.

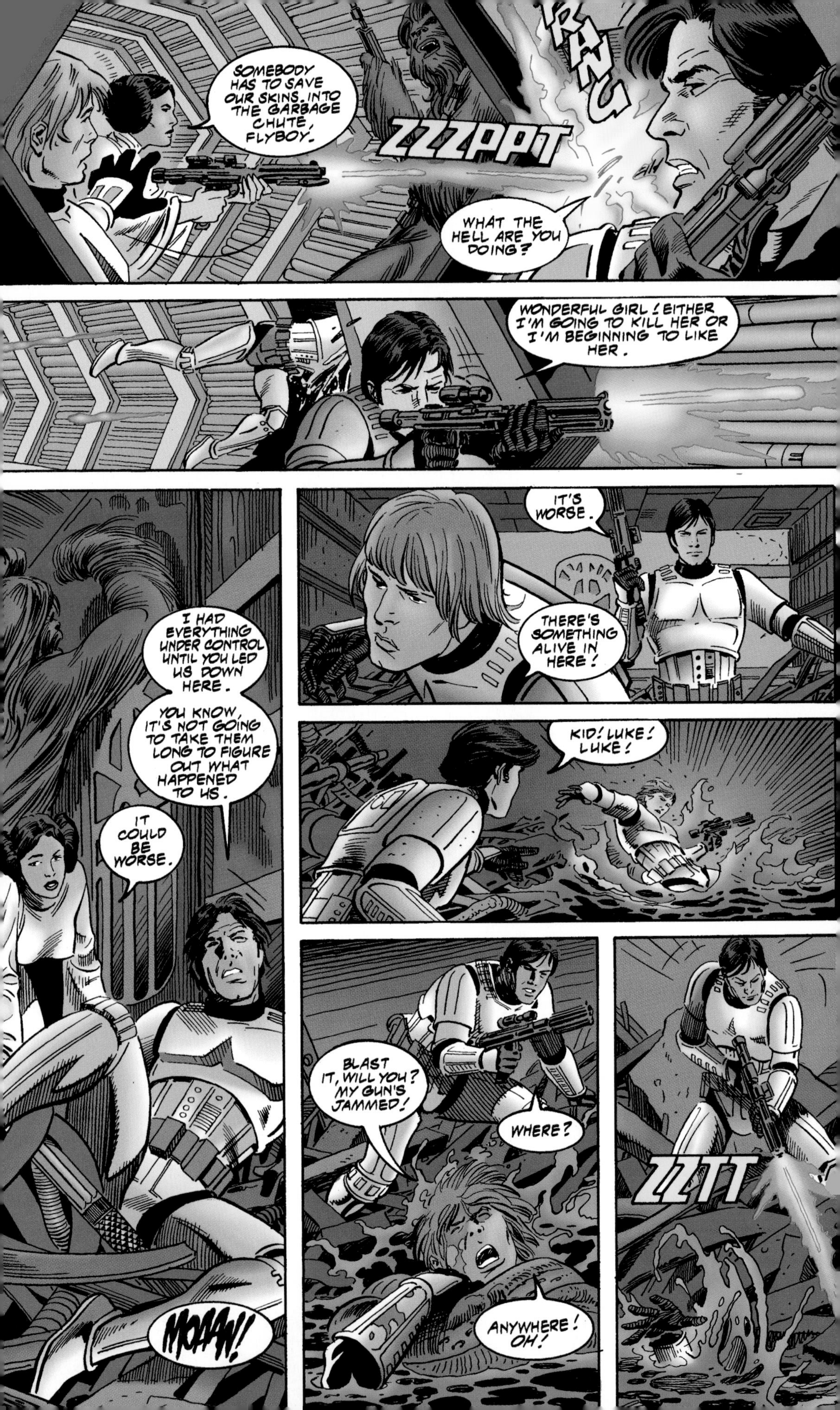
SOMEBODY HAS TO SAVE OUR SKINS. INTO THE GARBAGE CHUTE, FLYBOY.
ZZZPPT
KRANG
WHAT THE HELL ARE YOU DOING?
WONDERFUL GIRL! EITHER I'M GOING TO KILL HER OR I'M BEGINNING TO LIKE HER.
I HAD EVERYTHING UNDER CONTROL UNTIL YOU LED US DOWN HERE.
YOU KNOW, IT'S NOT GOING TO TAKE THEM LONG TO FIGURE OUT WHAT HAPPENED TO US.
IT COULD BE WORSE.
MOAAN!
IT'S WORSE.
THERE'S SOMETHING ALIVE IN HERE!
KID! LUKE! LUKE!
BLAST IT, WILL YOU? MY GUN'S JAMMED!
WHERE?
ANYWHERE! OH!
ZZTT

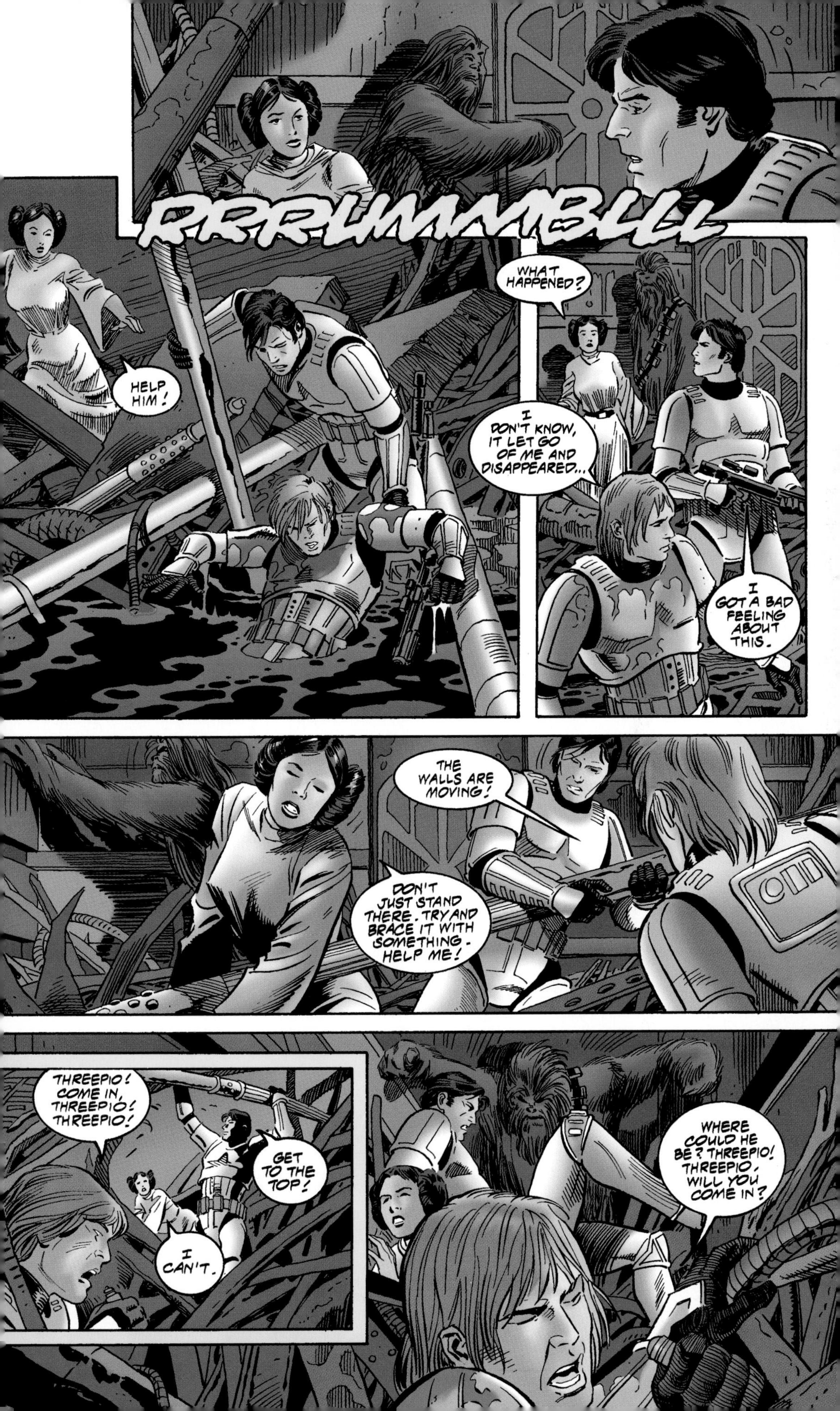

RRRUMMBULL
HELP HIM!
WHAT HAPPENED?
I DON'T KNOW, IT LET GO OF ME AND DISAPPEARED...
I GOT A BAD FEELING ABOUT THIS.
THE WALLS ARE MOVING!
DON'T JUST STAND THERE. TRY AND BRACE IT WITH SOMETHING. HELP ME!
THREEPIO! COME IN, THREEPIO! THREEPIO!
GET TO THE TOP!
I CAN'T.
WHERE COULD HE BE? THREEPIO! THREEPIO, WILL YOU COME IN?

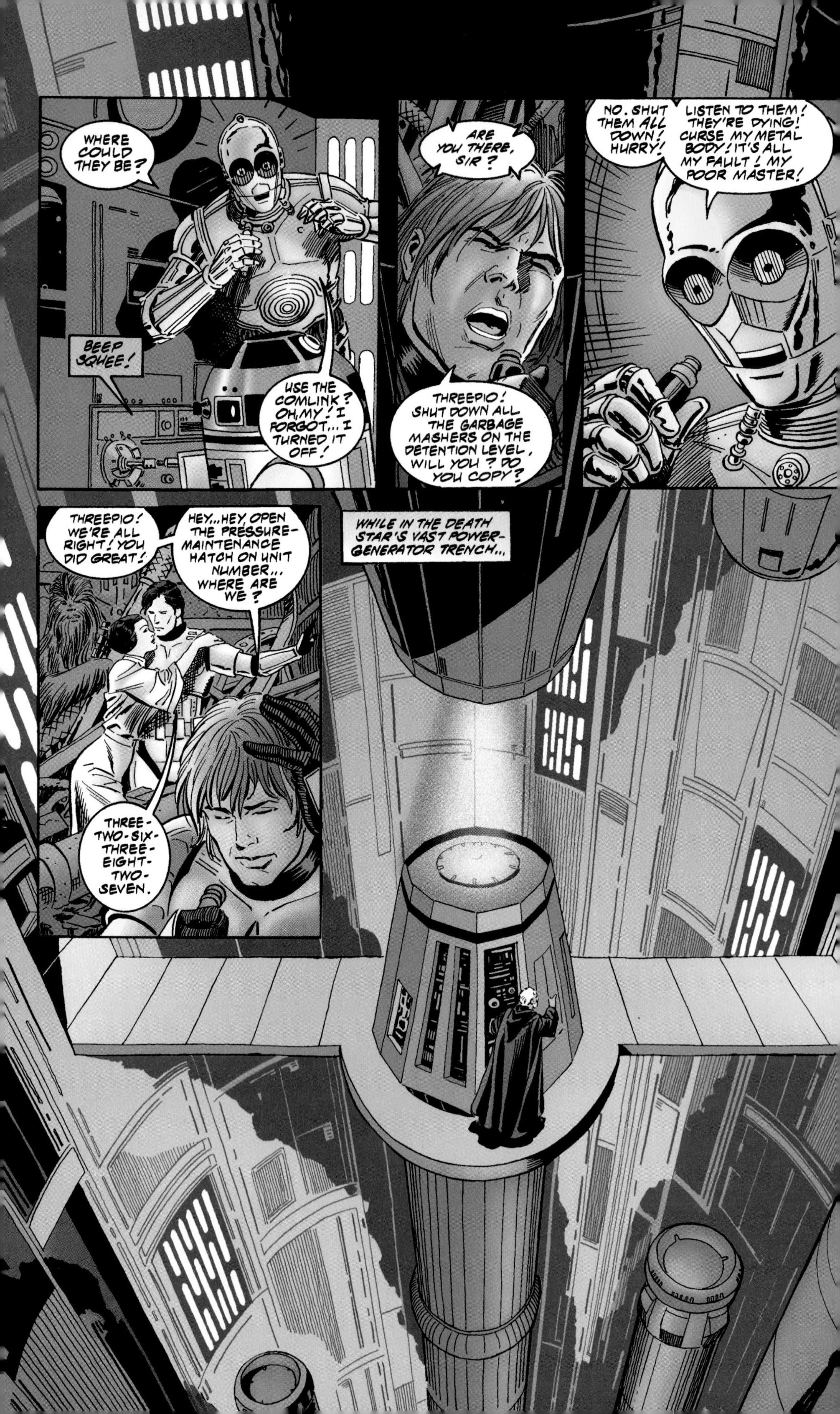

WHERE COULD THEY BE?
BEEP SQUEE!
USE THE COMLINK? OH, MY! I FORGOT... I TURNED IT OFF!
ARE YOU THERE, SIR?
THREEPIO! SHUT DOWN ALL THE GARBAGE MASHERS ON THE DETENTION LEVEL, WILL YOU? DO YOU COPY?
NO. SHUT THEM ALL DOWN! HURRY!
LISTEN TO THEM! THEY'RE DYING! CURSE MY METAL BODY! IT'S ALL MY FAULT! MY POOR MASTER!
THREEPIO! WE'RE ALL RIGHT! YOU DID GREAT!
HEY... HEY, OPEN THE PRESSURE-MAINTENANCE HATCH ON UNIT NUMBER... WHERE ARE WE?
THREE-TWO-SIX-THREE-EIGHT-TWO-SEVEN.
WHILE IN THE DEATH STAR'S VAST POWER-GENERATOR TRENCH...

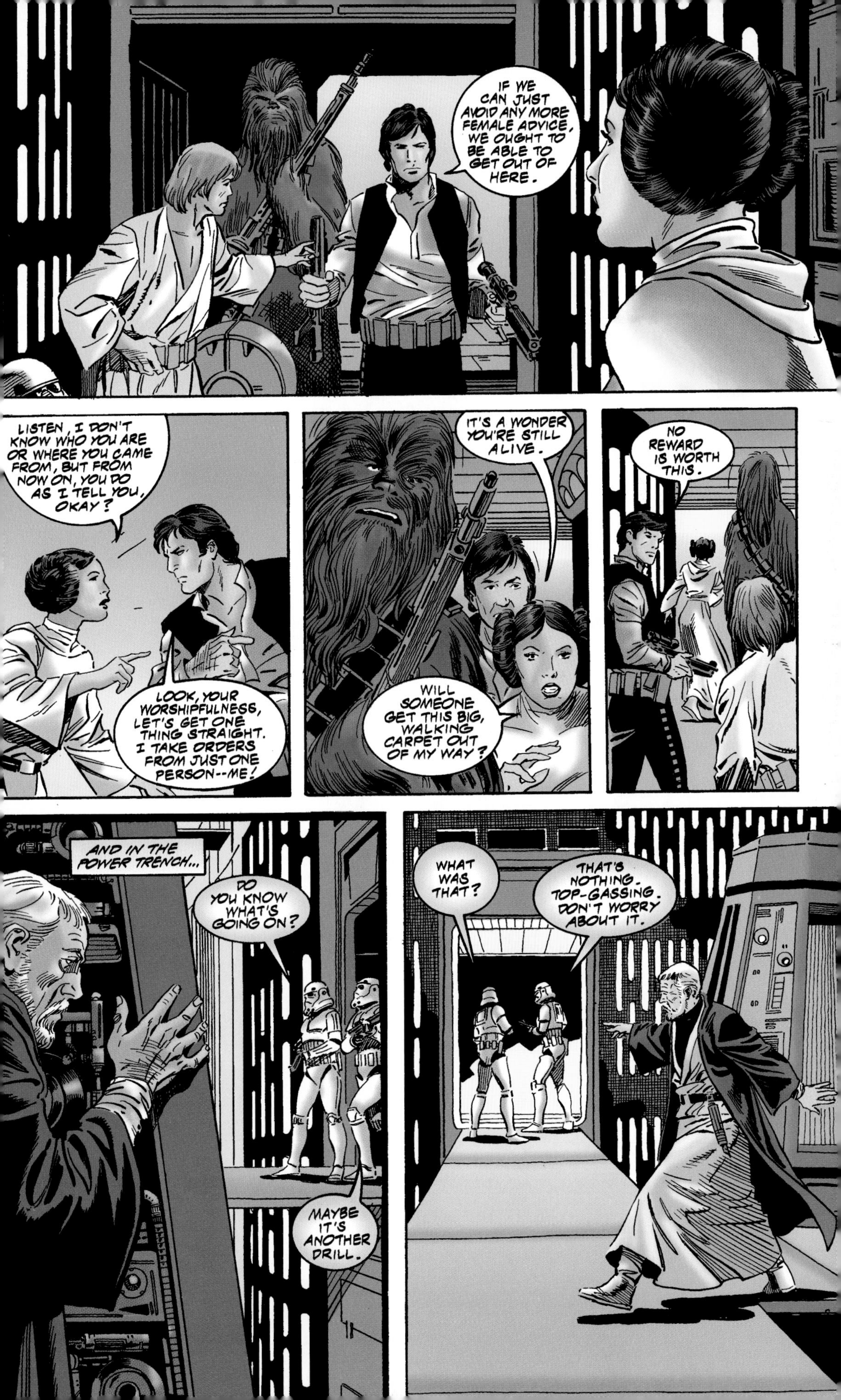
IF WE CAN JUST AVOID ANY MORE FEMALE ADVICE, WE OUGHT TO BE ABLE TO GET OUT OF HERE.
LISTEN, I DON'T KNOW WHO YOU ARE OR WHERE YOU CAME FROM, BUT FROM NOW ON, YOU DO AS I TELL YOU, OKAY?
LOOK, YOUR WORSHIPFULNESS, LET'S GET ONE THING STRAIGHT. I TAKE ORDERS FROM JUST ONE PERSON--ME!
IT'S A WONDER YOU'RE STILL ALIVE.
WILL SOMEONE GET THIS BIG, WALKING CARPET OUT OF MY WAY?
NO REWARD IS WORTH THIS.
AND IN THE POWER TRENCH...
DO YOU KNOW WHAT'S GOING ON?
MAYBE IT'S ANOTHER DRILL.
WHAT WAS THAT?
THAT'S NOTHING. TOP-GASSING. DON'T WORRY ABOUT IT.

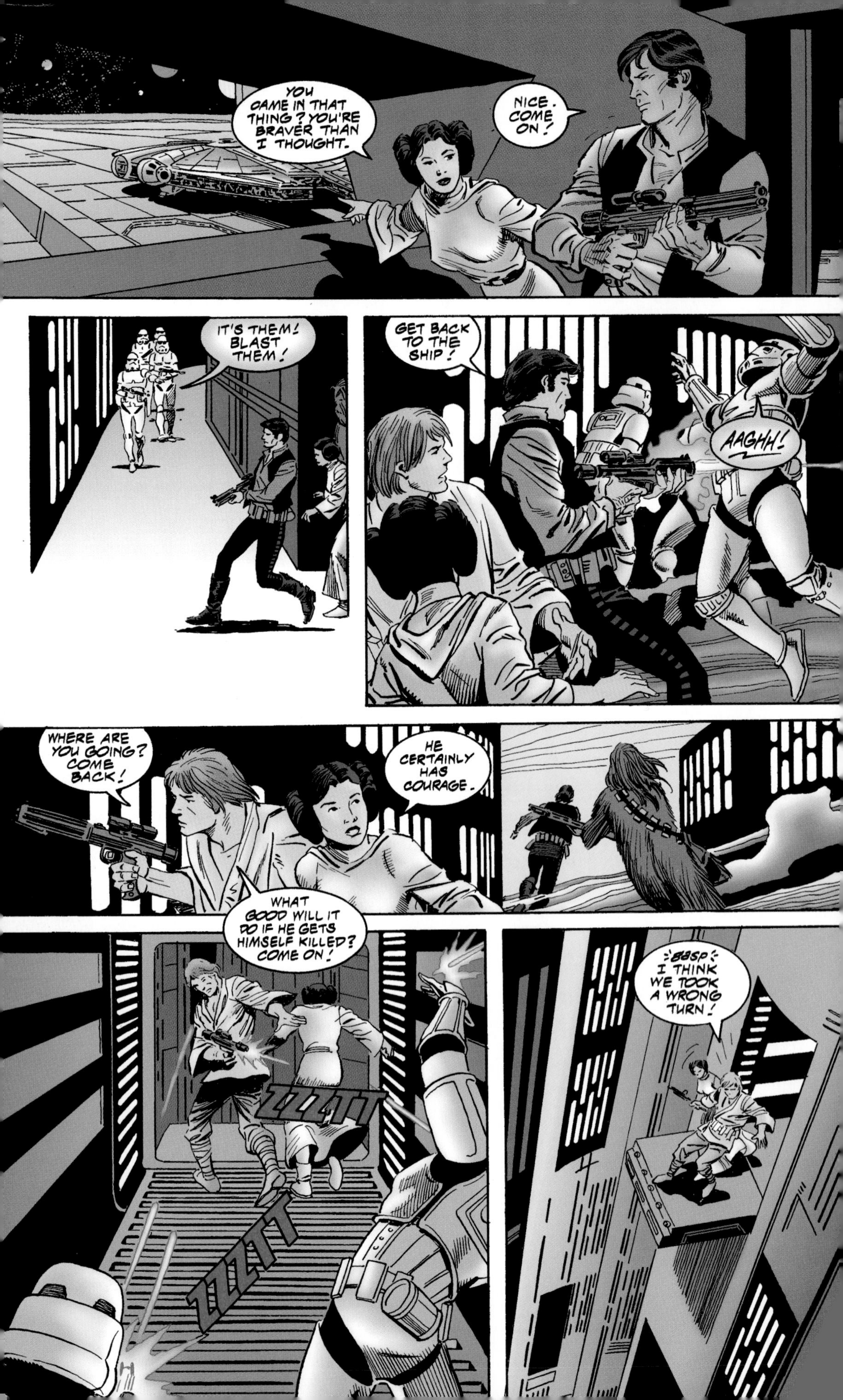

YOU CAME IN THAT THING? YOU'RE BRAVER THAN I THOUGHT.
NICE. COME ON!
IT'S THEM! BLAST THEM!
GET BACK TO THE SHIP!
AAGHH!
WHERE ARE YOU GOING? COME BACK!
HE CERTAINLY HAS COURAGE.
WHAT GOOD WILL IT DO IF HE GETS HIMSELF KILLED? COME ON!
ZZZTT
ZZZTT
GASP I THINK WE TOOK A WRONG TURN!

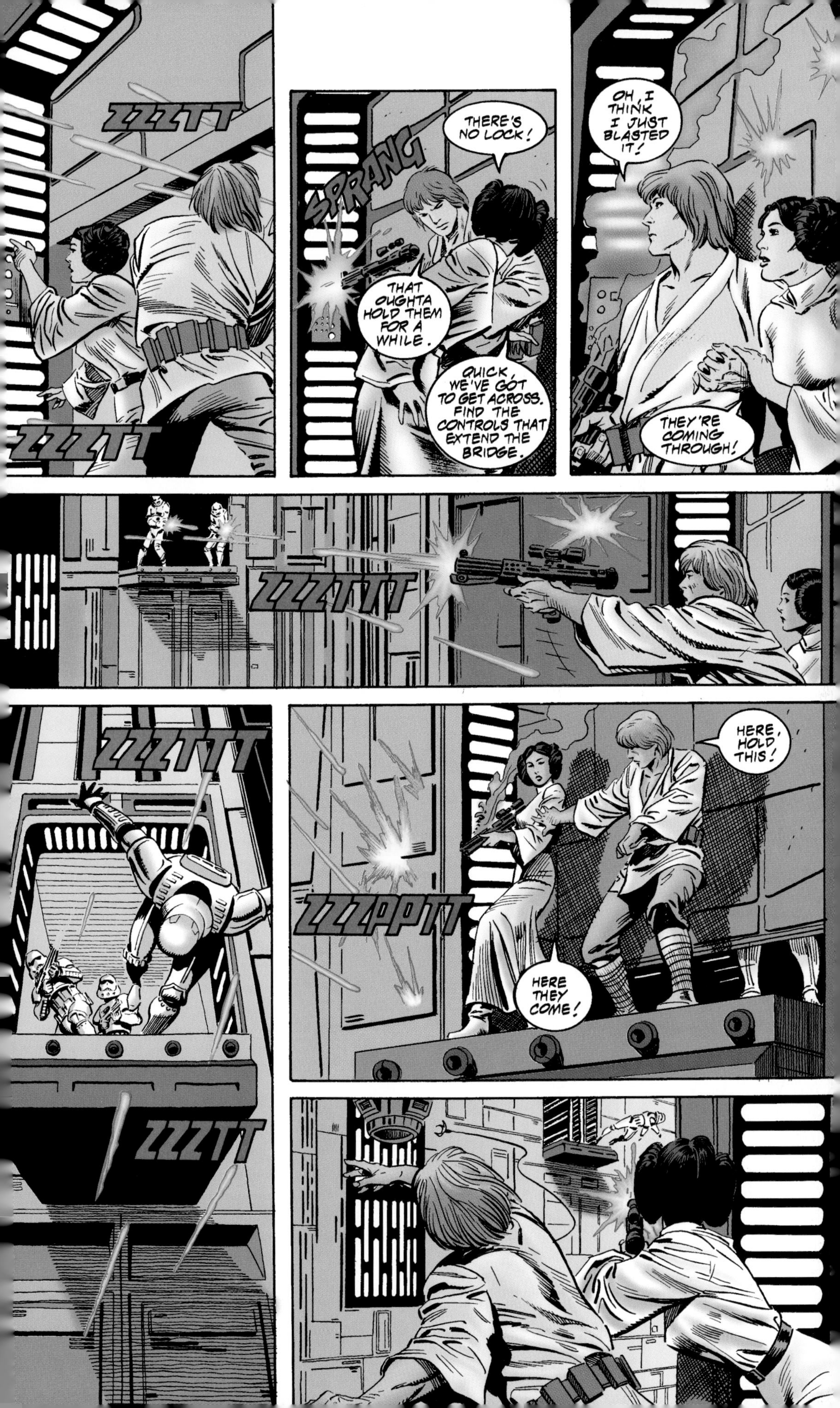
ZZZTT
ZZZTT
SPRANG
THERE'S NO LOCK!
THAT OUGHTA HOLD THEM FOR A WHILE.
QUICK, WE'VE GOT TO GET ACROSS. FIND THE CONTROLS THAT EXTEND THE BRIDGE.
OH, I THINK I JUST BLASTED IT!
THEY'RE COMING THROUGH!
ZZZTTT
ZZZTTT
ZZZTT
HERE, HOLD THIS!
ZZZPPTT
HERE THEY COME!

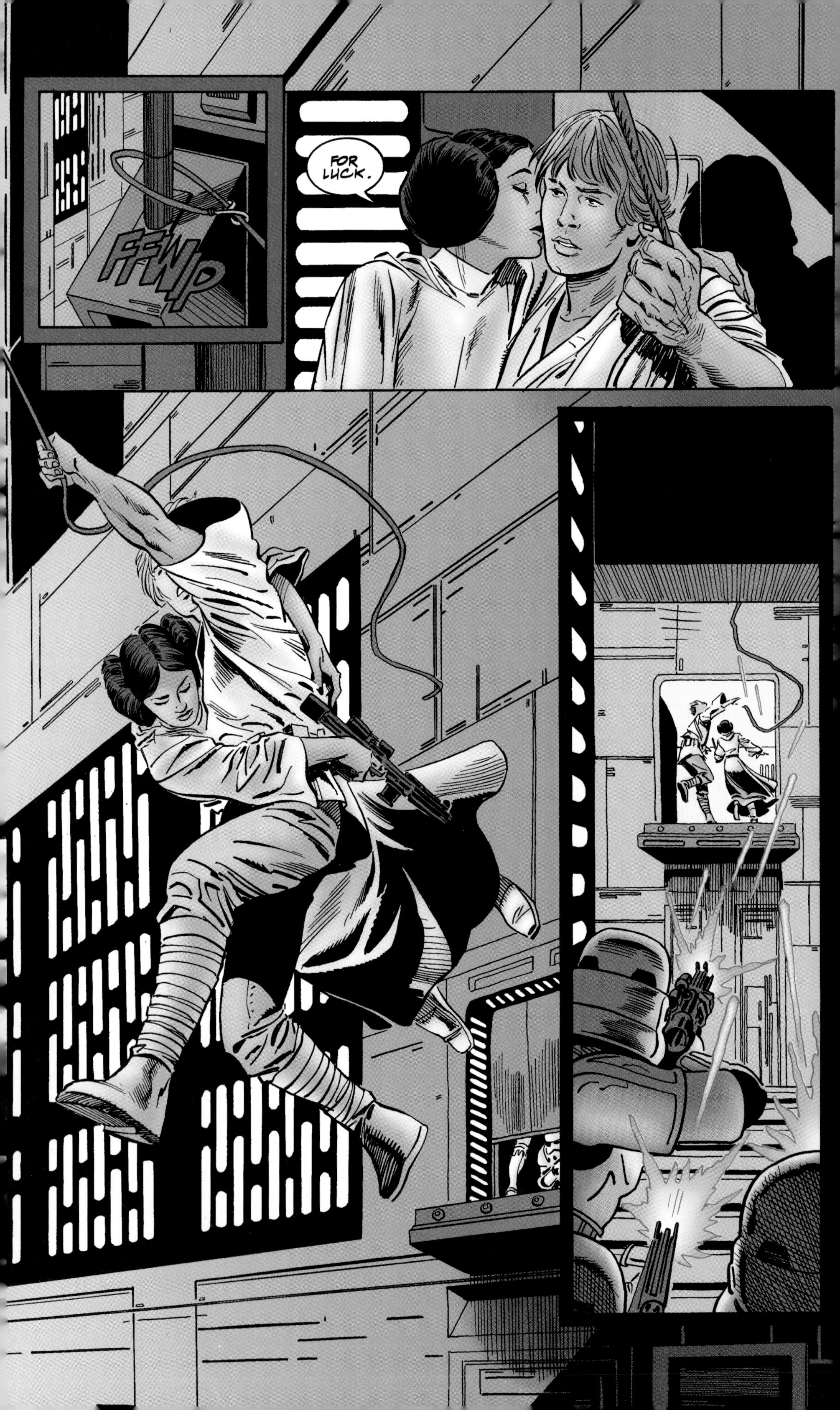
FFWIP
FOR LUCK.

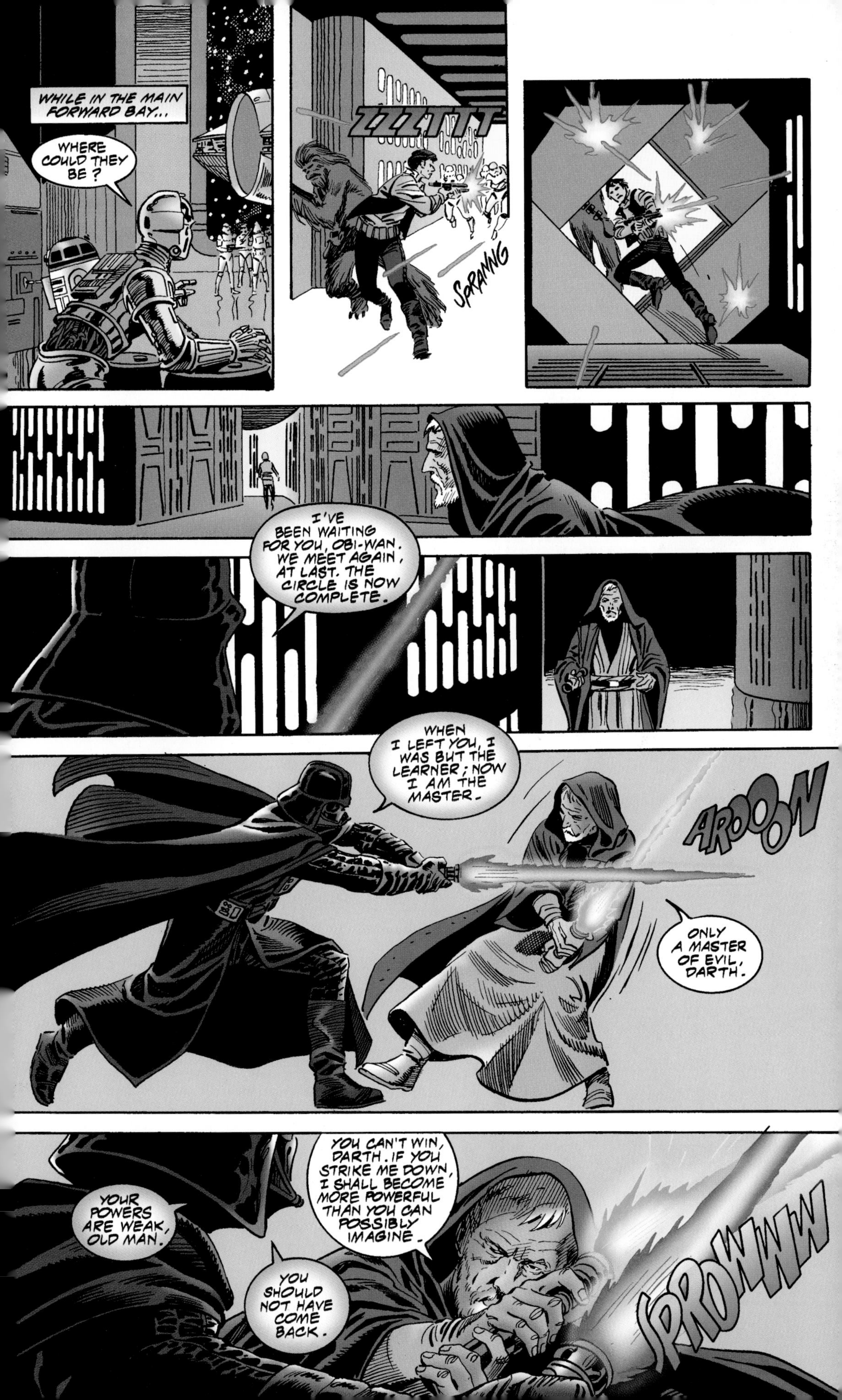
WHILE IN THE MAIN FORWARD BAY...
WHERE COULD THEY BE?
ZZZZTTT
SPRANNG
I'VE BEEN WAITING FOR YOU, OBI-WAN. WE MEET AGAIN, AT LAST. THE CIRCLE IS NOW COMPLETE.
WHEN I LEFT YOU, I WAS BUT THE LEARNER; NOW I AM THE MASTER.
AROOOON
ONLY A MASTER OF EVIL, DARTH.
YOUR POWERS ARE WEAK, OLD MAN.
YOU CAN'T WIN, DARTH. IF YOU STRIKE ME DOWN, I SHALL BECOME MORE POWERFUL THAN YOU CAN POSSIBLY IMAGINE.
YOU SHOULD NOT HAVE COME BACK.
SPROWWW

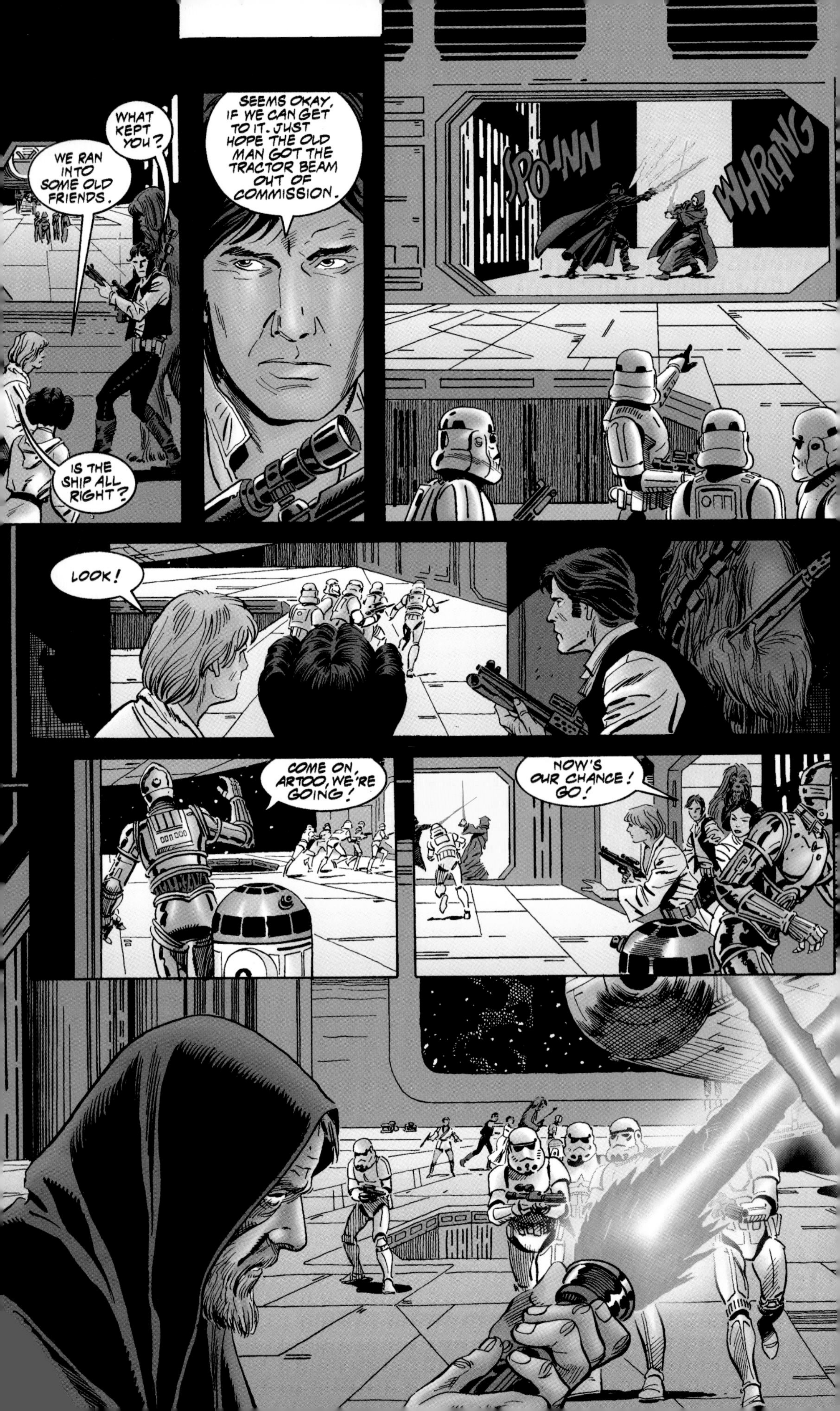
WHAT KEPT YOU?
WE RAN INTO SOME OLD FRIENDS.
IS THE SHIP ALL RIGHT?
SEEMS OKAY, IF WE CAN GET TO IT. JUST HOPE THE OLD MAN GOT THE TRACTOR BEAM OUT OF COMMISSION.
SPOHNN
WHRANG
LOOK!
COME ON, ARTOO, WE'RE GOING!
NOW'S OUR CHANCE! GO!

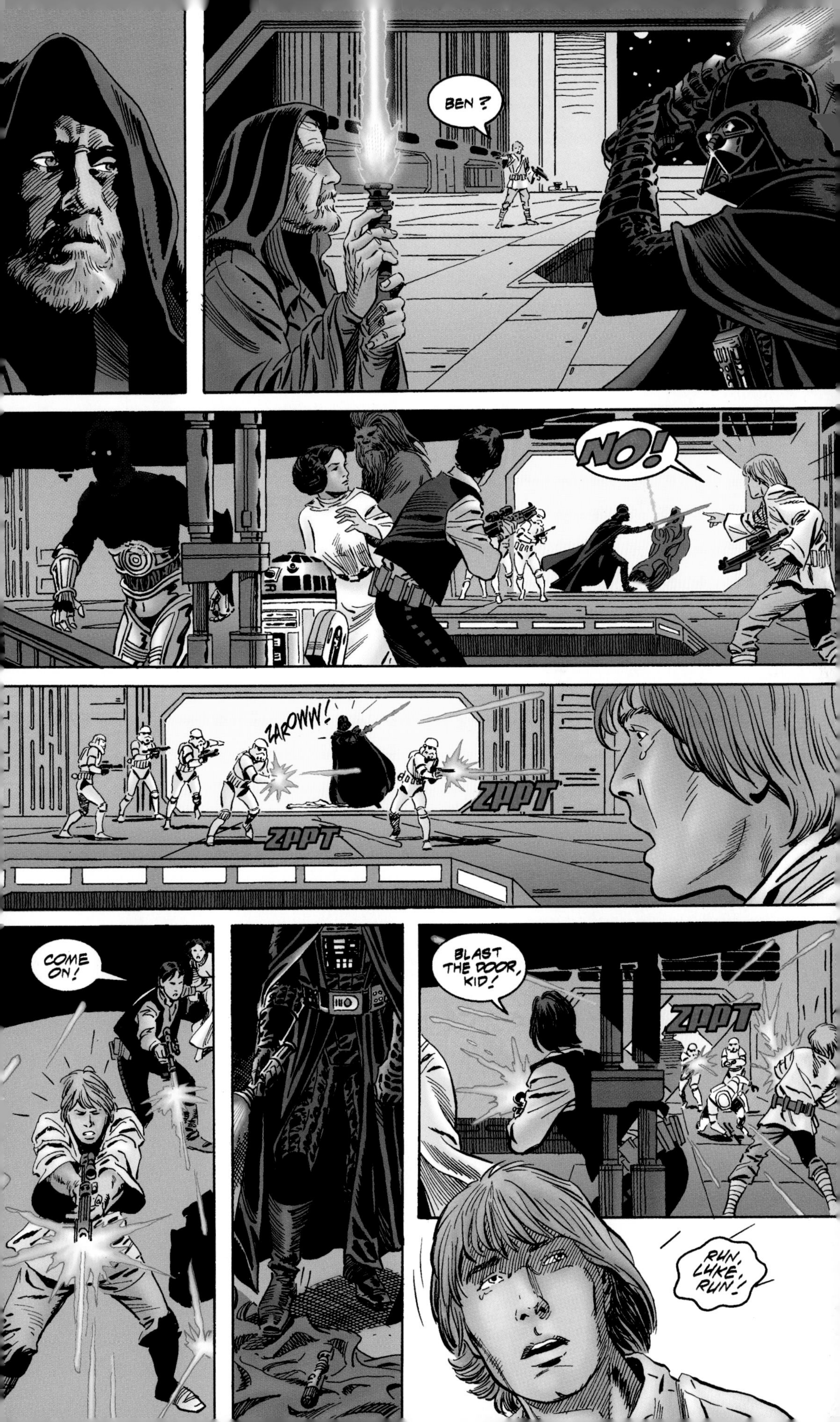
BEN ?
NO!
ZAROWW!
ZPPT
ZPPT
COME ON!
BLAST THE DOOR, KID!
ZPPT
RUN, LUKE, RUN!

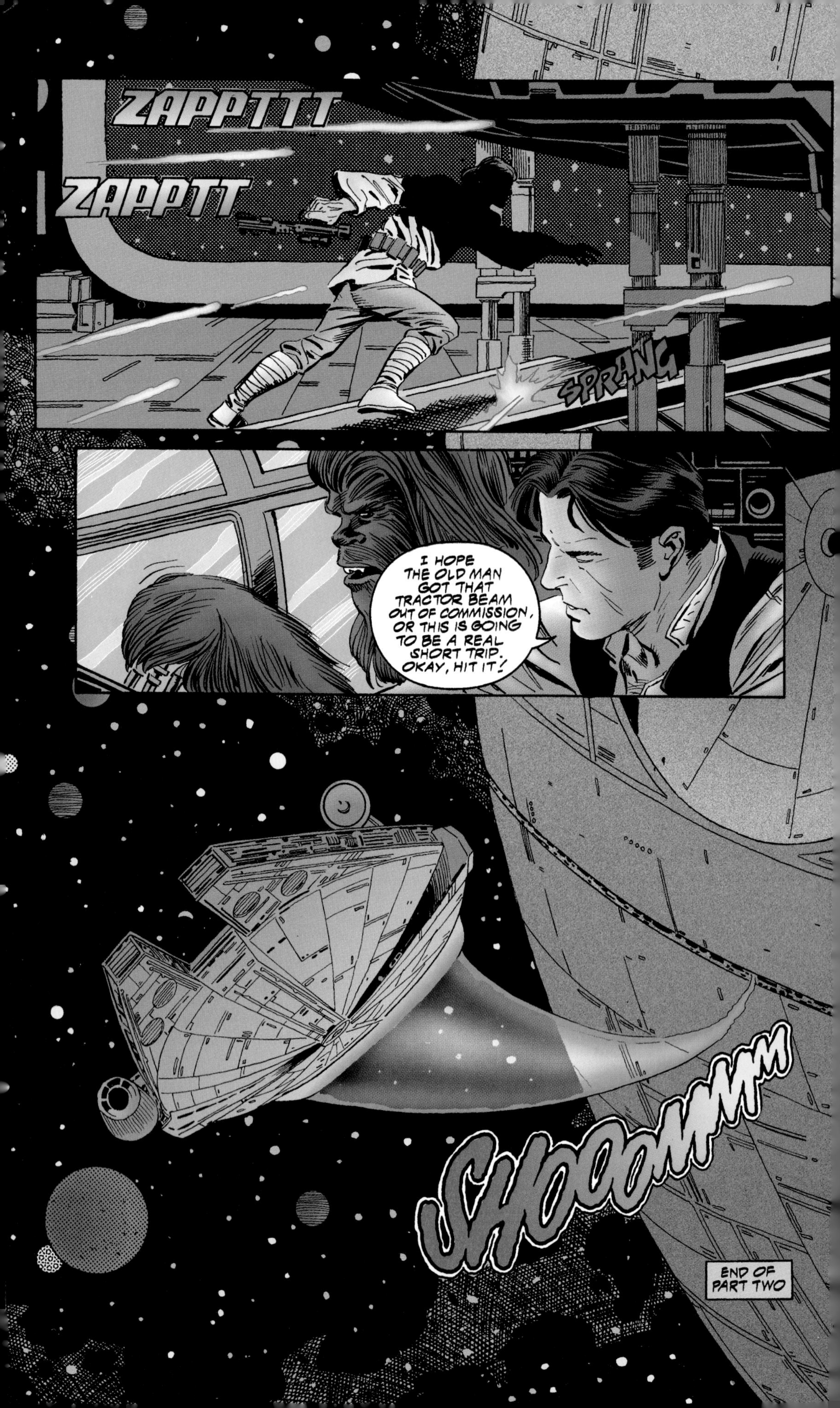
ZAPPTTT
ZAPPTT
SPRANG
I HOPE THE OLD MAN GOT THAT TRACTOR BEAM OUT OF COMMISSION, OR THIS IS GOING TO BE A REAL SHORT TRIP. OKAY, HIT IT!
SHOOOMMM
END OF PART TWO

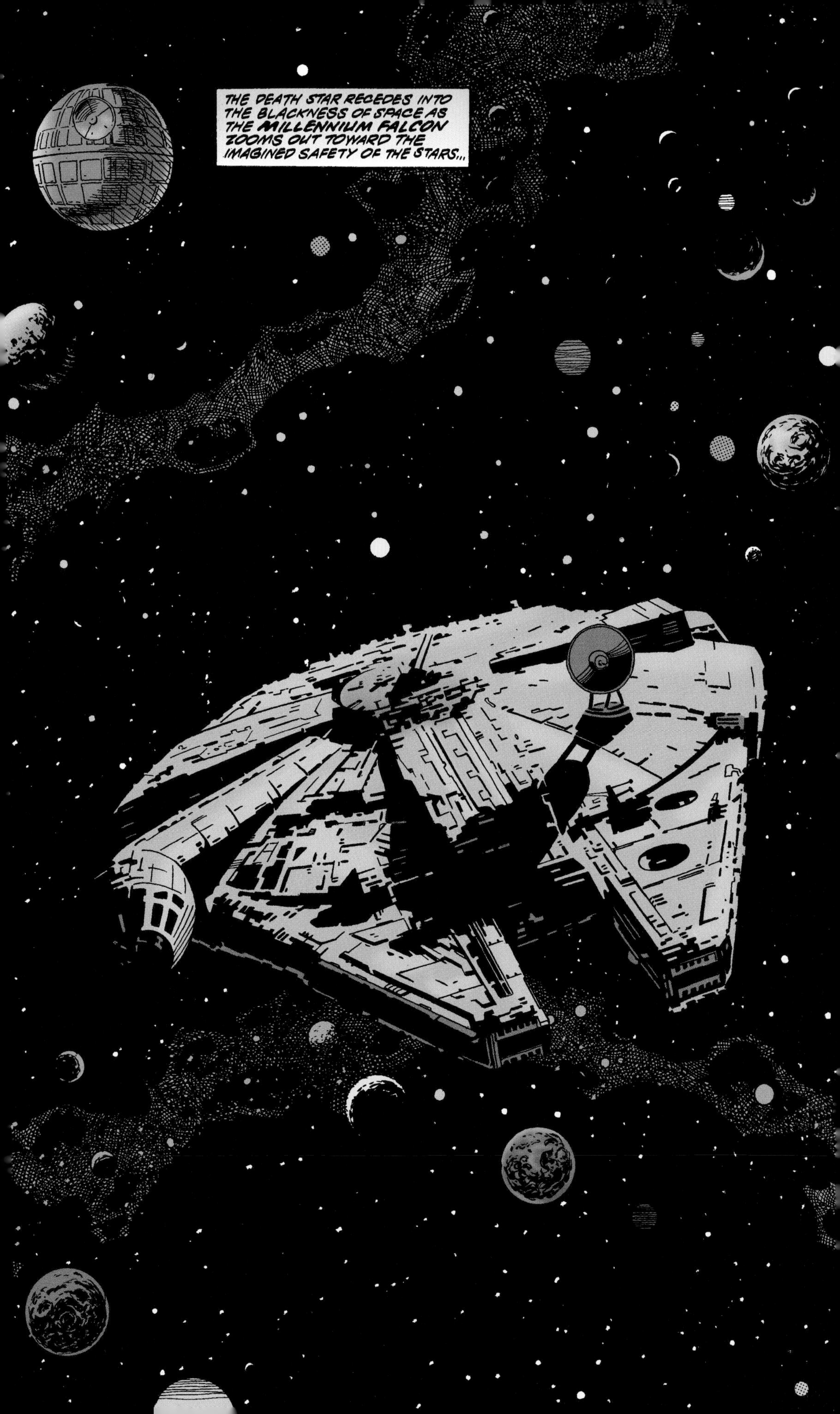
THE DEATH STAR RECEDES INTO THE BLACKNESS OF SPACE AS THE MILLENNIUM FALCON ZOOMS OUT TOWARD THE IMAGINED SAFETY OF THE STARS...

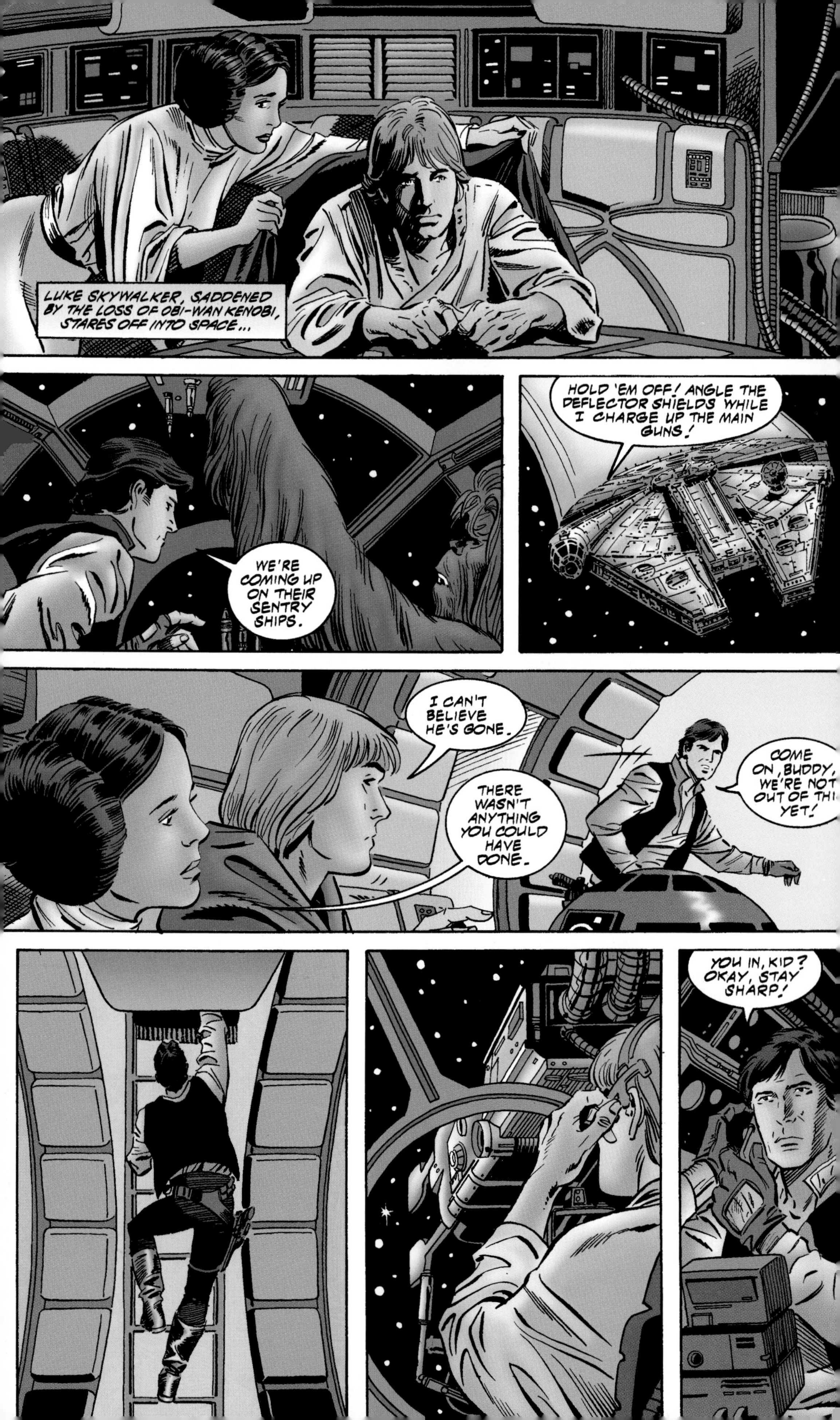
LUKE SKYWALKER, SADDENED BY THE LOSS OF OBI-WAN KENOBI, STARES OFF INTO SPACE...
WE'RE COMING UP ON THEIR SENTRY SHIPS.
HOLD 'EM OFF! ANGLE THE DEFLECTOR SHIELDS WHILE I CHARGE UP THE MAIN GUNS!
I CAN'T BELIEVE HE'S GONE.
THERE WASN'T ANYTHING YOU COULD HAVE DONE.
COME ON, BUDDY, WE'RE NOT OUT OF THI YET!
YOU IN, KID? OKAY, STAY SHARP!

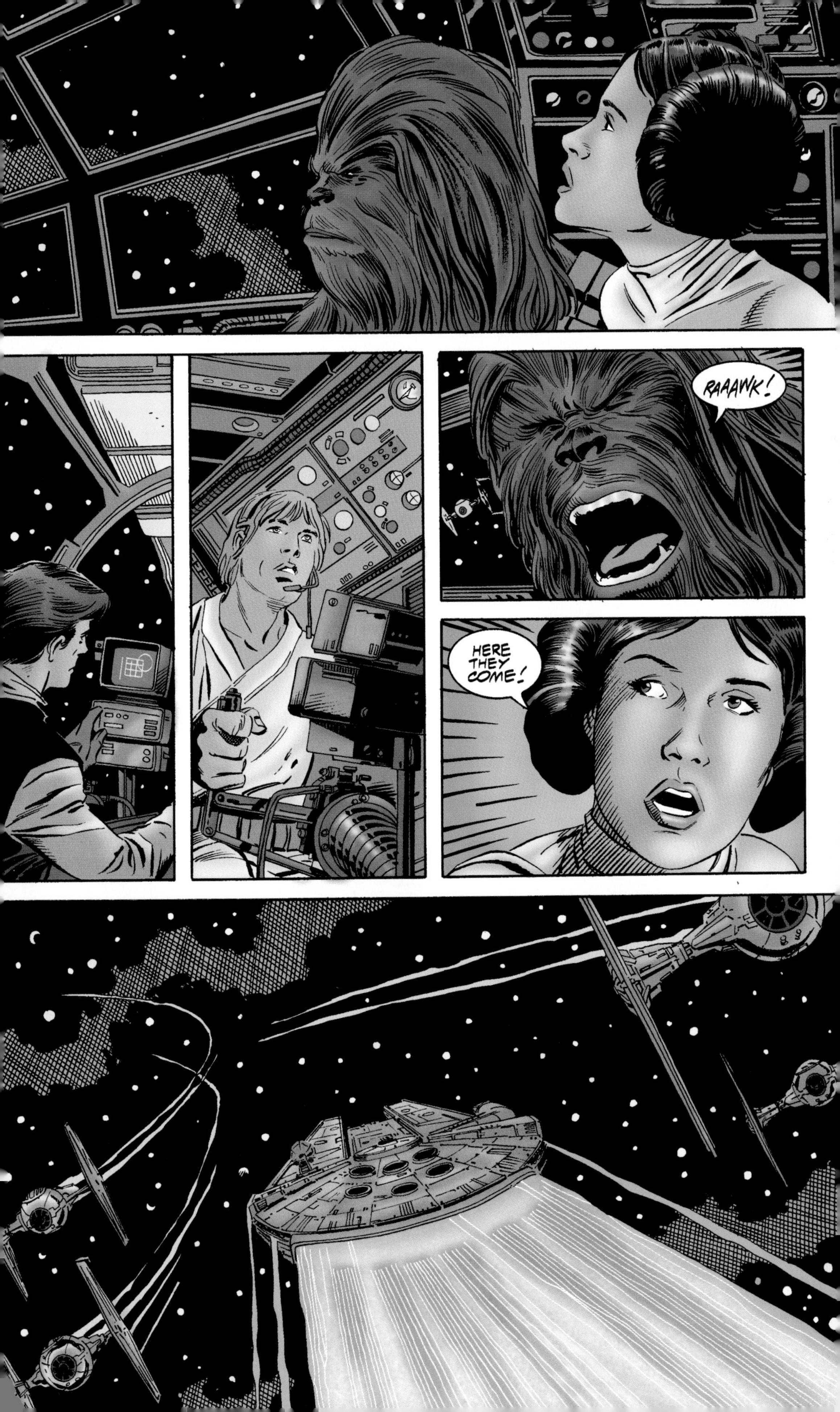
RAAAWK!
HERE THEY COME!

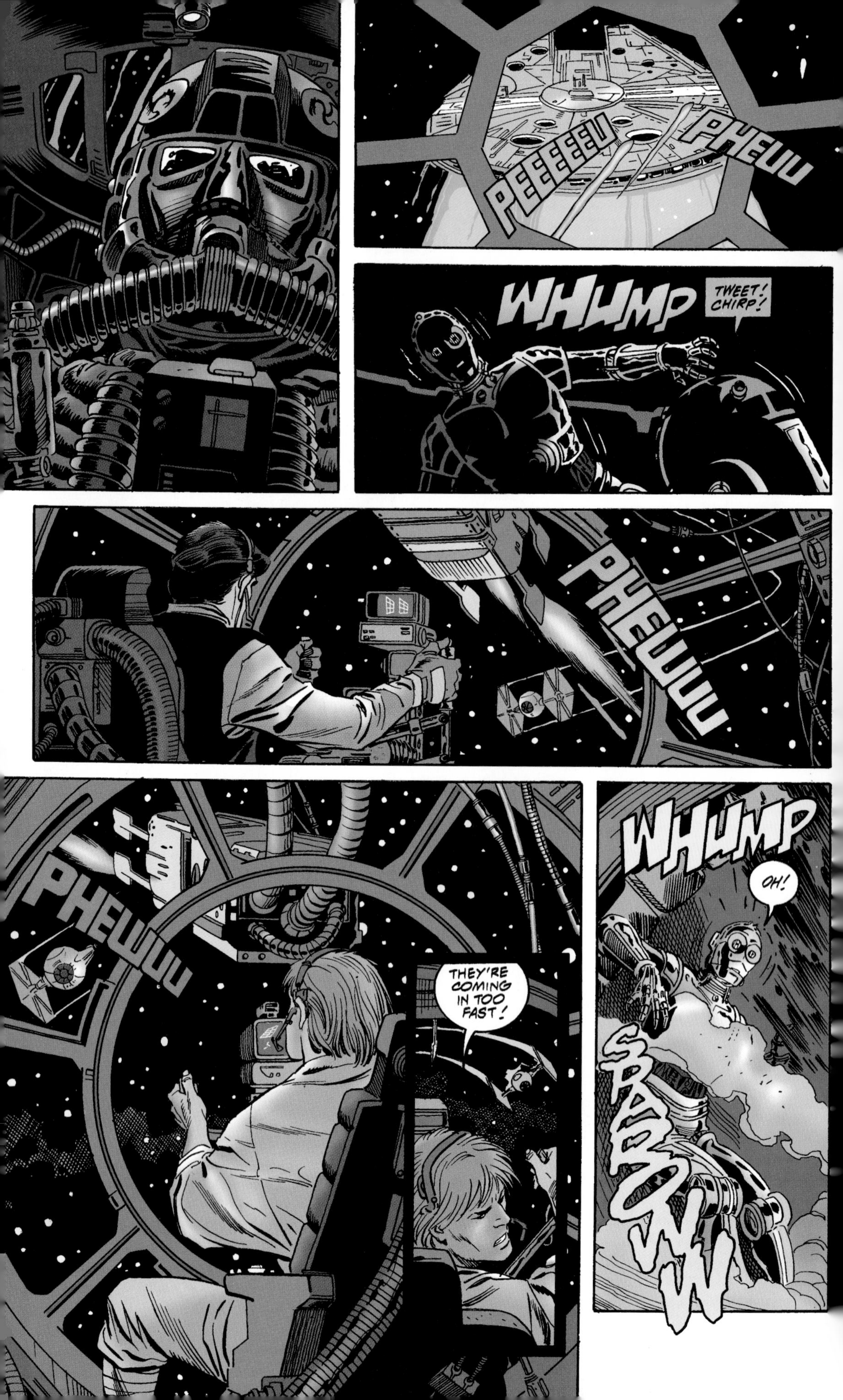
PEEEEEU
PHEUU
WHUMP
TWEET! CHIRP!
PHEUUU
PHEUUU
THEY'RE COMING IN TOO FAST!
WHUMP
OH!
SPABOWW

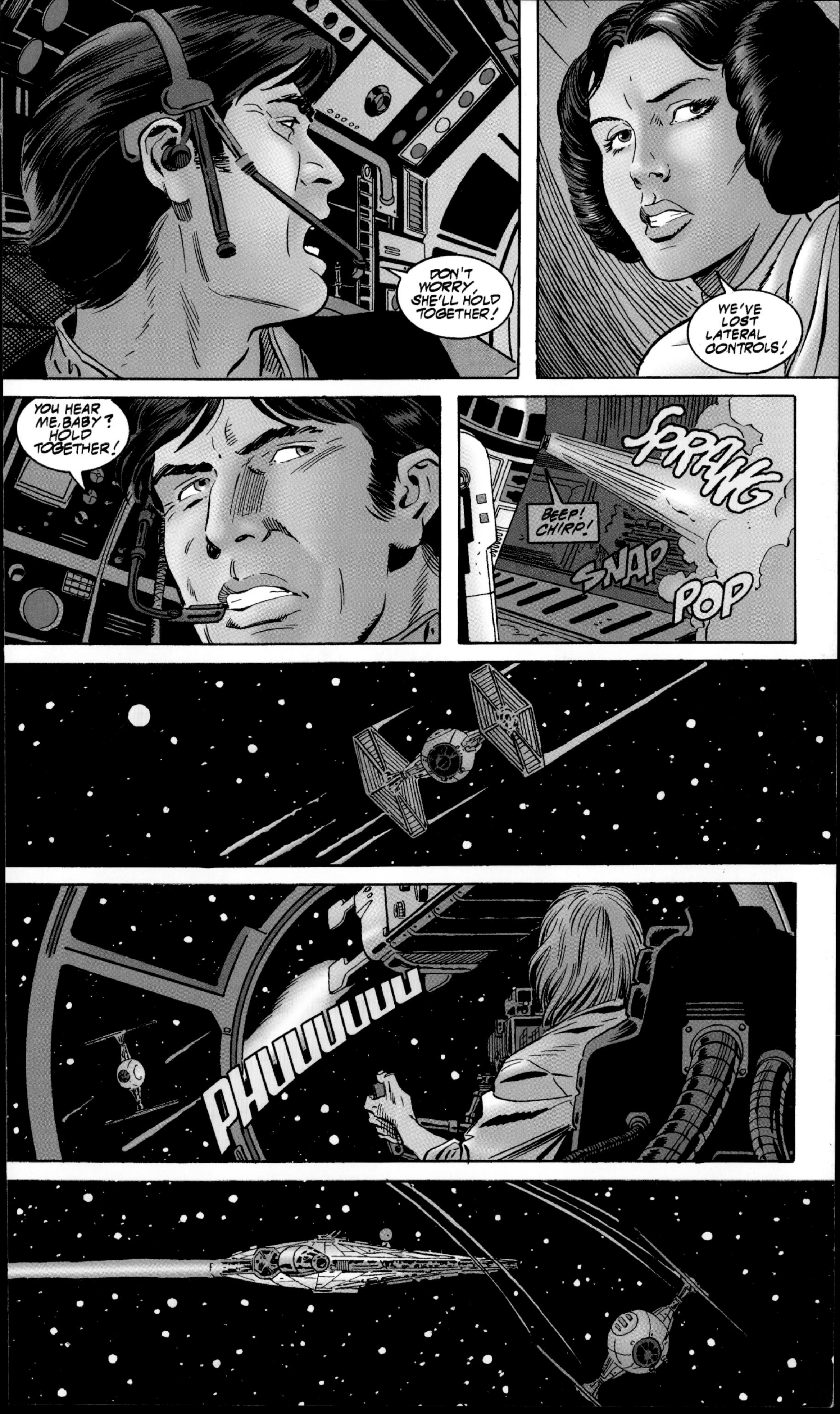
DON'T WORRY, SHE'LL HOLD TOGETHER!
WE'VE LOST LATERAL CONTROLS!
YOU HEAR ME, BABY? HOLD TOGETHER!
BEEP! CHIRP!
SPRANG
SNAP
POP
PHUUUUUUU

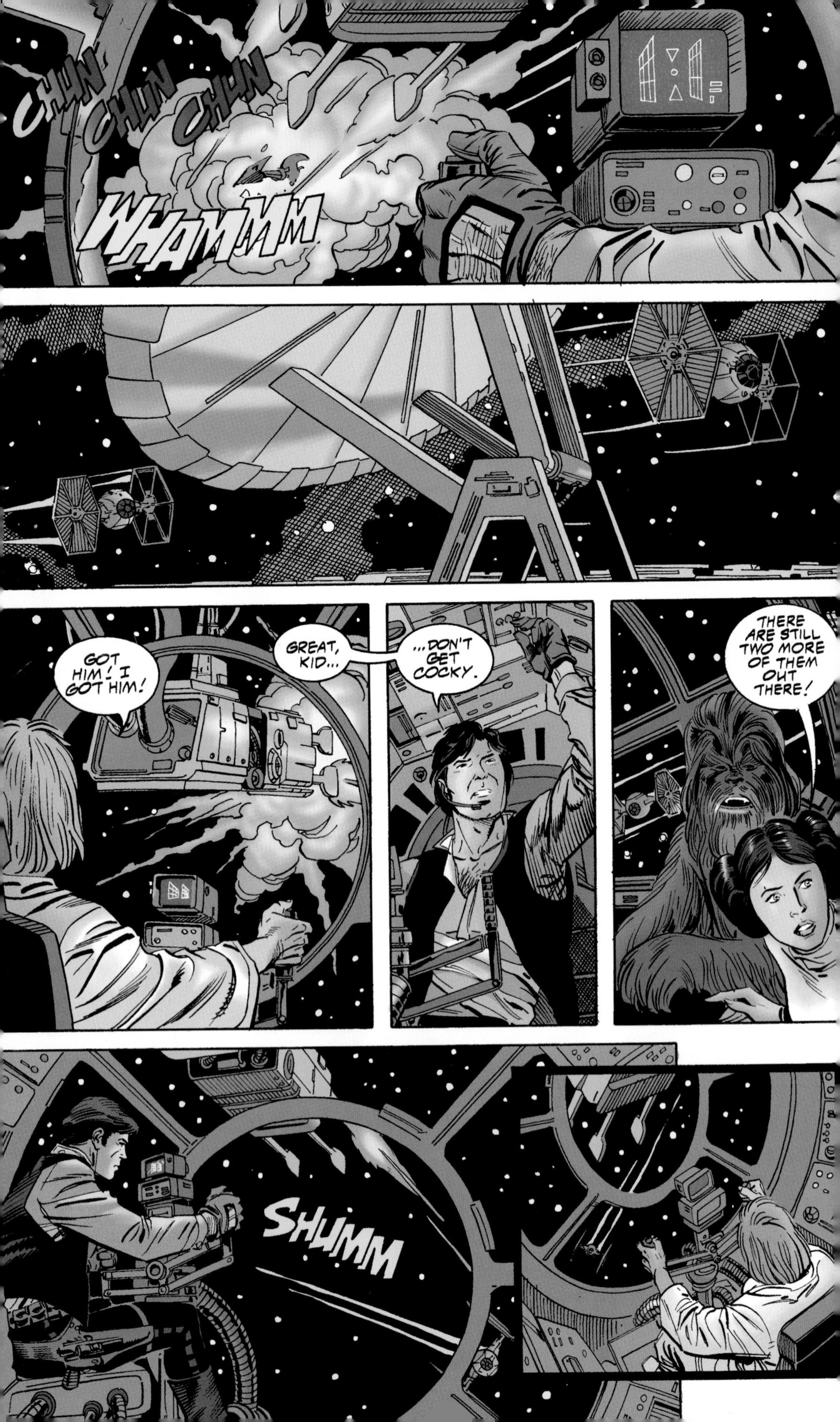
CHUN CHUN CHUN
WHAMMM
GOT HIM! I GOT HIM!
GREAT, KID...
...DON'T GET COCKY.
THERE ARE STILL TWO MORE OF THEM OUT THERE!
SHUMM

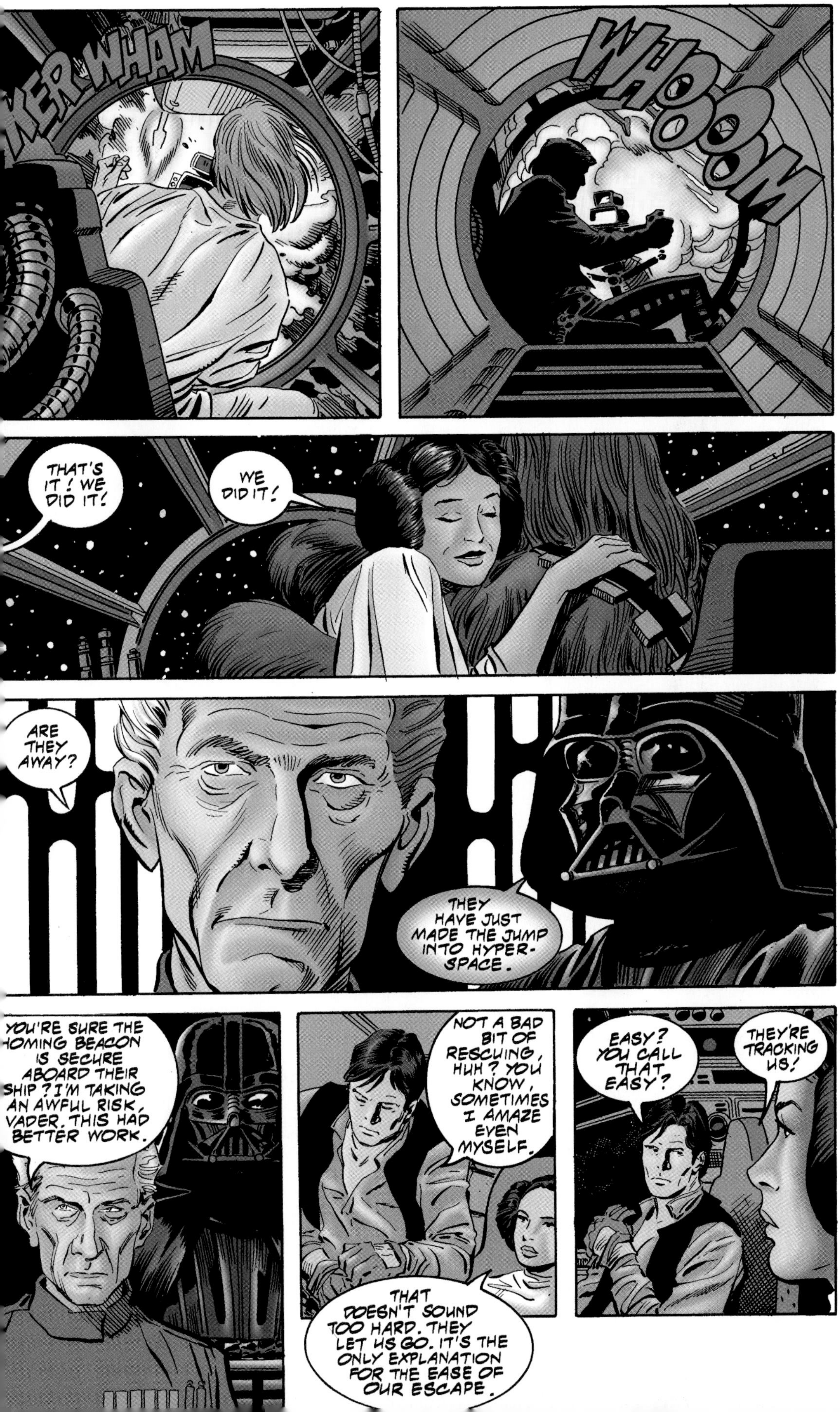
KER-WHAM
WHOOOOM
THAT'S IT! WE DID IT!
WE DID IT!
ARE THEY AWAY?
THEY HAVE JUST MADE THE JUMP INTO HYPER-SPACE.
YOU'RE SURE THE HOMING BEACON IS SECURE ABOARD THEIR SHIP? I'M TAKING AN AWFUL RISK, VADER. THIS HAD BETTER WORK.
NOT A BAD BIT OF RESCUING, HUH? YOU KNOW, SOMETIMES I AMAZE EVEN MYSELF.
THAT DOESN'T SOUND TOO HARD. THEY LET US GO. IT'S THE ONLY EXPLANATION FOR THE EASE OF OUR ESCAPE.
EASY? YOU CALL THAT EASY?
THEY'RE TRACKING US!

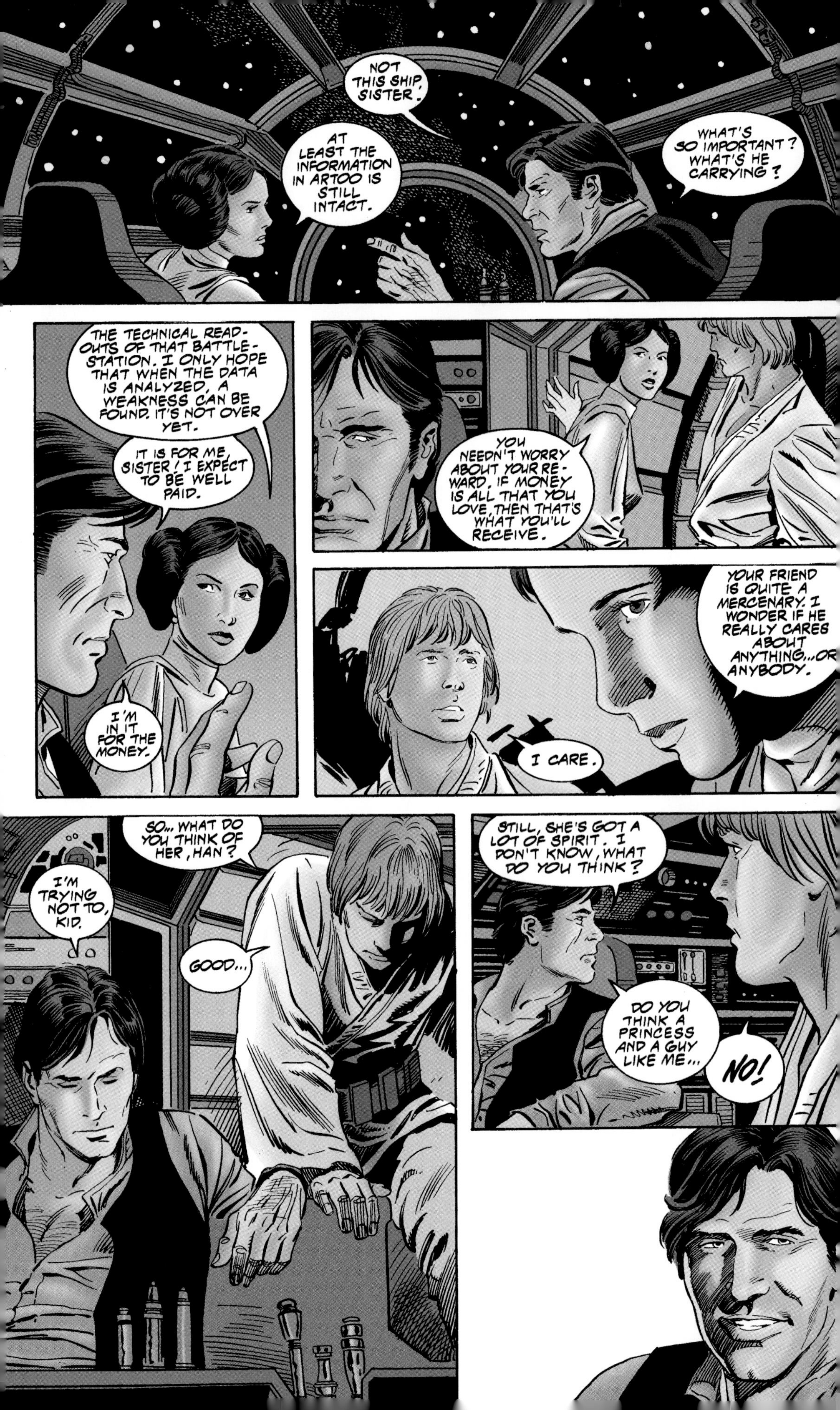
NOT THIS SHIP, SISTER.
AT LEAST THE INFORMATION IN ARTOO IS STILL INTACT.
WHAT'S SO IMPORTANT? WHAT'S HE CARRYING?
THE TECHNICAL READ-OUTS OF THAT BATTLE-STATION. I ONLY HOPE THAT WHEN THE DATA IS ANALYZED, A WEAKNESS CAN BE FOUND. IT'S NOT OVER YET.
IT IS FOR ME, SISTER! I EXPECT TO BE WELL PAID.
I'M IN IT FOR THE MONEY.
YOU NEEDN'T WORRY ABOUT YOUR RE-WARD. IF MONEY IS ALL THAT YOU LOVE, THEN THAT'S WHAT YOU'LL RECEIVE.
YOUR FRIEND IS QUITE A MERCENARY. I WONDER IF HE REALLY CARES ABOUT ANYTHING...OR ANYBODY.
I CARE.
SO... WHAT DO YOU THINK OF HER, HAN?
I'M TRYING NOT TO, KID.
GOOD...
STILL, SHE'S GOT A LOT OF SPIRIT. I DON'T KNOW, WHAT DO YOU THINK?
DO YOU THINK A PRINCESS AND A GUY LIKE ME...
NO!

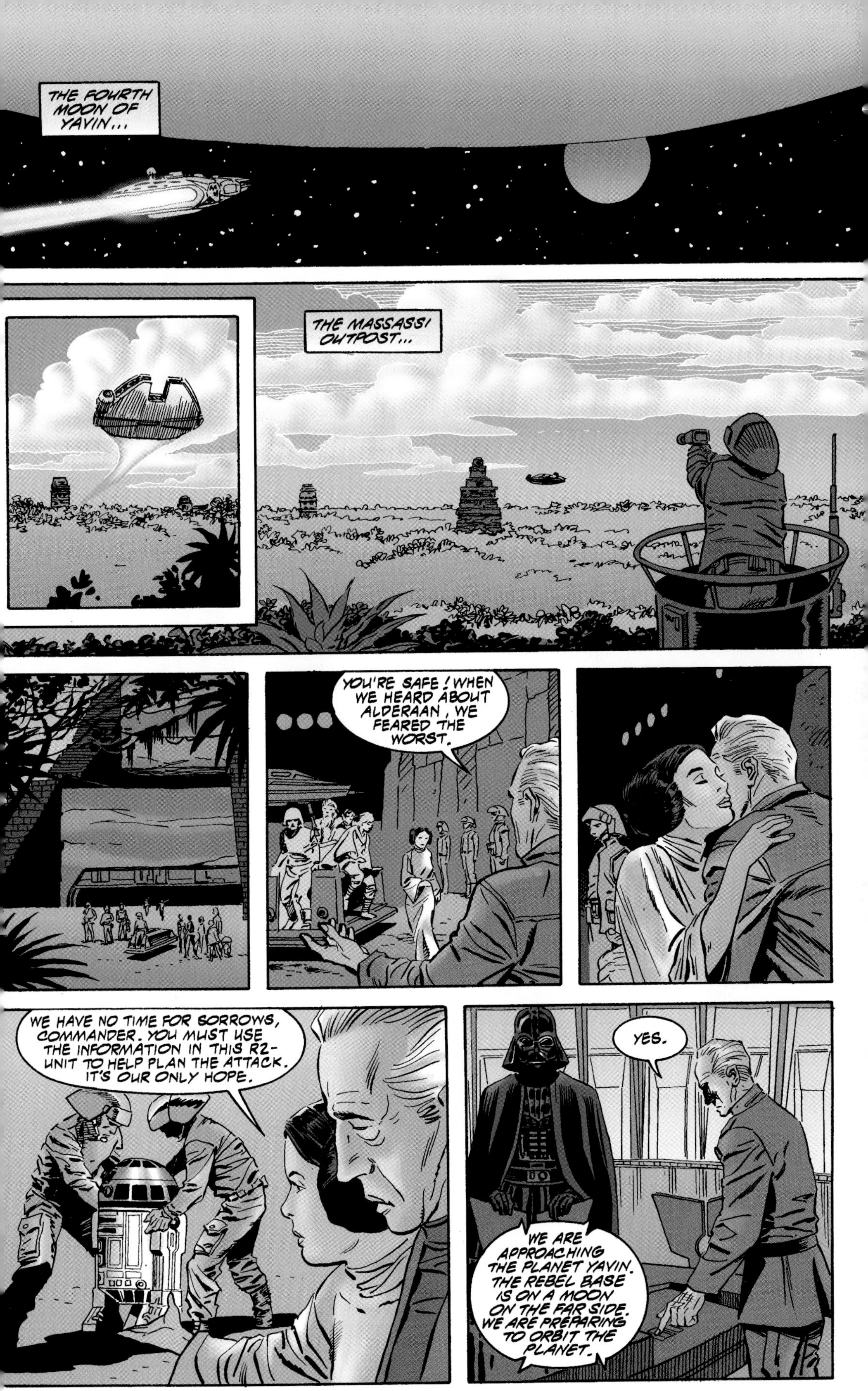
THE FOURTH MOON OF YAVIN...
THE MASSASSI OUTPOST...
YOU'RE SAFE! WHEN WE HEARD ABOUT ALDERAAN, WE FEARED THE WORST.
WE HAVE NO TIME FOR SORROWS, COMMANDER. YOU MUST USE THE INFORMATION IN THIS R2-UNIT TO HELP PLAN THE ATTACK. IT'S OUR ONLY HOPE.
WE ARE APPROACHING THE PLANET YAVIN. THE REBEL BASE IS ON A MOON ON THE FAR SIDE. WE ARE PREPARING TO ORBIT THE PLANET.
YES.

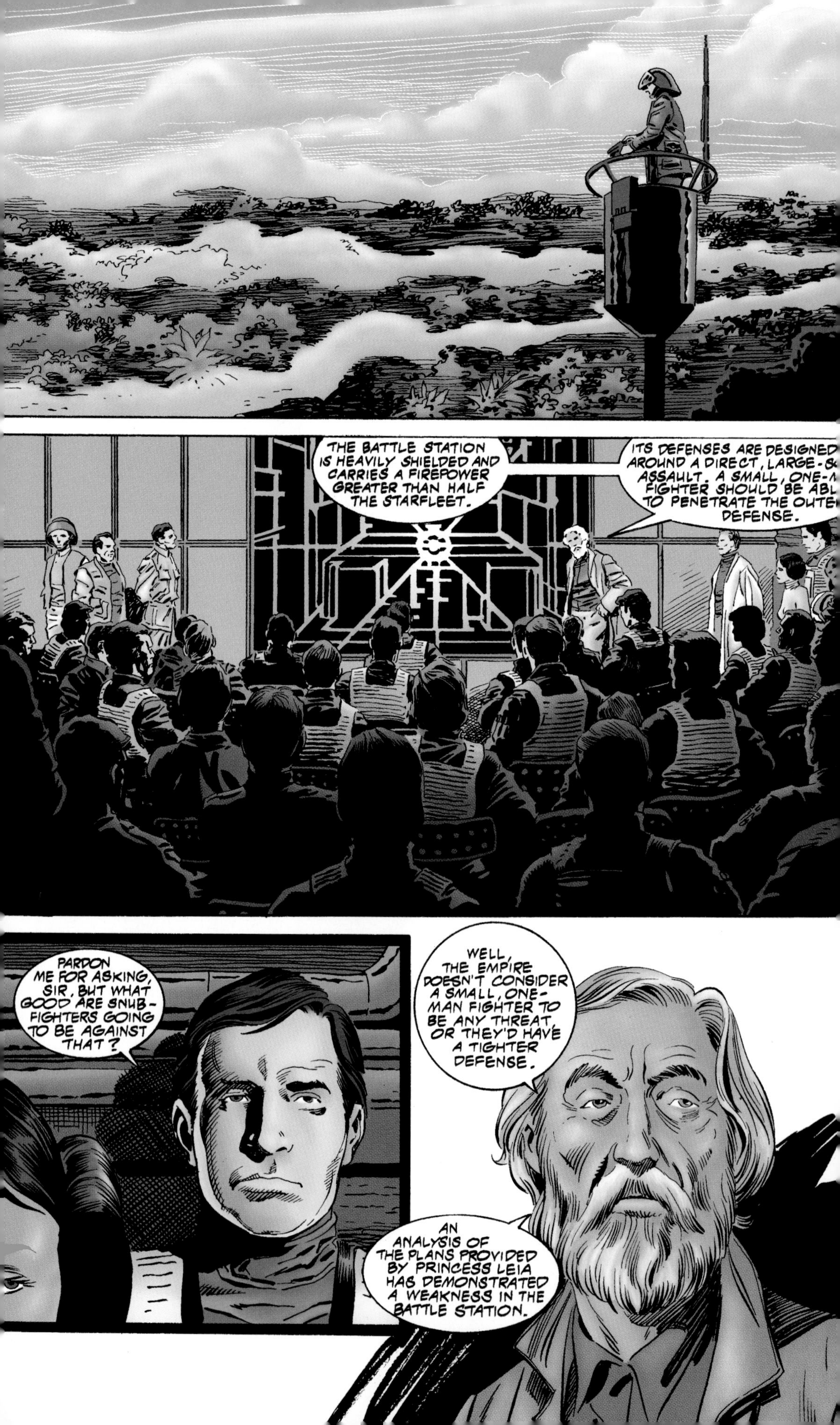
THE BATTLE STATION IS HEAVILY SHIELDED AND CARRIES A FIREPOWER GREATER THAN HALF THE STARFLEET.
ITS DEFENSES ARE DESIGNED AROUND A DIRECT, LARGE-SC ASSAULT. A SMALL, ONE-M FIGHTER SHOULD BE ABL TO PENETRATE THE OUTE DEFENSE.
PARDON ME FOR ASKING, SIR, BUT WHAT GOOD ARE SNUB-FIGHTERS GOING TO BE AGAINST THAT?
WELL, THE EMPIRE DOESN'T CONSIDER A SMALL, ONE-MAN FIGHTER TO BE ANY THREAT, OR THEY'D HAVE A TIGHTER DEFENSE.
AN ANALYSIS OF THE PLANS PROVIDED BY PRINCESS LEIA HAS DEMONSTRATED A WEAKNESS IN THE BATTLE STATION.

THE APPROACH WILL NOT BE EASY. YOU ARE REQUIRED TO MANEUVER STRAIGHT DOWN THIS TRENCH AND SKIM THE SURFACE TO THIS POINT...

...THE TARGET AREA IS ONLY TWO METERS WIDE. IT'S A SMALL, THERMAL-EXHAUST PORT, RIGHT BELOW THE MAIN PORT.

THE SHAFT LEADS DIRECTLY TO THE REACTOR SYSTEM.

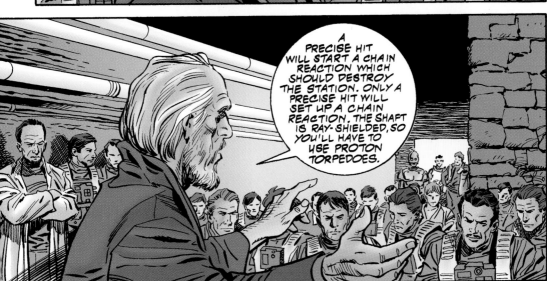

A PRECISE HIT WILL START A CHAIN REACTION WHICH SHOULD DESTROY THE STATION. ONLY A PRECISE HIT WILL SET UP A CHAIN REACTION. THE SHAFT IS RAY-SHIELDED, SO YOU'LL HAVE TO USE PROTON TORPEDOES.

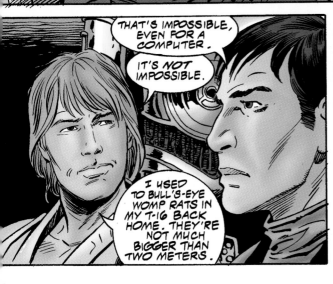

THAT'S IMPOSSIBLE, EVEN FOR A COMPUTER.

IT'S NOT IMPOSSIBLE.

I USED TO BULL'S-EYE WOMP RATS IN MY T-16 BACK HOME. THEY'RE NOT MUCH BIGGER THAN TWO METERS.

THEN MAN YOUR SHIPS! AND MAY THE FORCE BE WITH YOU!

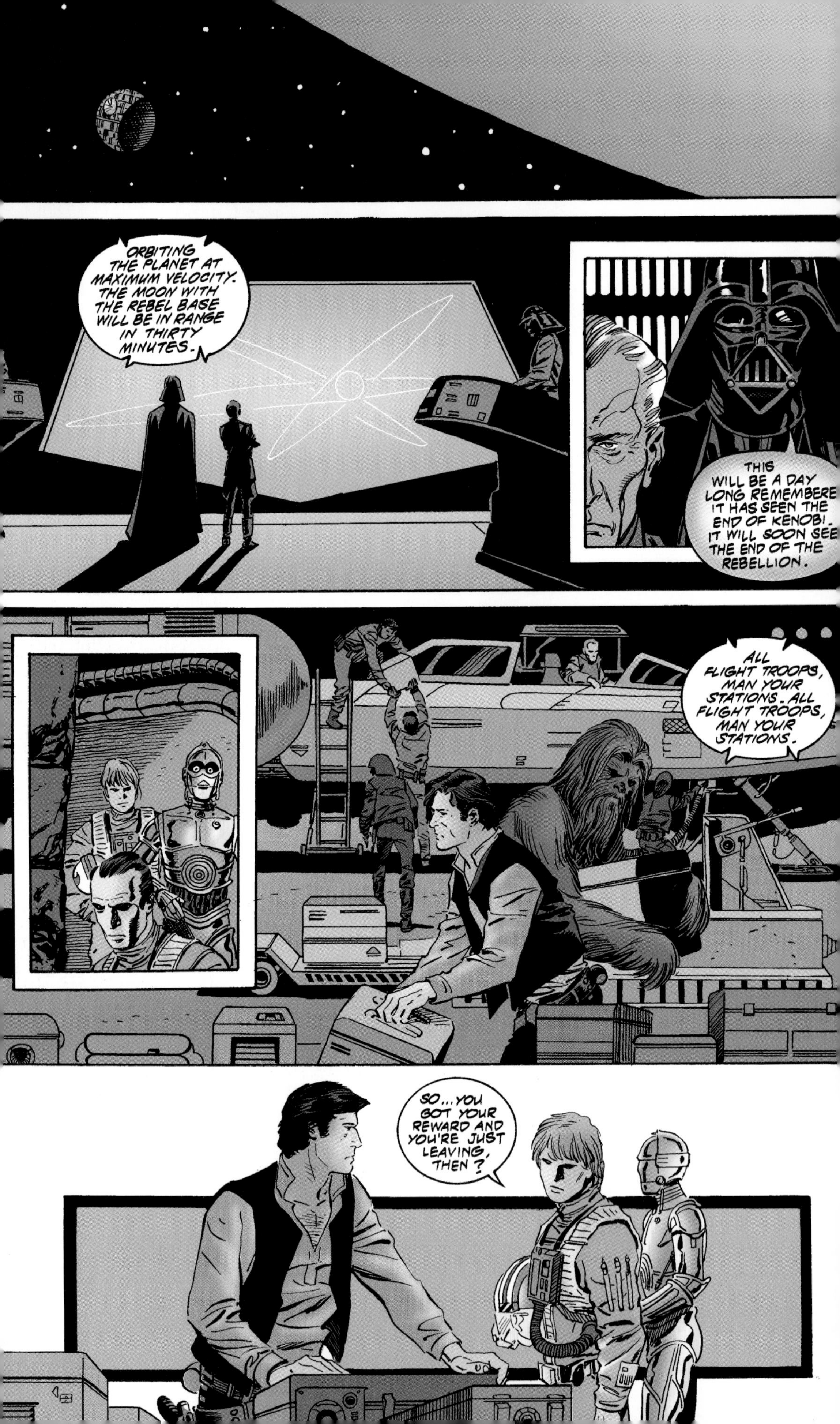
ORBITING THE PLANET AT MAXIMUM VELOCITY. THE MOON WITH THE REBEL BASE WILL BE IN RANGE IN THIRTY MINUTES.
THIS WILL BE A DAY LONG REMEMBERE IT HAS SEEN THE END OF KENOBI. IT WILL SOON SEE THE END OF THE REBELLION.
ALL FLIGHT TROOPS, MAN YOUR STATIONS. ALL FLIGHT TROOPS, MAN YOUR STATIONS.
SO... YOU GOT YOUR REWARD AND YOU'RE JUST LEAVING, THEN?

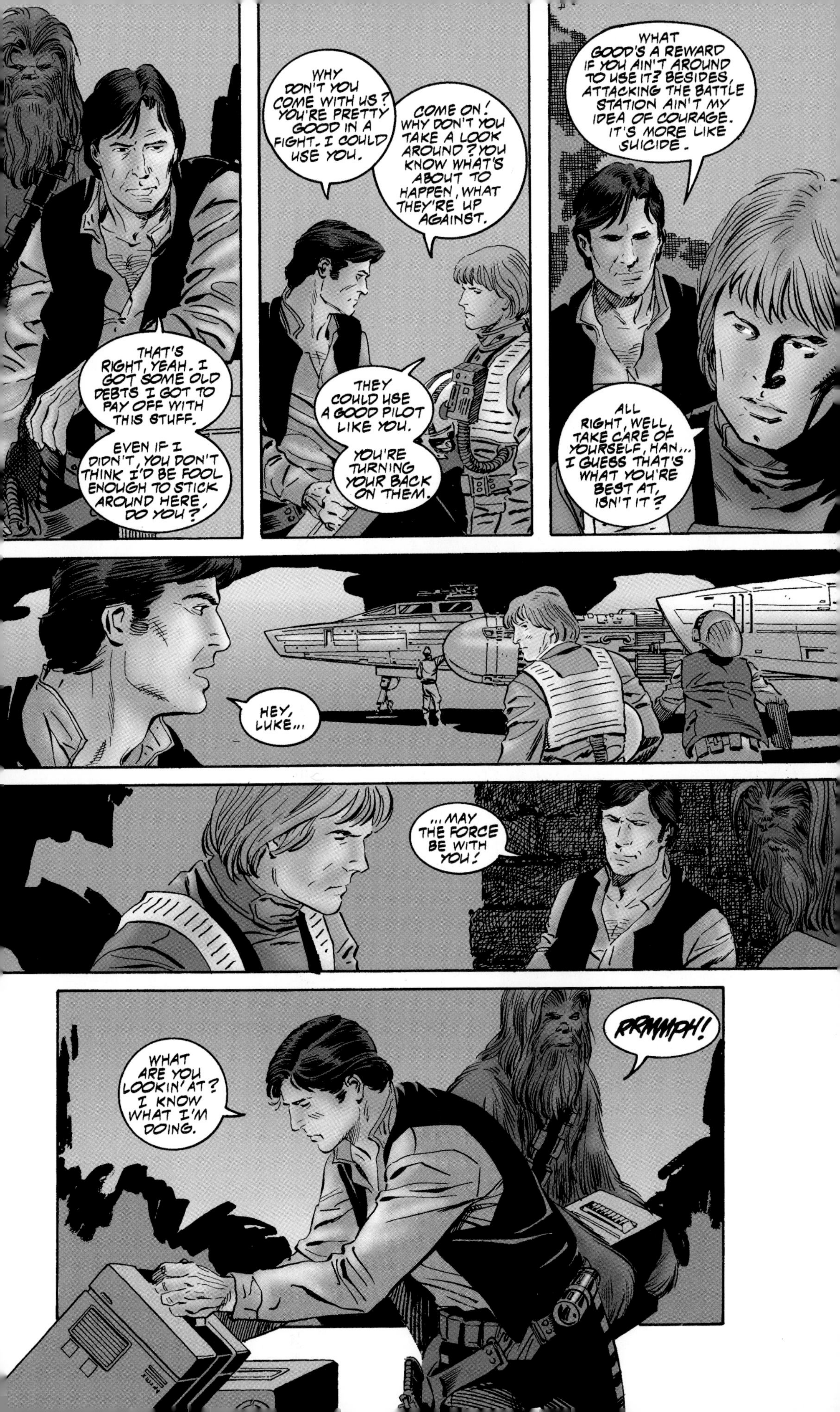
THAT'S RIGHT, YEAH. I GOT SOME OLD DEBTS I GOT TO PAY OFF WITH THIS STUFF.
EVEN IF I DIDN'T, YOU DON'T THINK I'D BE FOOL ENOUGH TO STICK AROUND HERE, DO YOU?
WHY DON'T YOU COME WITH US? YOU'RE PRETTY GOOD IN A FIGHT. I COULD USE YOU.
COME ON! WHY DON'T YOU TAKE A LOOK AROUND? YOU KNOW WHAT'S ABOUT TO HAPPEN, WHAT THEY'RE UP AGAINST.
THEY COULD USE A GOOD PILOT LIKE YOU.
YOU'RE TURNING YOUR BACK ON THEM.
WHAT GOOD'S A REWARD IF YOU AIN'T AROUND TO USE IT? BESIDES, ATTACKING THE BATTLE STATION AIN'T MY IDEA OF COURAGE. IT'S MORE LIKE SUICIDE.
ALL RIGHT, WELL, TAKE CARE OF YOURSELF, HAN... I GUESS THAT'S WHAT YOU'RE BEST AT, ISN'T IT?
HEY, LUKE...
...MAY THE FORCE BE WITH YOU!
WHAT ARE YOU LOOKIN' AT? I KNOW WHAT I'M DOING.
RRWMPH!

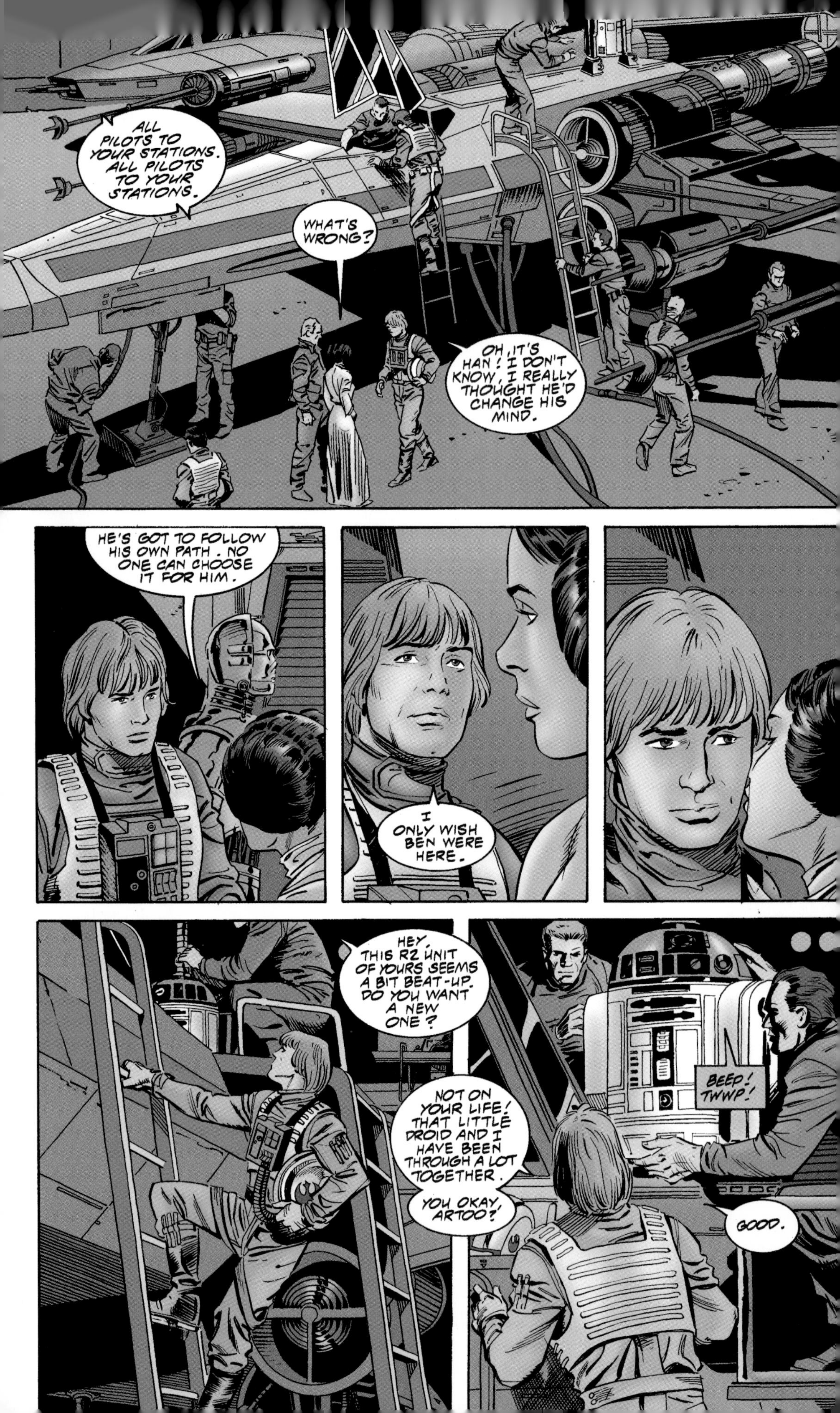
ALL PILOTS TO YOUR STATIONS. ALL PILOTS TO YOUR STATIONS.
WHAT'S WRONG?
OH, IT'S HAN! I DON'T KNOW, I REALLY THOUGHT HE'D CHANGE HIS MIND.
HE'S GOT TO FOLLOW HIS OWN PATH. NO ONE CAN CHOOSE IT FOR HIM.
I ONLY WISH BEN WERE HERE.
HEY, THIS R2 UNIT OF YOURS SEEMS A BIT BEAT-UP. DO YOU WANT A NEW ONE?
NOT ON YOUR LIFE! THAT LITTLE DROID AND I HAVE BEEN THROUGH A LOT TOGETHER.
YOU OKAY, ARTOO?
BEEP! TWWP!
GOOD.

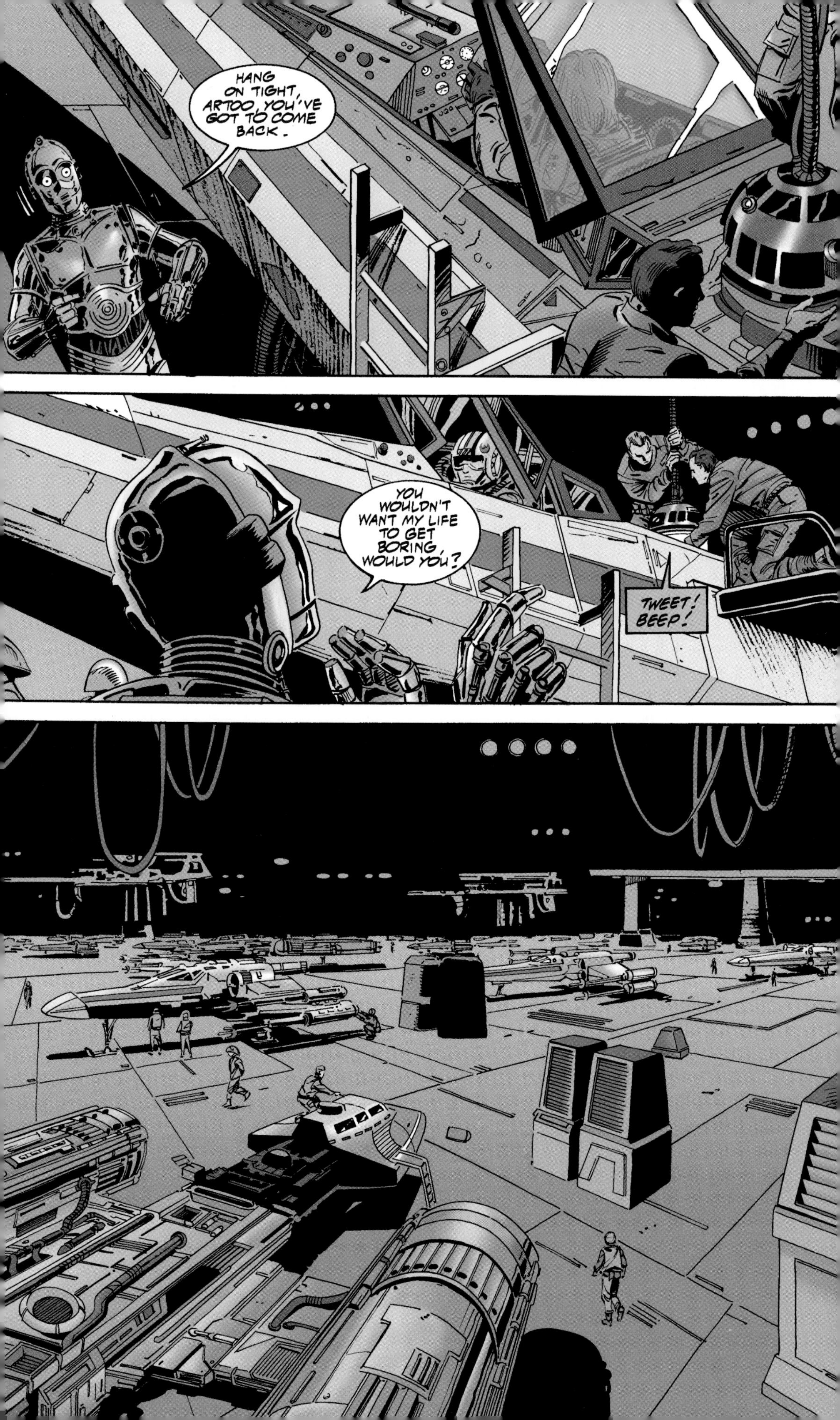
HANG ON TIGHT, ARTOO, YOU'VE GOT TO COME BACK.
YOU WOULDN'T WANT MY LIFE TO GET BORING, WOULD YOU?
TWEET! BEEP!

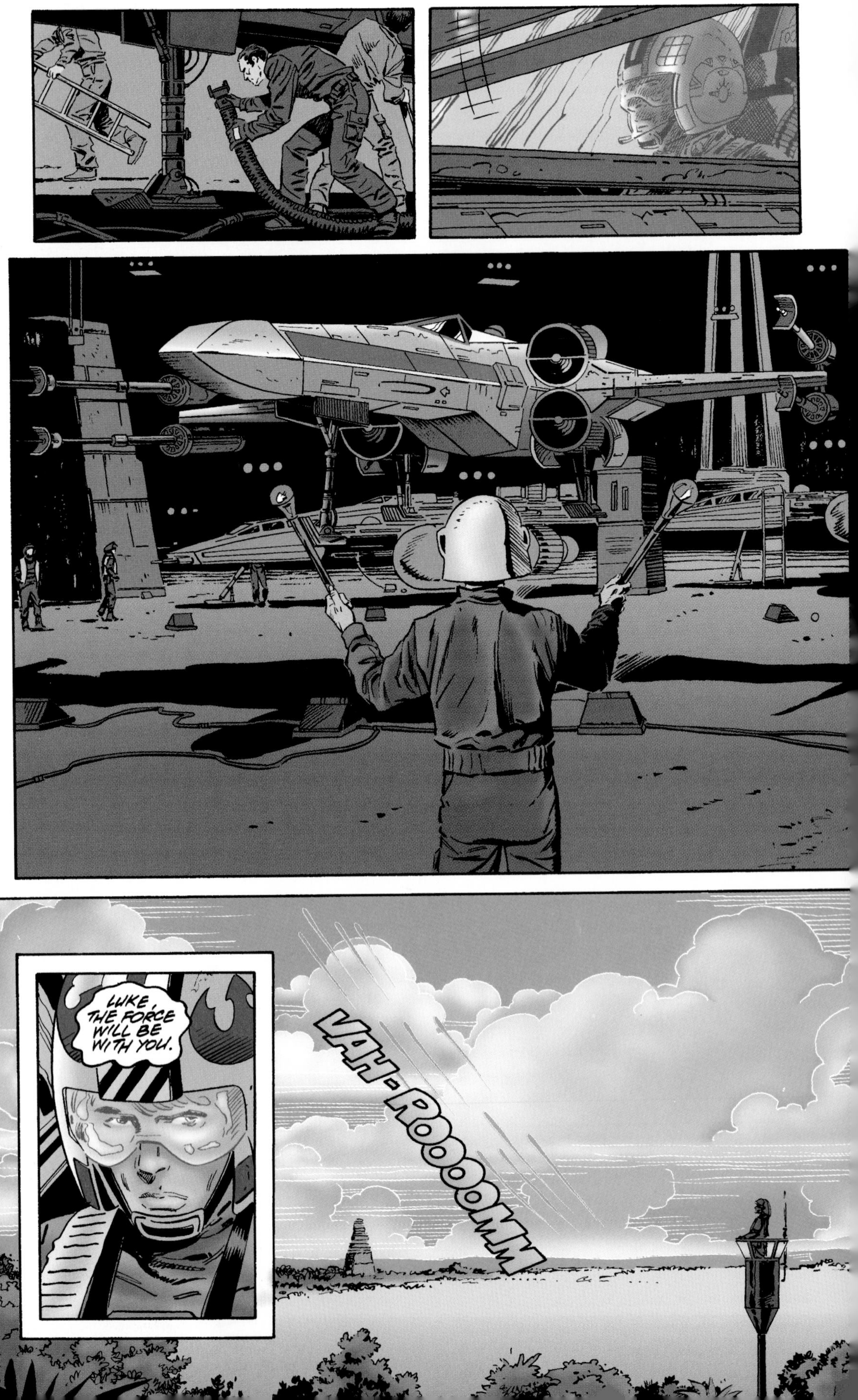
LUKE, THE FORCE WILL BE WITH YOU.
VAH-ROOOOMM

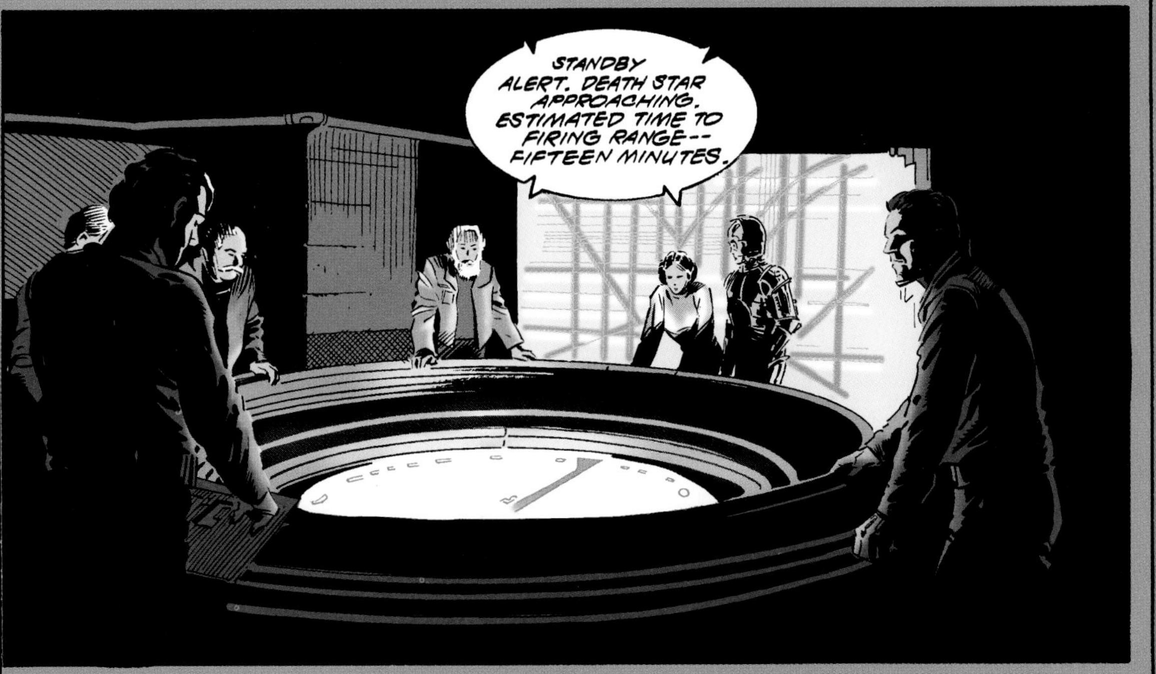
STANDBY ALERT. DEATH STAR APPROACHING. ESTIMATED TIME TO FIRING RANGE-- FIFTEEN MINUTES.

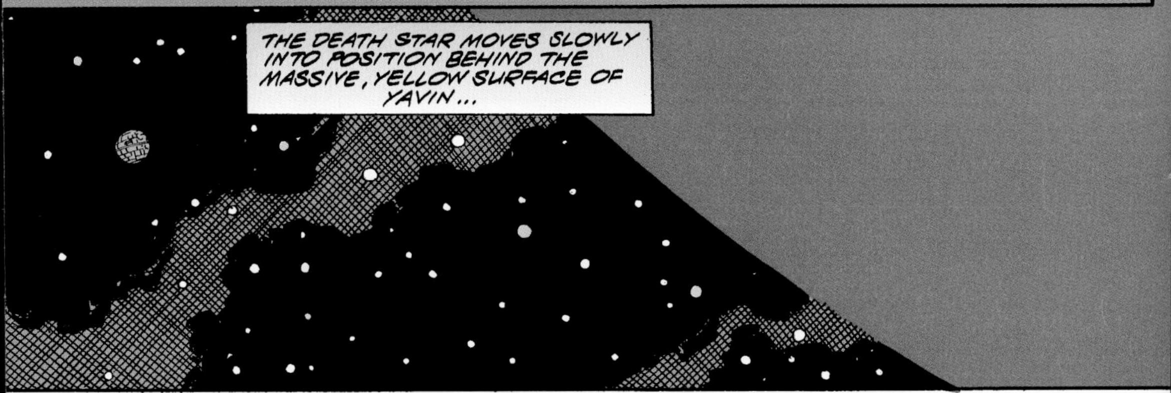
THE DEATH STAR MOVES SLOWLY INTO POSITION BEHIND THE MASSIVE, YELLOW SURFACE OF YAVIN...

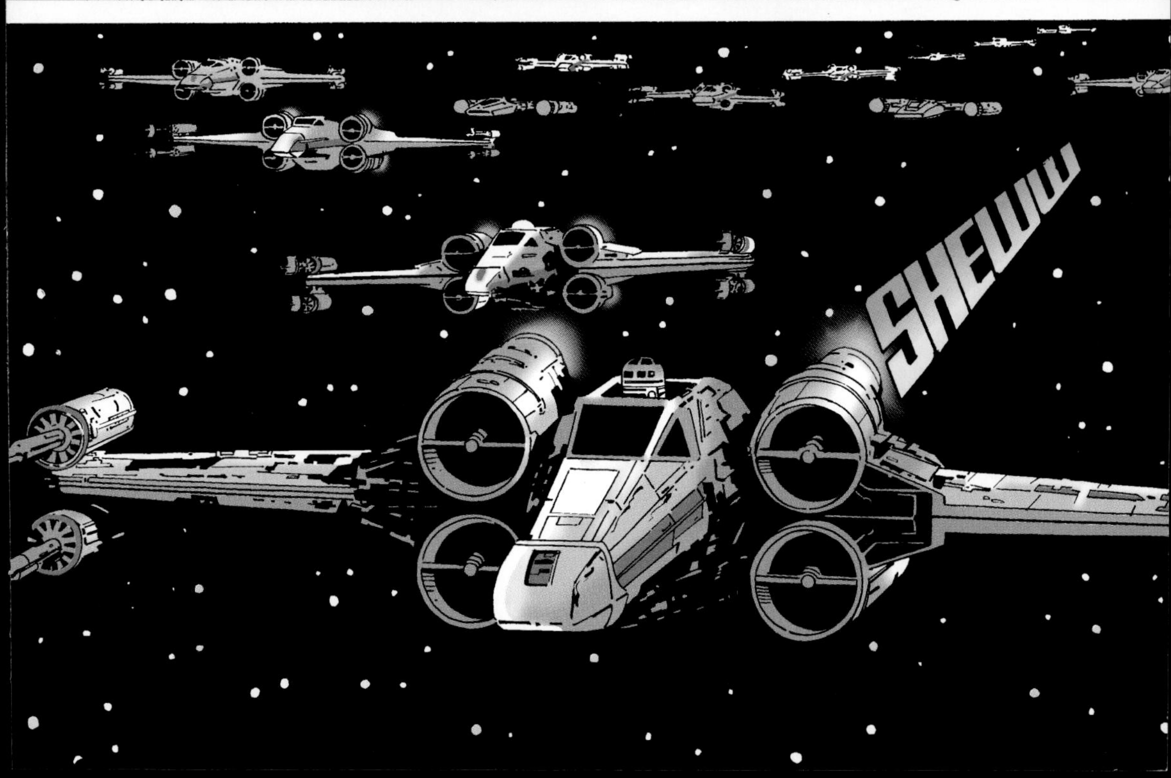
SHEWW

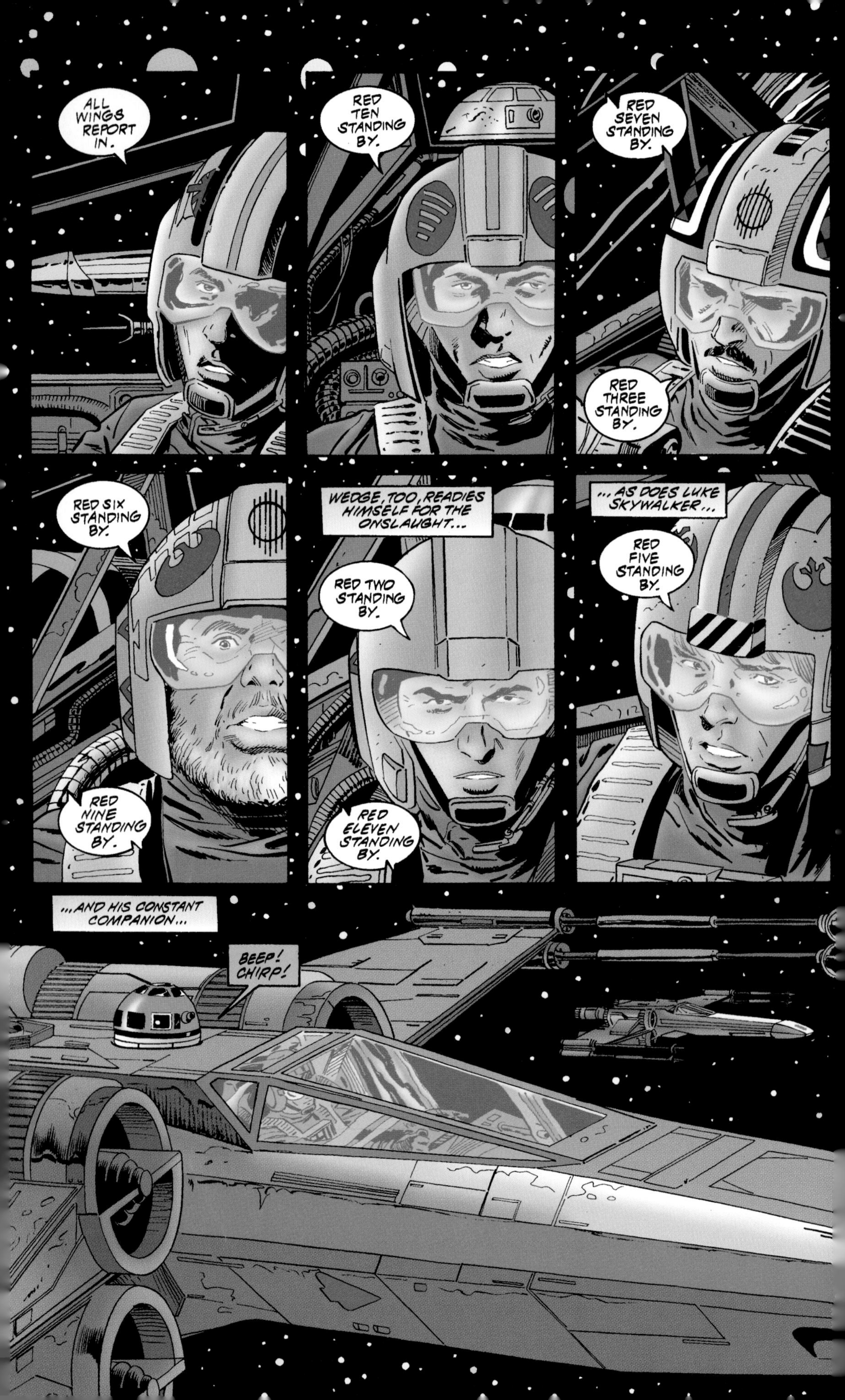

ALL WINGS REPORT IN.
RED TEN STANDING BY.
RED SEVEN STANDING BY.
RED THREE STANDING BY.
RED SIX STANDING BY.
RED NINE STANDING BY.
WEDGE, TOO, READIES HIMSELF FOR THE ONSLAUGHT...
RED TWO STANDING BY.
RED ELEVEN STANDING BY.
...AS DOES LUKE SKYWALKER...
RED FIVE STANDING BY.
...AND HIS CONSTANT COMPANION...
BEEP! CHIRP!

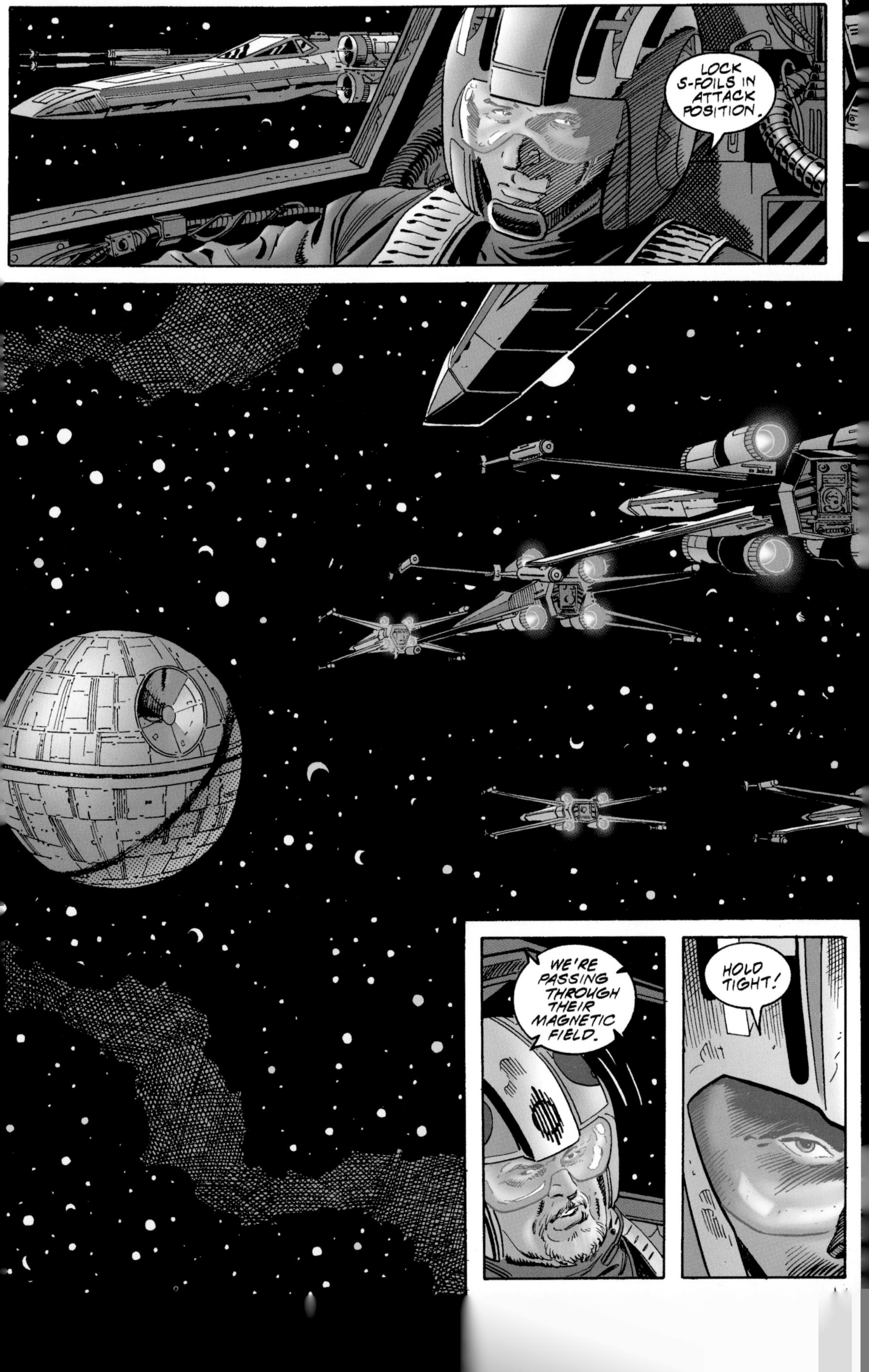
LOCK S-FOILS IN ATTACK POSITION.
WE'RE PASSING THROUGH THEIR MAGNETIC FIELD.
HOLD TIGHT!

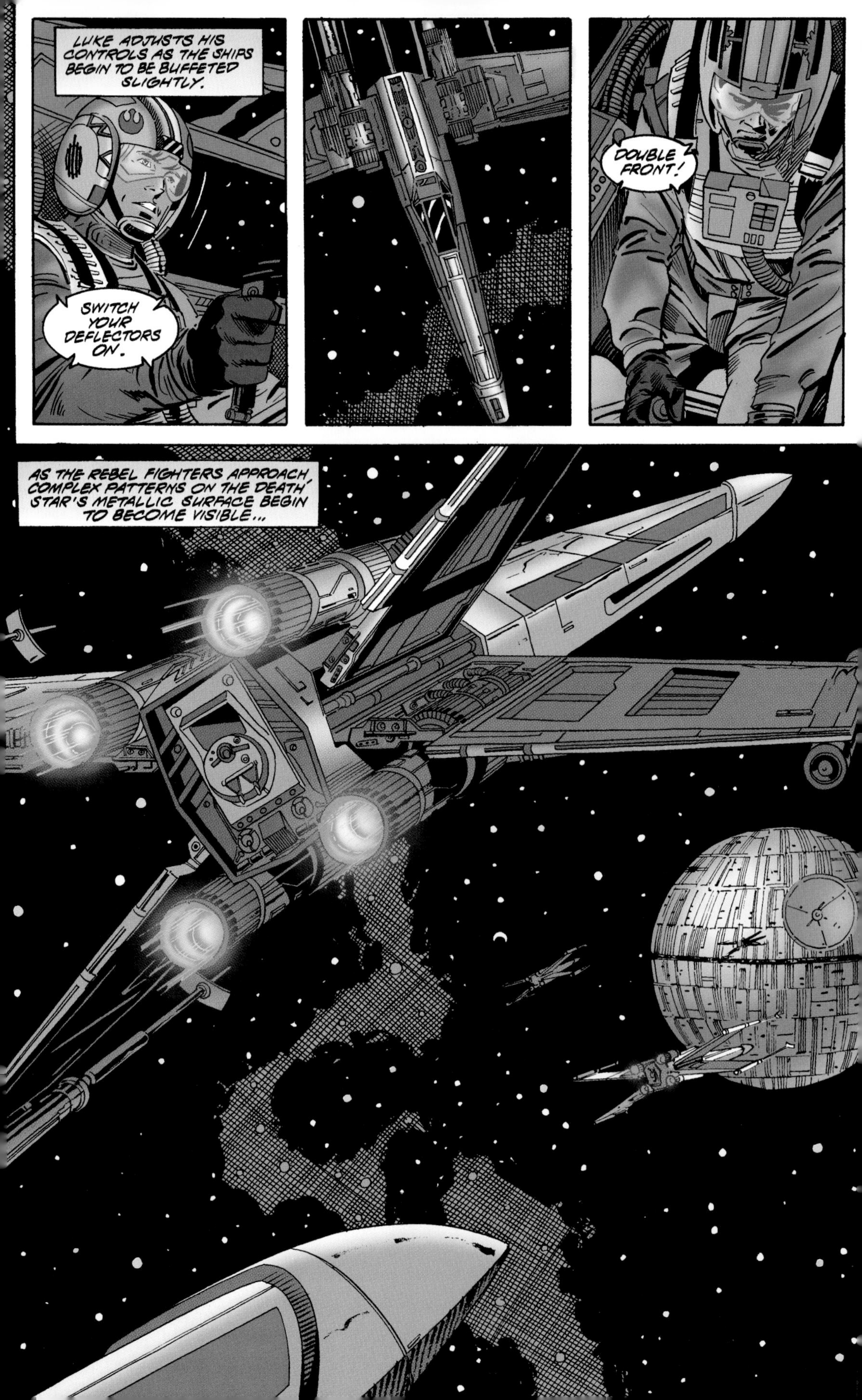
LUKE ADJUSTS HIS CONTROLS AS THE SHIPS BEGIN TO BE BUFFETED SLIGHTLY.
SWITCH YOUR DEFLECTORS ON.
DOUBLE FRONT!
AS THE REBEL FIGHTERS APPROACH, COMPLEX PATTERNS ON THE DEATH STAR'S METALLIC SURFACE BEGIN TO BECOME VISIBLE...

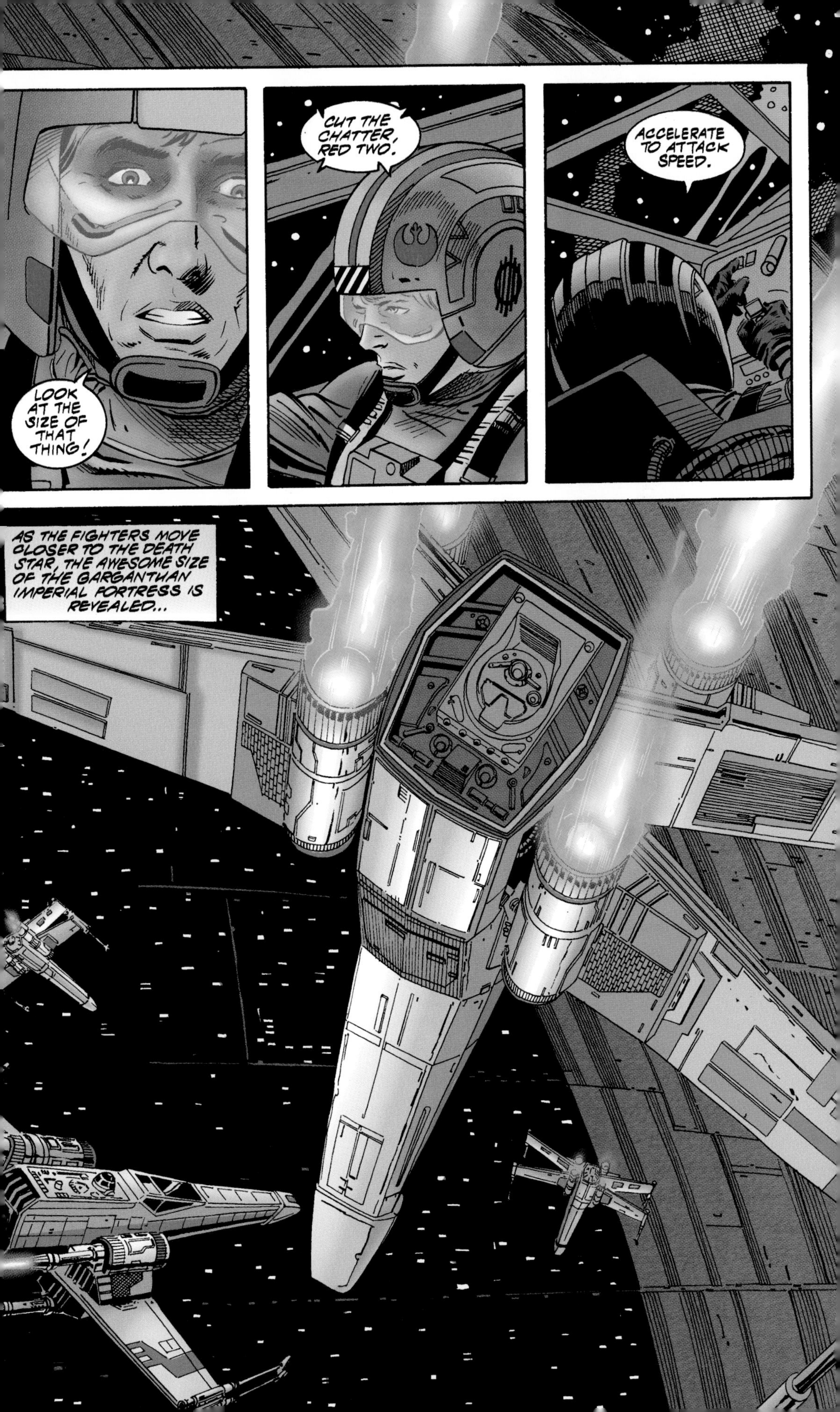
LOOK AT THE SIZE OF THAT THING!
CUT THE CHATTER, RED TWO.
ACCELERATE TO ATTACK SPEED.
AS THE FIGHTERS MOVE CLOSER TO THE DEATH STAR, THE AWESOME SIZE OF THE GARGANTUAN IMPERIAL FORTRESS IS REVEALED...

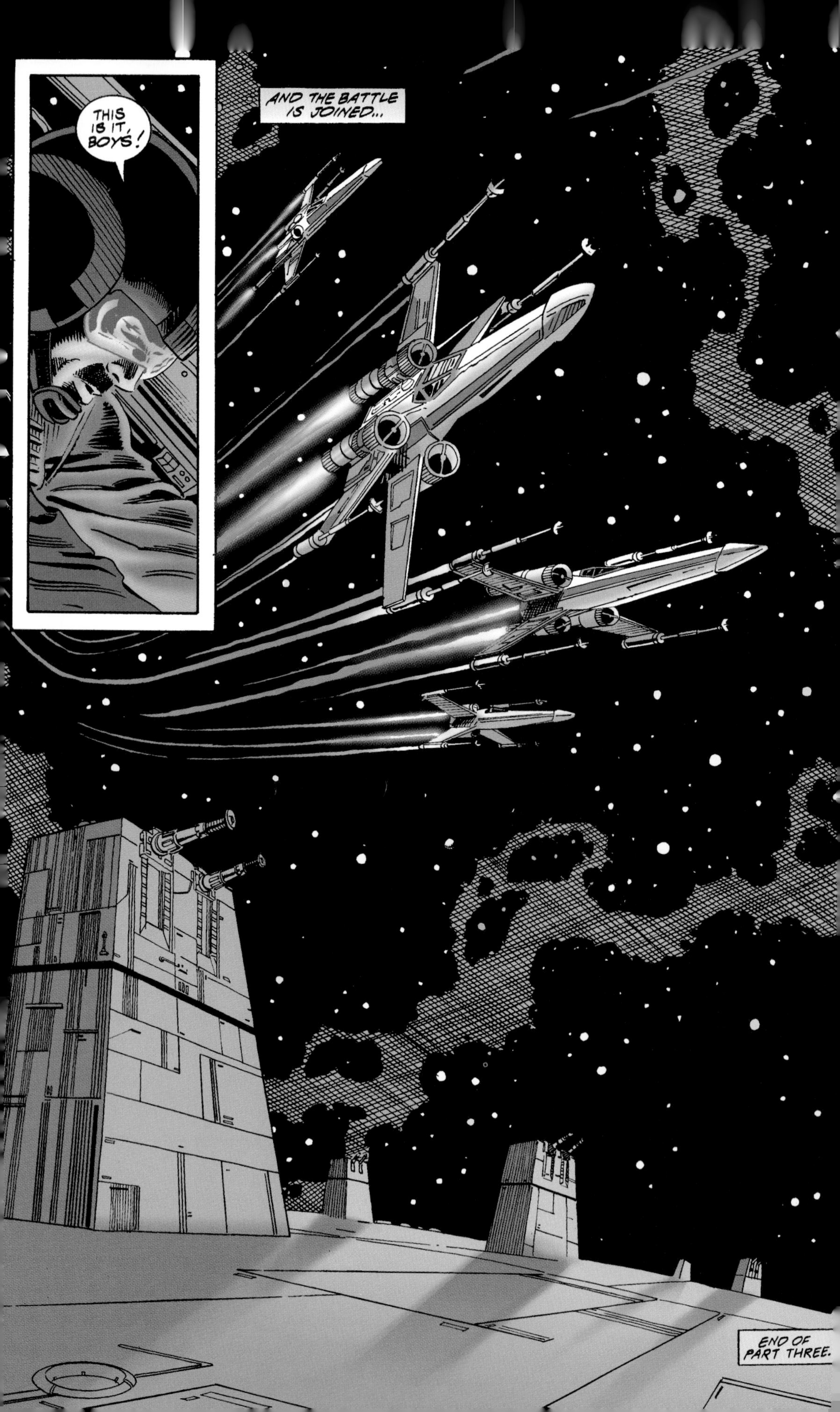
THIS IS IT, BOYS!
AND THE BATTLE IS JOINED...
END OF PART THREE.

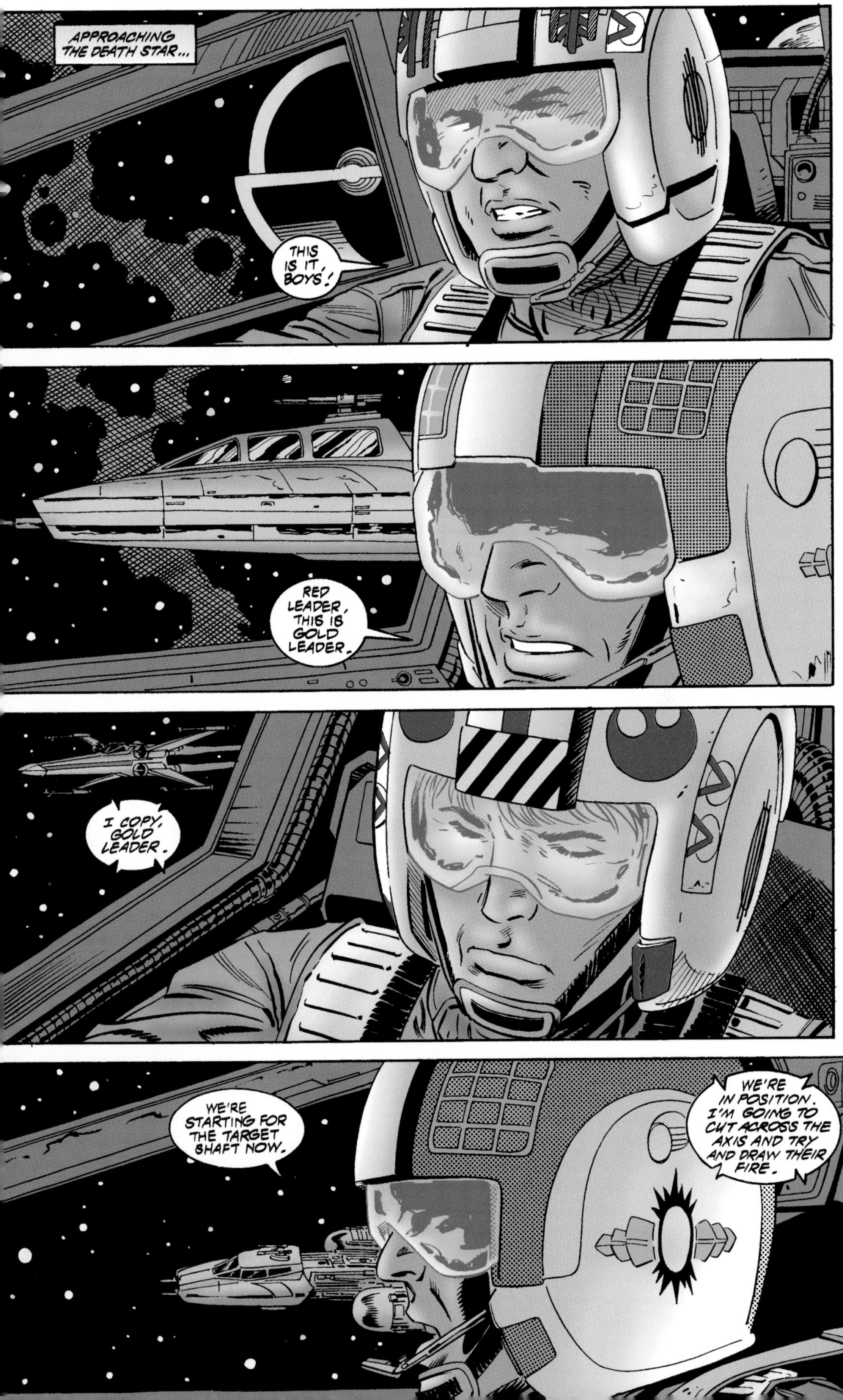
APPROACHING THE DEATH STAR...
THIS IS IT, BOYS!
RED LEADER, THIS IS GOLD LEADER.
I COPY, GOLD LEADER.
WE'RE STARTING FOR THE TARGET SHAFT NOW.
WE'RE IN POSITION. I'M GOING TO CUT ACROSS THE AXIS AND TRY AND DRAW THEIR FIRE.

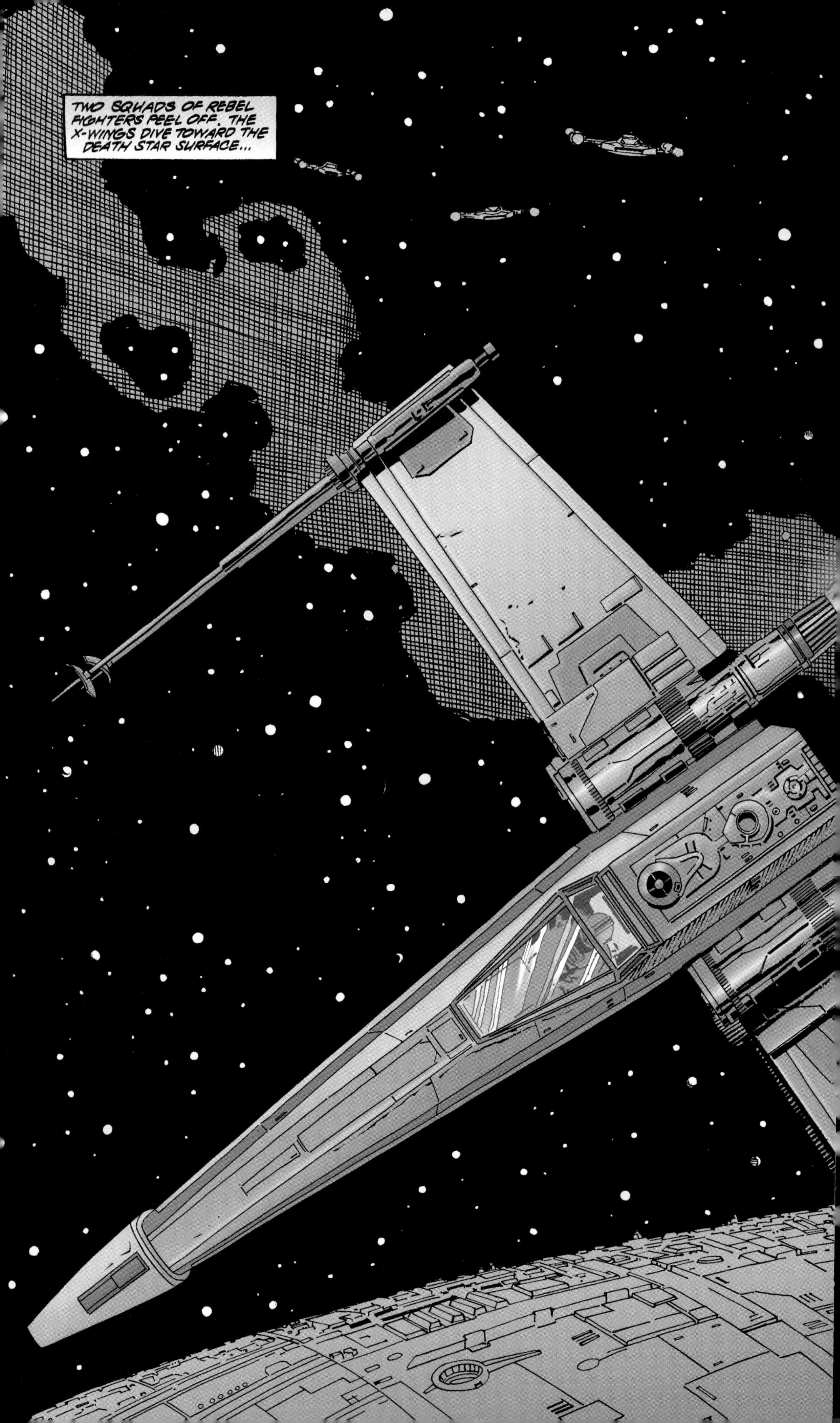
TWO SQUADS OF REBEL FIGHTERS PEEL OFF. THE X-WINGS DIVE TOWARD THE DEATH STAR SURFACE...

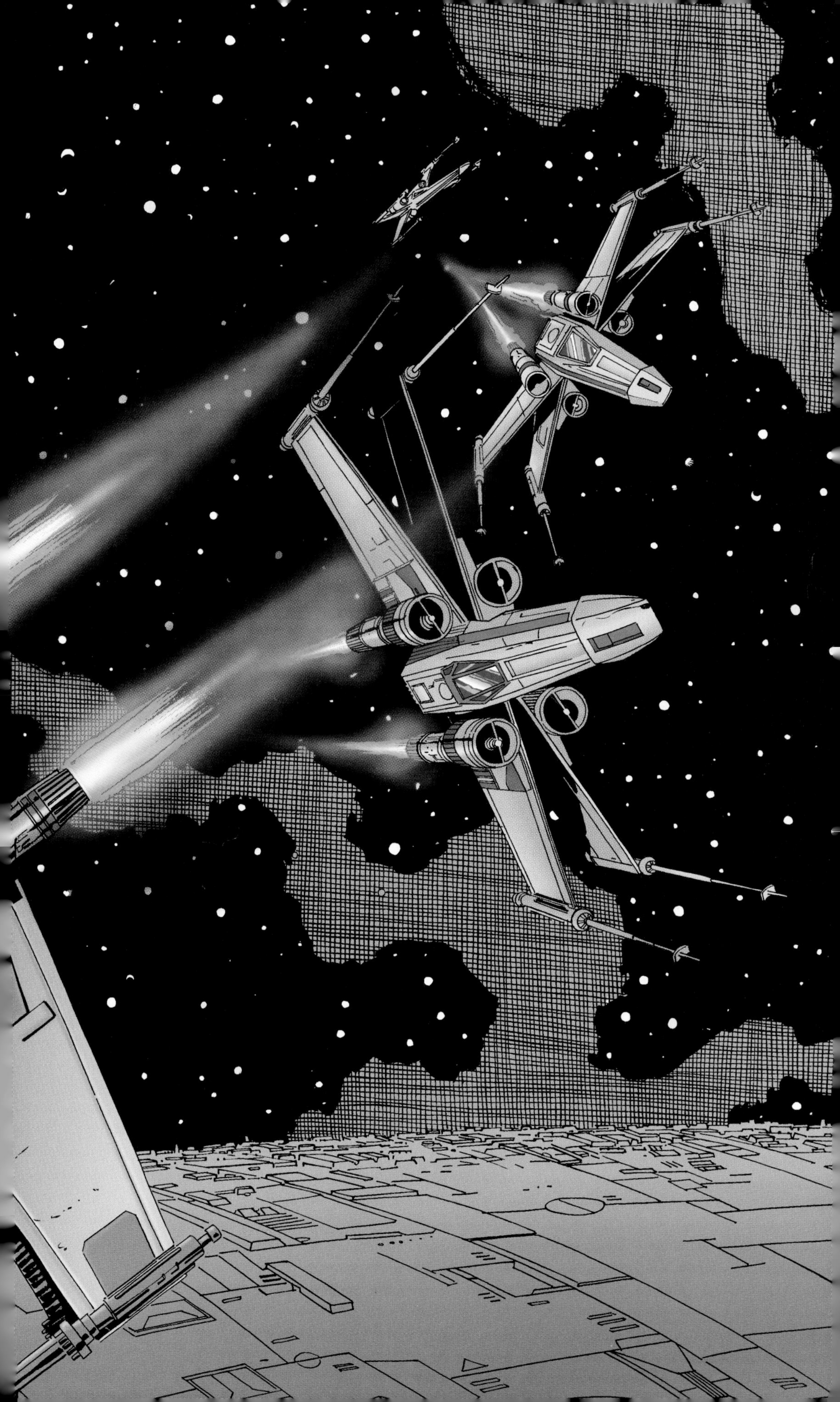

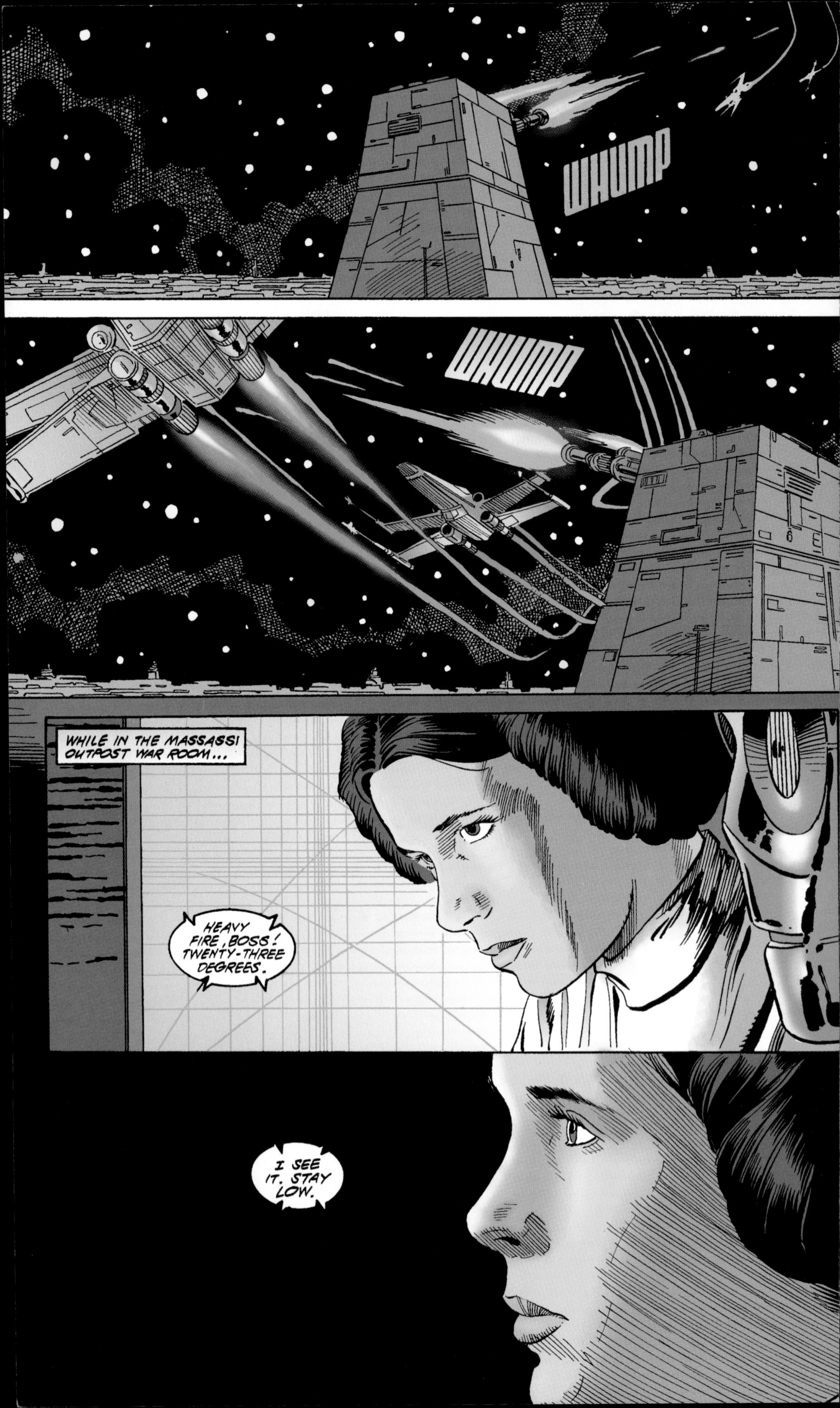
WHUMP
WHUMP
WHILE IN THE MASSASSI OUTPOST WAR ROOM...
HEAVY FIRE, BOSS! TWENTY-THREE DEGREES.
I SEE IT. STAY LOW.

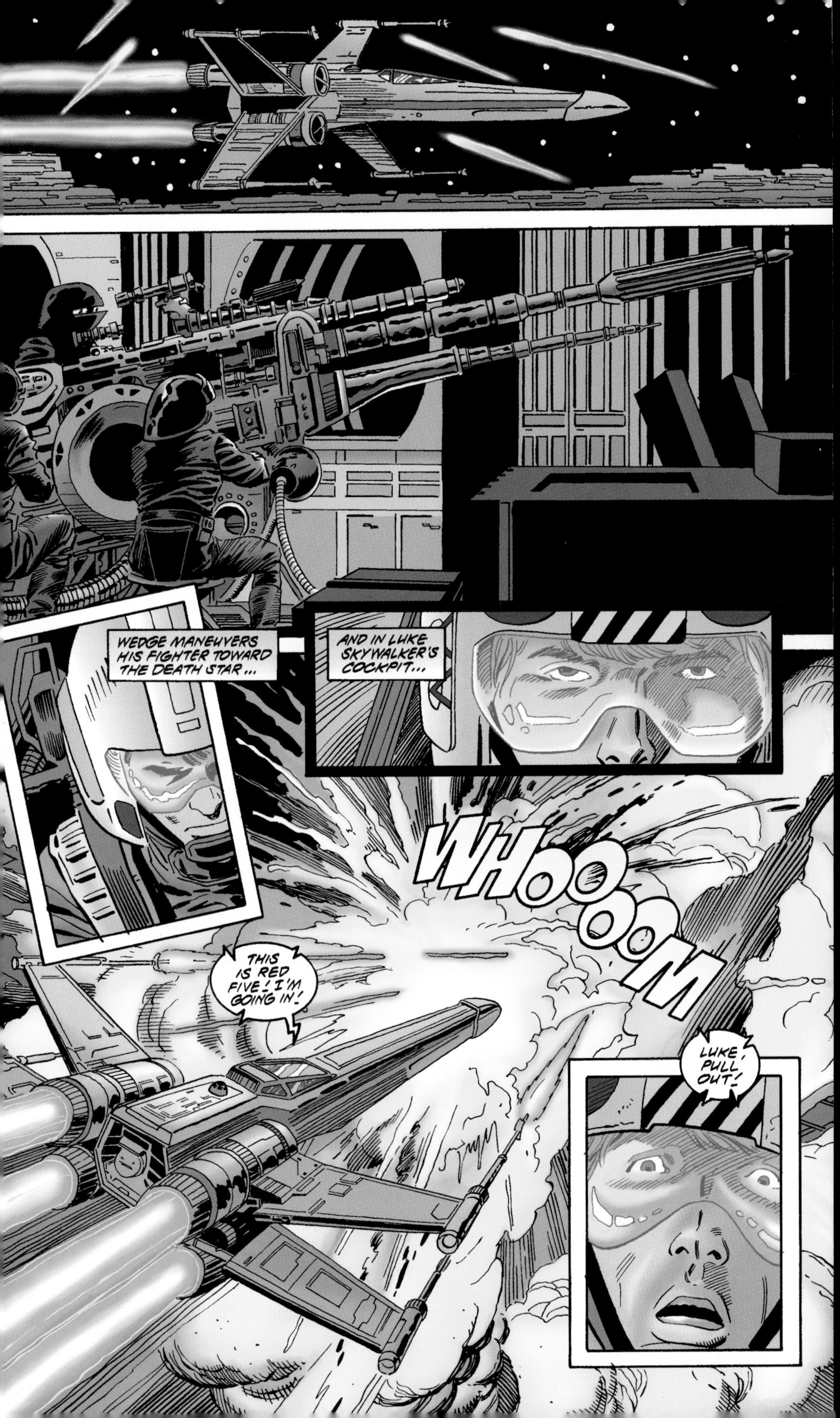
WEDGE MANEUVERS HIS FIGHTER TOWARD THE DEATH STAR...
AND IN LUKE SKYWALKER'S COCKPIT...
WHOOOOOM
THIS IS RED FIVE! I'M GOING IN!
LUKE, PULL OUT!

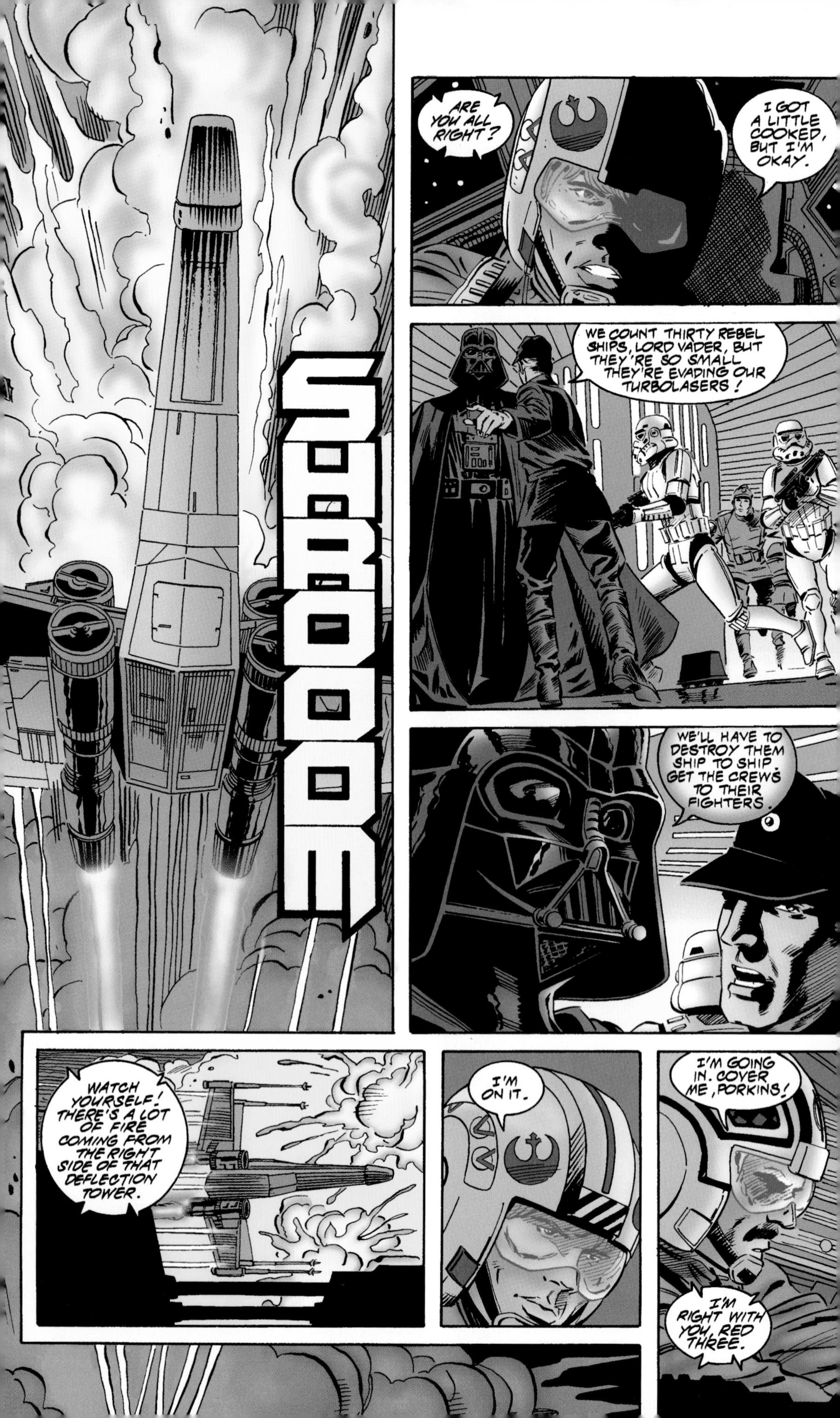
SHROOM
ARE YOU ALL RIGHT?
I GOT A LITTLE COOKED, BUT I'M OKAY.
WE COUNT THIRTY REBEL SHIPS, LORD VADER, BUT THEY'RE SO SMALL THEY'RE EVADING OUR TURBOLASERS!
WE'LL HAVE TO DESTROY THEM SHIP TO SHIP. GET THE CREWS TO THEIR FIGHTERS.
WATCH YOURSELF! THERE'S A LOT OF FIRE COMING FROM THE RIGHT SIDE OF THAT DEFLECTION TOWER.
I'M ON IT.
I'M GOING IN. COVER ME, PORKINS!
I'M RIGHT WITH YOU, RED THREE.

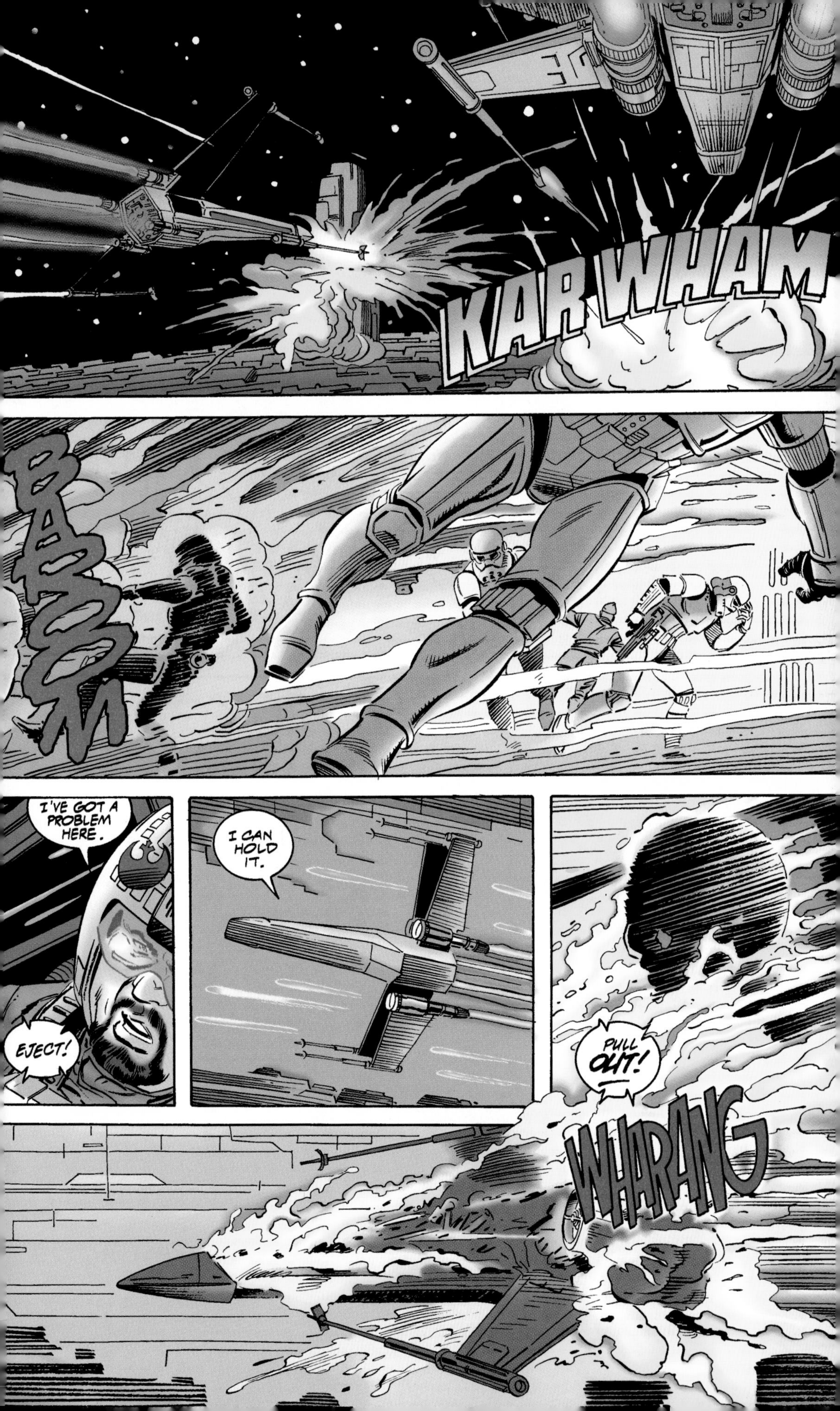
KARWHAM
BABOOM
I'VE GOT A PROBLEM HERE.
EJECT!
I CAN HOLD IT.
PULL OUT!
WHARANG

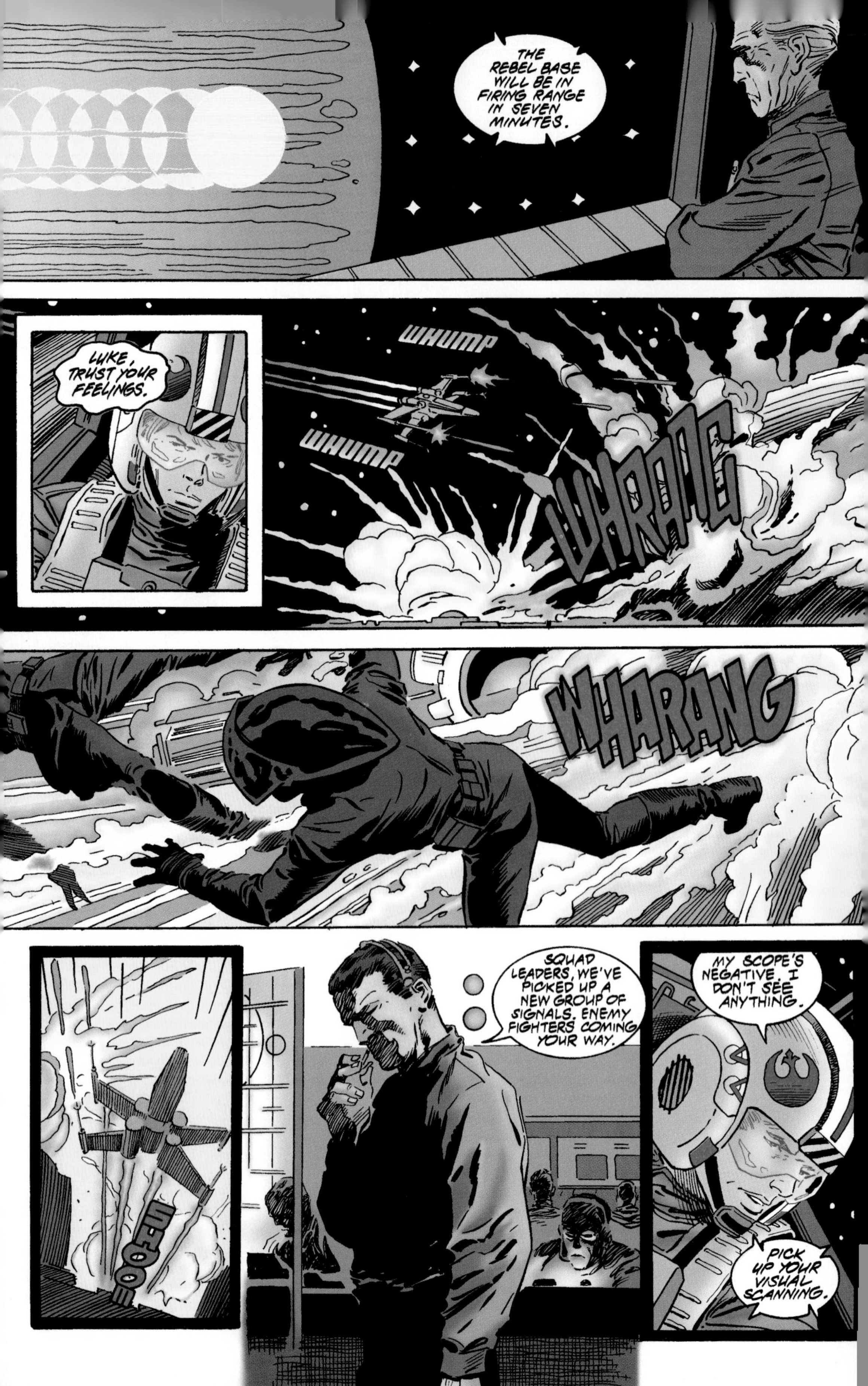
THE REBEL BASE WILL BE IN FIRING RANGE IN SEVEN MINUTES.
LUKE, TRUST YOUR FEELINGS.
WHUMP
WHUMP
WHRANG
WHARANG
SQUAD LEADERS, WE'VE PICKED UP A NEW GROUP OF SIGNALS. ENEMY FIGHTERS COMING YOUR WAY.
MY SCOPE'S NEGATIVE. I DON'T SEE ANYTHING.
PICK UP YOUR VISUAL SCANNING.

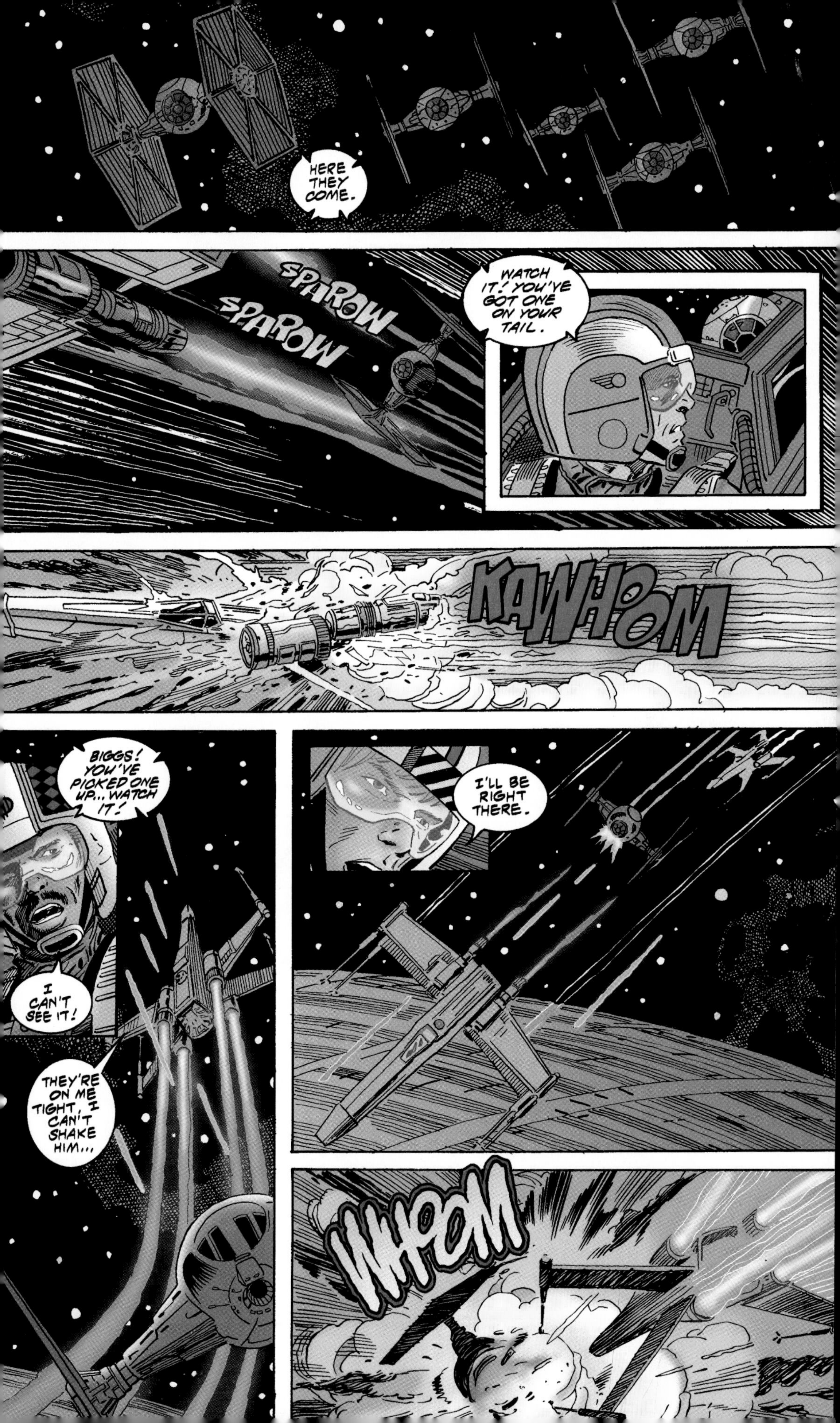
HERE THEY COME.
SPAROW
SPAROW
WATCH IT! YOU'VE GOT ONE ON YOUR TAIL.
KAWHOOM
BIGGS! YOU'VE PICKED ONE UP... WATCH IT!
I CAN'T SEE IT!
THEY'RE ON ME TIGHT, I CAN'T SHAKE HIM...
I'LL BE RIGHT THERE.
WHOOM

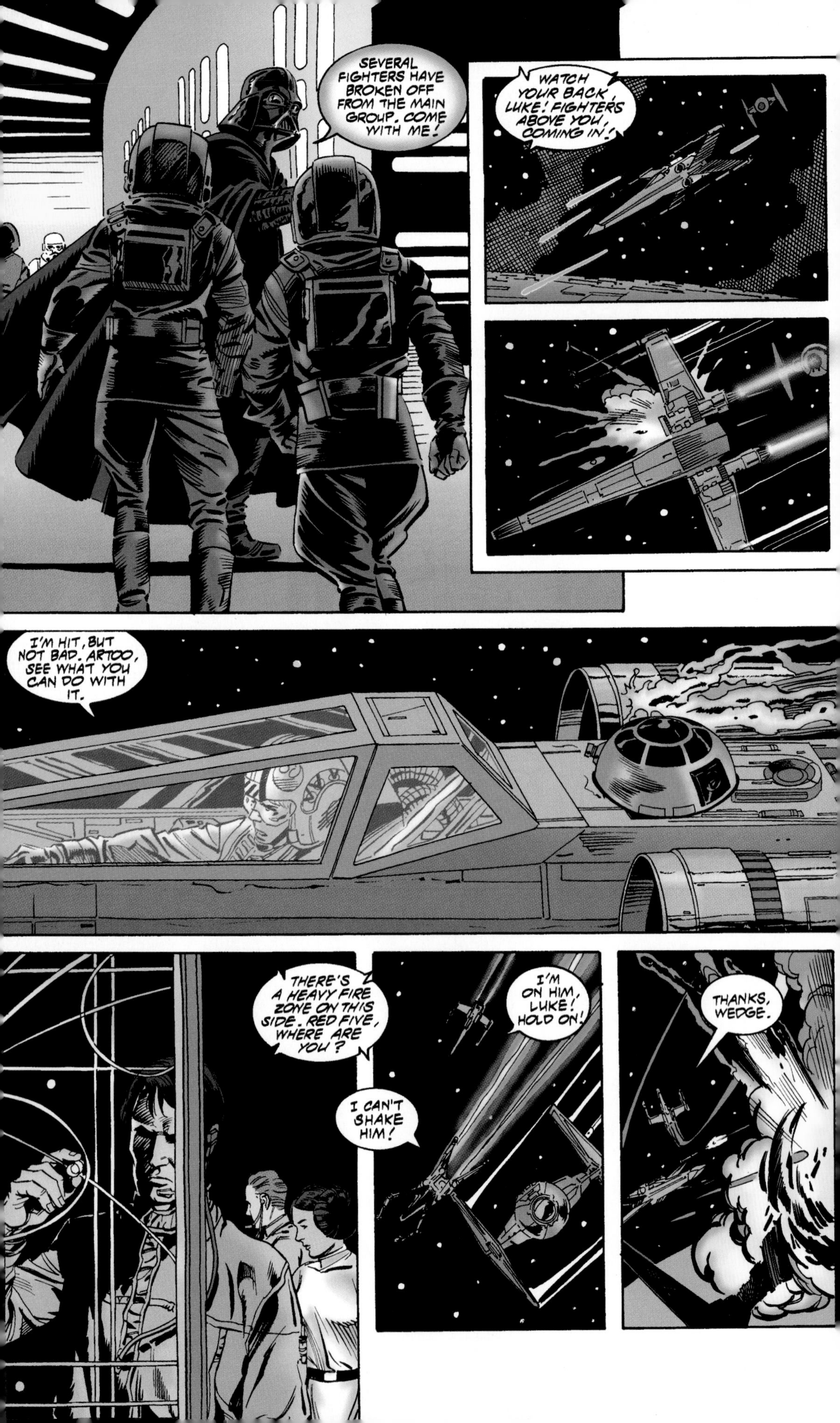
SEVERAL FIGHTERS HAVE BROKEN OFF FROM THE MAIN GROUP. COME WITH ME!
WATCH YOUR BACK, LUKE! FIGHTERS ABOVE YOU, COMING IN!
I'M HIT, BUT NOT BAD. ARTOO, SEE WHAT YOU CAN DO WITH IT.
THERE'S A HEAVY FIRE ZONE ON THIS SIDE. RED FIVE, WHERE ARE YOU?
I CAN'T SHAKE HIM!
I'M ON HIM, LUKE! HOLD ON!
THANKS, WEDGE.

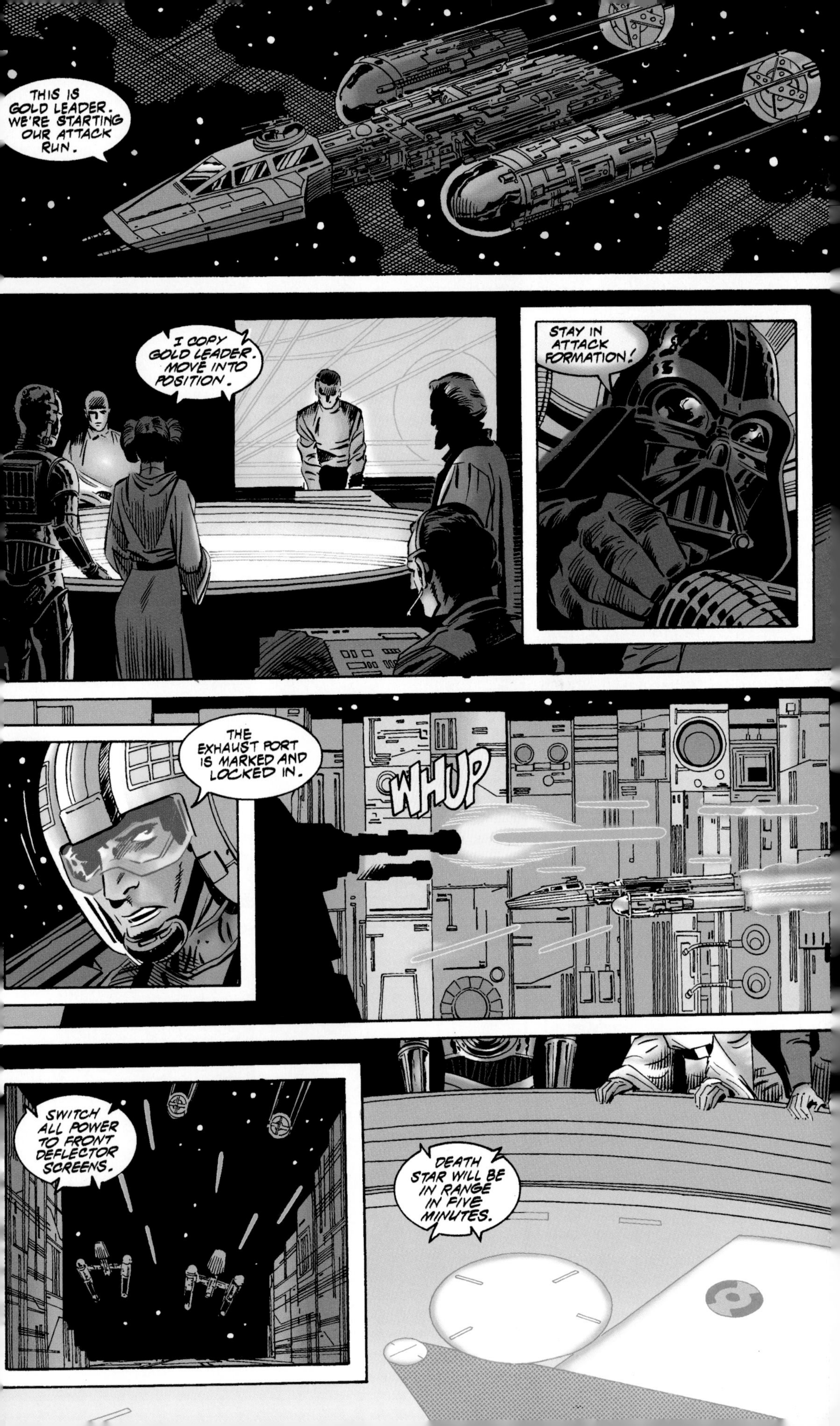
THIS IS GOLD LEADER. WE'RE STARTING OUR ATTACK RUN.
I COPY GOLD LEADER. MOVE INTO POSITION.
STAY IN ATTACK FORMATION!
THE EXHAUST PORT IS MARKED AND LOCKED IN.
WHUP
SWITCH ALL POWER TO FRONT DEFLECTOR SCREENS.
DEATH STAR WILL BE IN RANGE IN FIVE MINUTES.

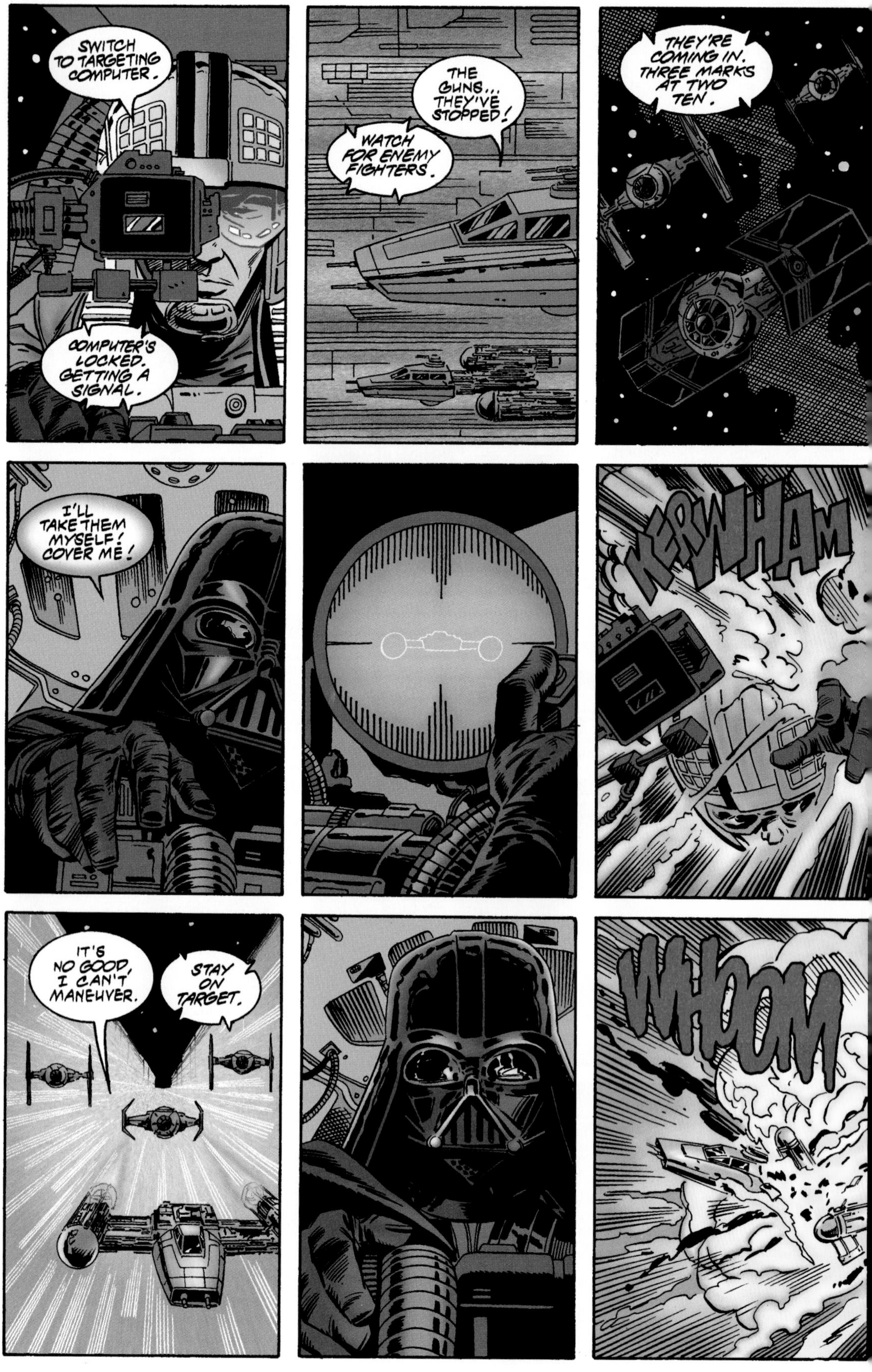
SWITCH TO TARGETING COMPUTER.
COMPUTER'S LOCKED. GETTING A SIGNAL.
THE GUNS... THEY'VE STOPPED!
WATCH FOR ENEMY FIGHTERS.
THEY'RE COMING IN. THREE MARKS AT TWO TEN.
I'LL TAKE THEM MYSELF! COVER ME!
KERWHAM
IT'S NO GOOD, I CAN'T MANEUVER.
STAY ON TARGET.
WHOOM

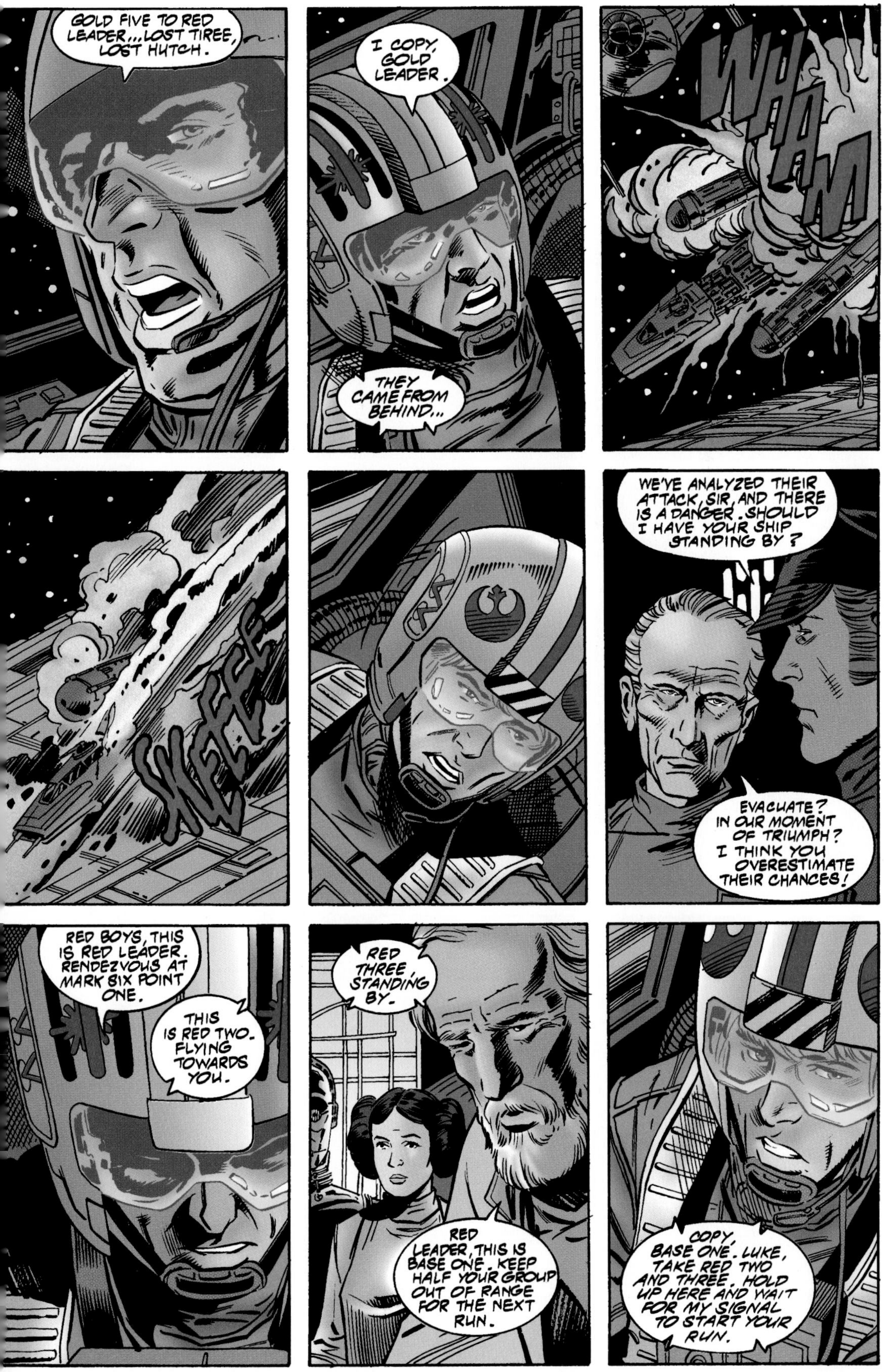
GOLD FIVE TO RED LEADER... LOST TIREE, LOST HUTCH.
I COPY, GOLD LEADER.
THEY CAME FROM BEHIND...
WHAM
WE'VE ANALYZED THEIR ATTACK, SIR, AND THERE IS A DANGER. SHOULD I HAVE YOUR SHIP STANDING BY?
EVACUATE? IN OUR MOMENT OF TRIUMPH? I THINK YOU OVERESTIMATE THEIR CHANCES!
RED BOYS, THIS IS RED LEADER. RENDEZVOUS AT MARK SIX POINT ONE.
THIS IS RED TWO. FLYING TOWARDS YOU.
RED THREE, STANDING BY.
RED LEADER, THIS IS BASE ONE. KEEP HALF YOUR GROUP OUT OF RANGE FOR THE NEXT RUN.
COPY, BASE ONE. LUKE, TAKE RED TWO AND THREE. HOLD UP HERE AND WAIT FOR MY SIGNAL TO START YOUR RUN.

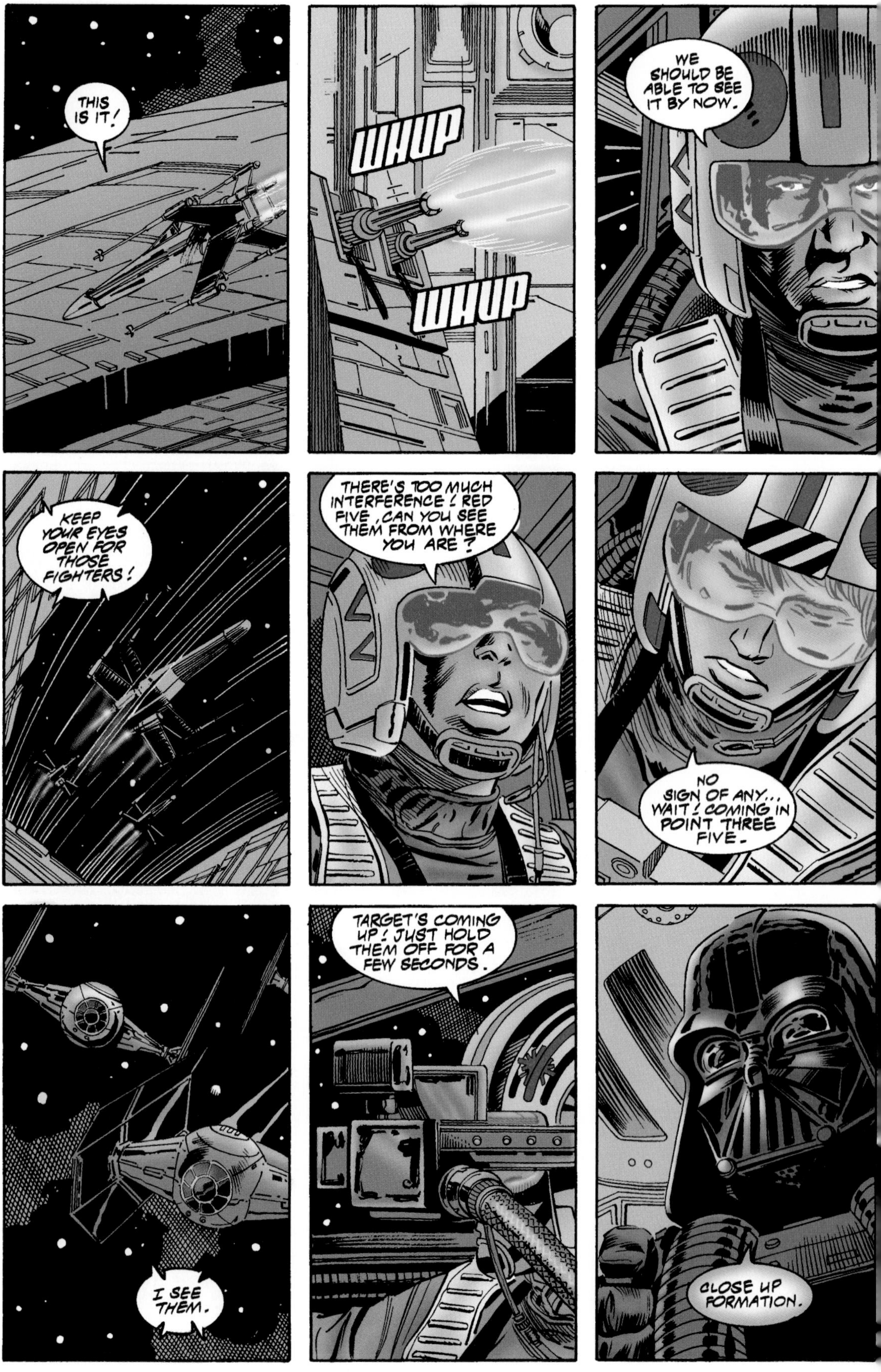
THIS IS IT!
WHUP
WHUP
WE SHOULD BE ABLE TO SEE IT BY NOW.
KEEP YOUR EYES OPEN FOR THOSE FIGHTERS!
THERE'S TOO MUCH INTERFERENCE! RED FIVE, CAN YOU SEE THEM FROM WHERE YOU ARE?
NO SIGN OF ANY... WAIT! COMING IN POINT THREE FIVE.
I SEE THEM.
TARGET'S COMING UP! JUST HOLD THEM OFF FOR A FEW SECONDS.
CLOSE UP FORMATION.

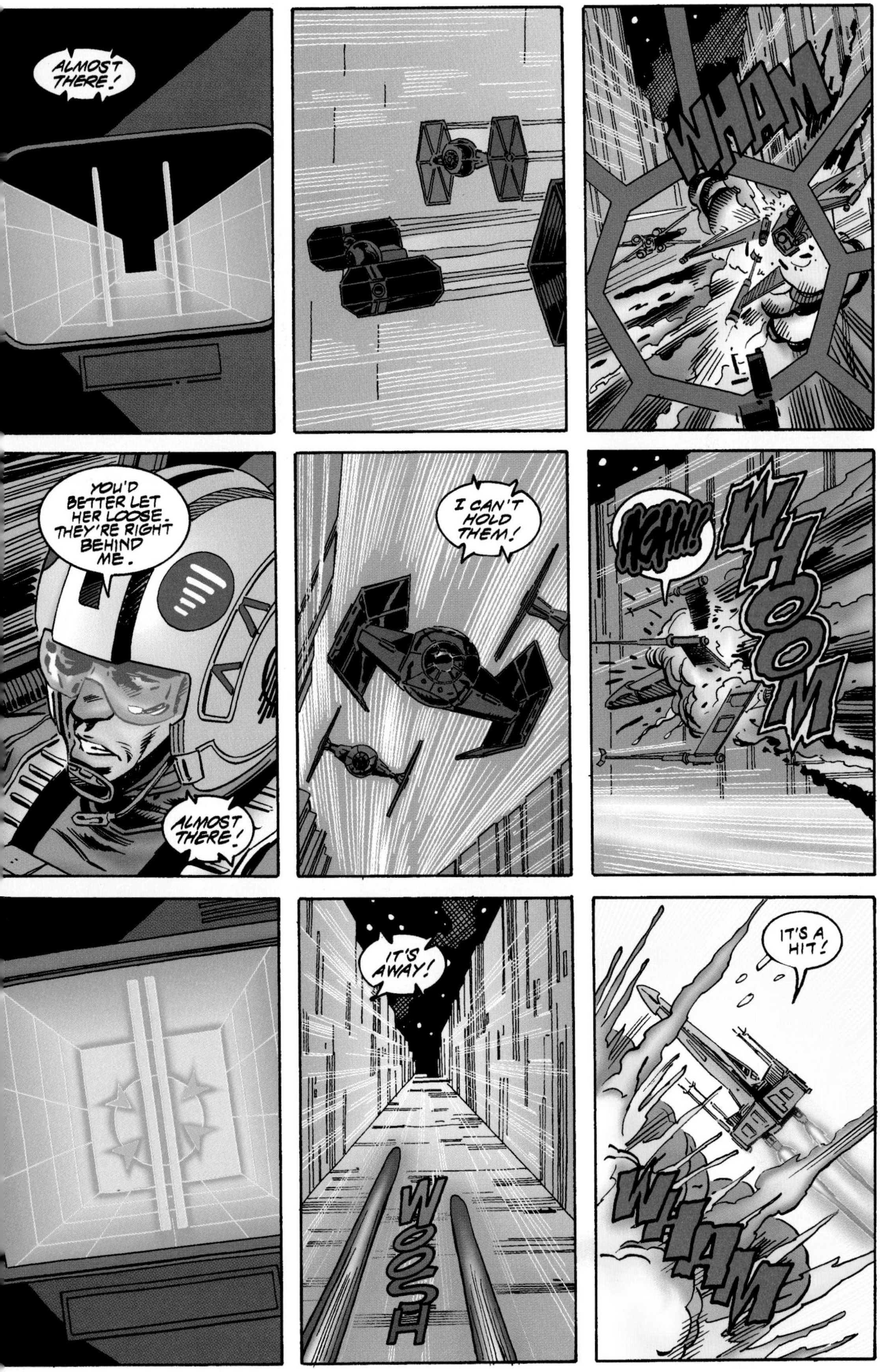
ALMOST THERE!
WHAM!
YOU'D BETTER LET HER LOOSE. THEY'RE RIGHT BEHIND ME.
ALMOST THERE!
I CAN'T HOLD THEM!
AGHH!
WHOOM
IT'S AWAY!
WOOSH
IT'S A HIT!
WHAM

NEGATIVE. IT DIDN'T GO IN, JUST IMPACTED ON THE SURFACE.

I JUST LOST MY STARBOARD ENGINE. GET SET UP FOR YOUR ATTACK RUN.

VIP

VIP

WHOOM

REBEL BASE, ONE MINUTE AND CLOSING.

BIGGS, WEDGE, LET'S CLOSE IT UP. WE'RE GOING IN FULL THROTTLE. THAT OUGHT TO KEEP THOSE FIGHTERS OFF OUR BACKS.

RIGHT WITH YOU, BOSS.

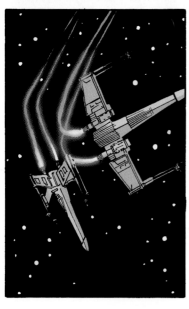

LUKE, AT THAT SPEED WILL YOU BE ABLE TO PULL OUT IN TIME?

IT'LL BE JUST LIKE BEGGAR'S CANYON BACK HOME.

WATCH YOURSELF! INCREASE SPEED FULL THROTTLE!

WHAT ABOUT THAT TOWER?

YOU WORRY ABOUT THOSE FIGHTERS! I'LL WORRY ABOUT THE TOWER!

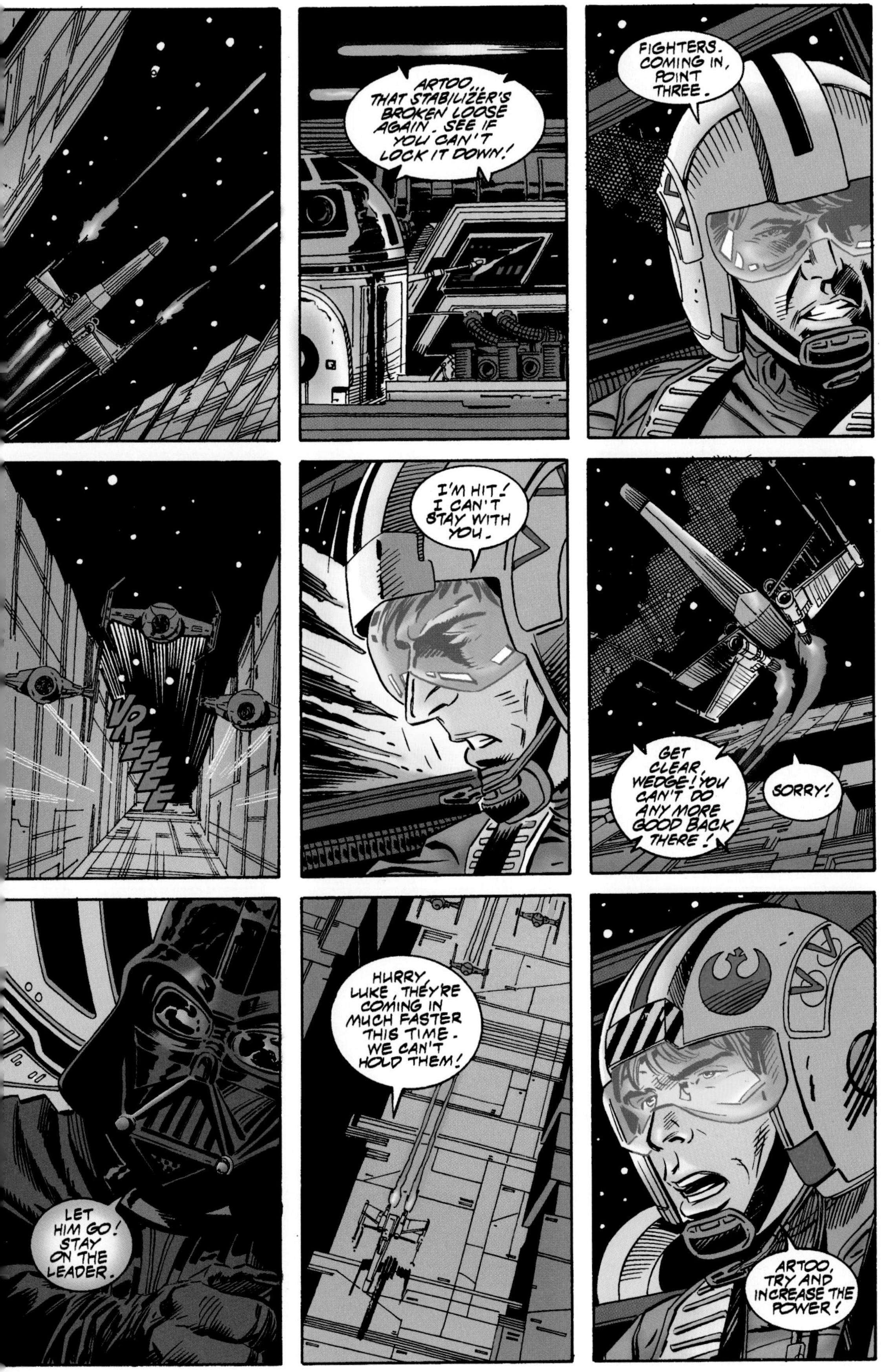
ARTOO... THAT STABILIZER'S BROKEN LOOSE AGAIN. SEE IF YOU CAN'T LOCK IT DOWN!
FIGHTERS. COMING IN, POINT THREE.
VREEEE
I'M HIT! I CAN'T STAY WITH YOU.
GET CLEAR, WEDGE! YOU CAN'T DO ANY MORE GOOD BACK THERE!
SORRY!
LET HIM GO! STAY ON THE LEADER.
HURRY, LUKE, THEY'RE COMING IN MUCH FASTER THIS TIME. WE CAN'T HOLD THEM!
ARTOO, TRY AND INCREASE THE POWER!

HURRY UP, LUKE! WAIT!
BLAM
REBEL BASE, THIRTY SECONDS AND CLOSING.
I'M ON THE LEADER.
HANG ON, ARTOO!

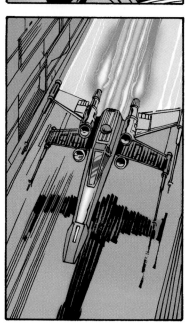

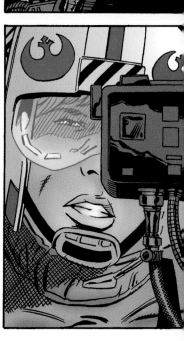

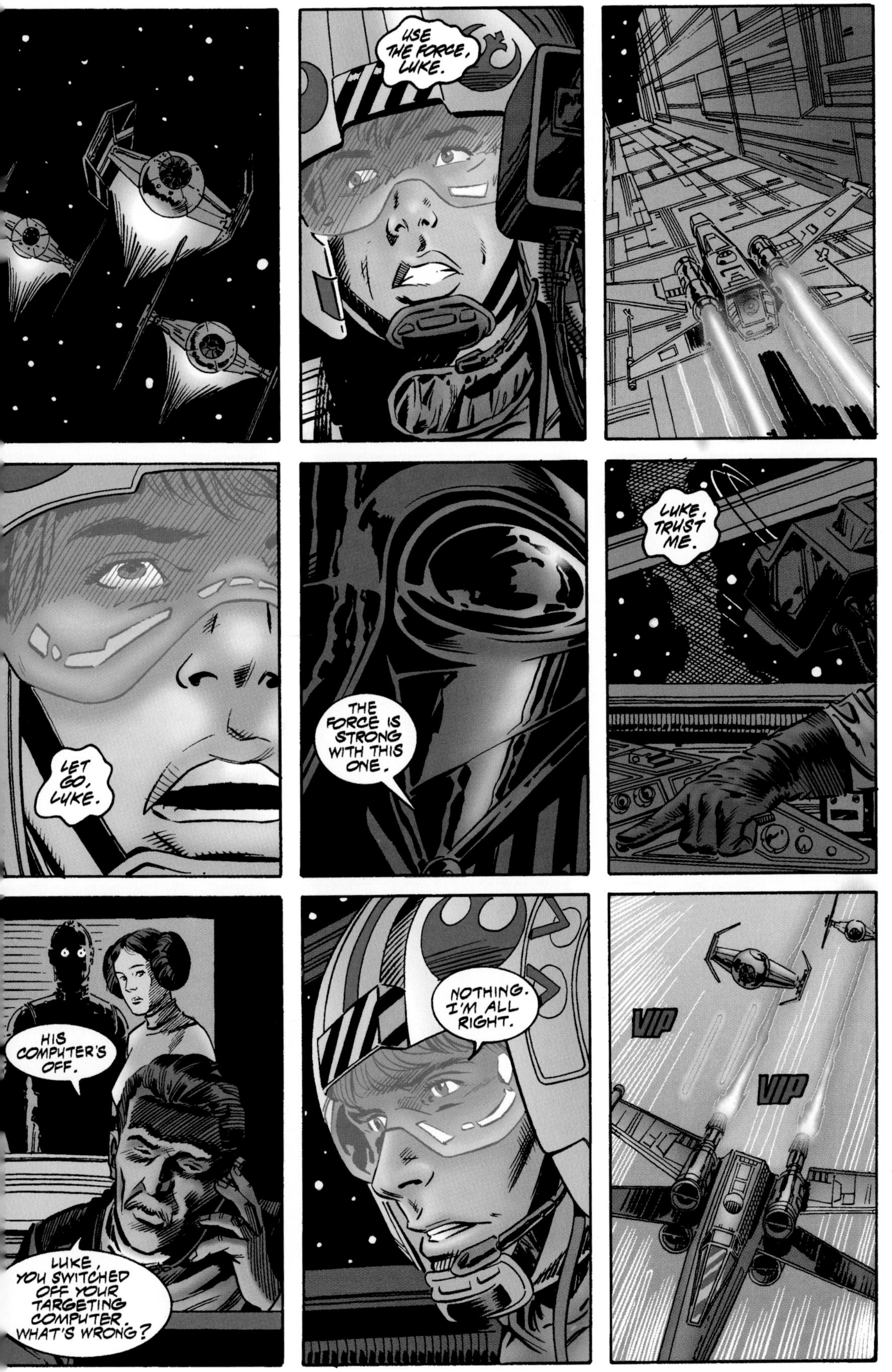
USE THE FORCE, LUKE.
LET GO, LUKE.
THE FORCE IS STRONG WITH THIS ONE.
LUKE, TRUST ME.
HIS COMPUTER'S OFF.
LUKE, YOU SWITCHED OFF YOUR TARGETING COMPUTER. WHAT'S WRONG?
NOTHING. I'M ALL RIGHT.
VIP
VIP

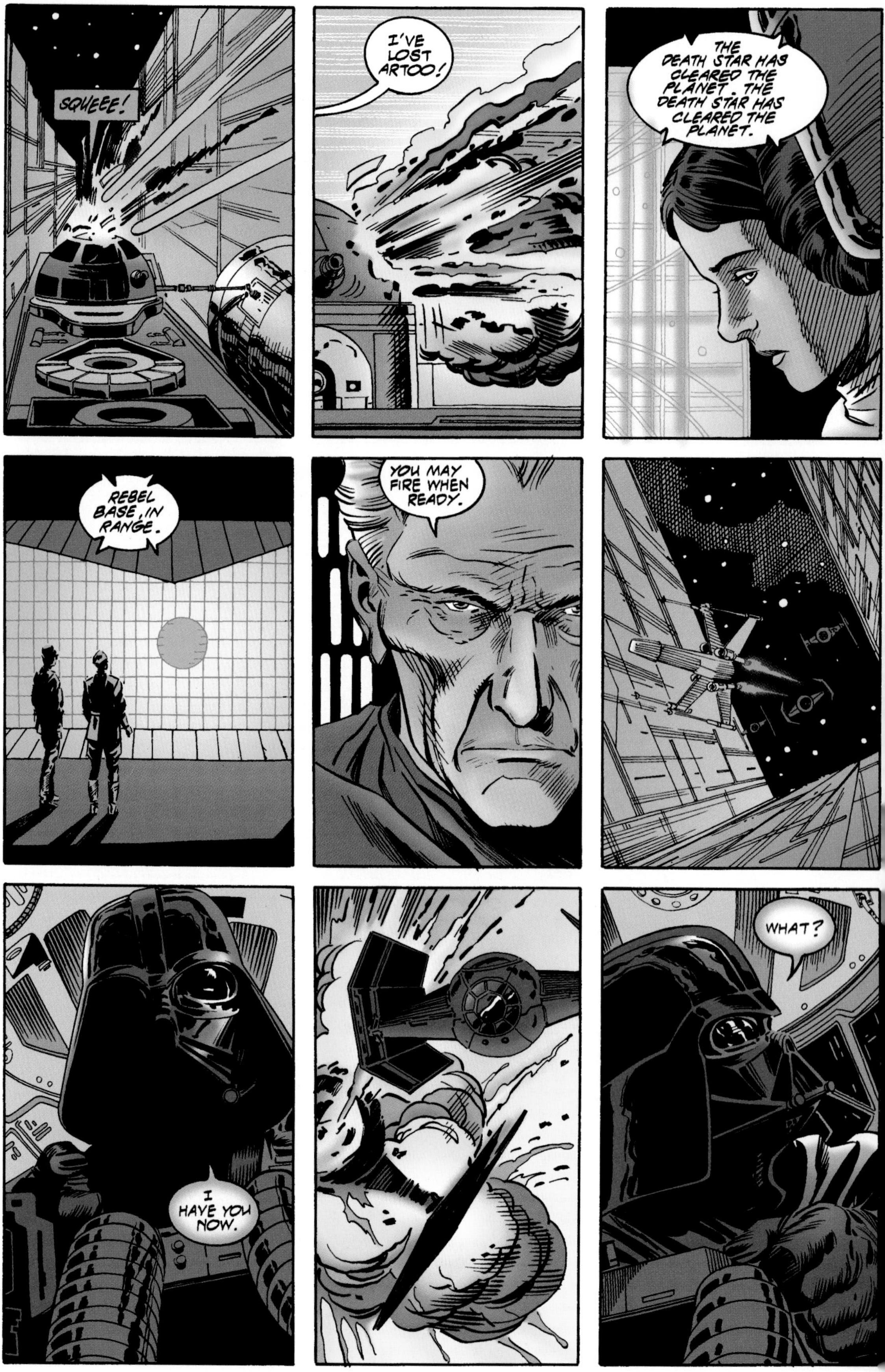
SQUEEE!
I'VE LOST ARTOO!
THE DEATH STAR HAS CLEARED THE PLANET. THE DEATH STAR HAS CLEARED THE PLANET.
REBEL BASE, IN RANGE.
YOU MAY FIRE WHEN READY.
I HAVE YOU NOW.
WHAT?

YAHOO!

KHARANG!

WHOOM

YOU'RE ALL CLEAR, KID! NOW LET'S BLOW THIS THING AND GO HOME!

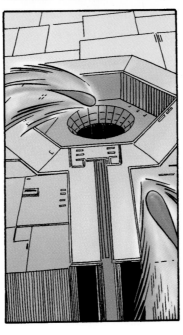

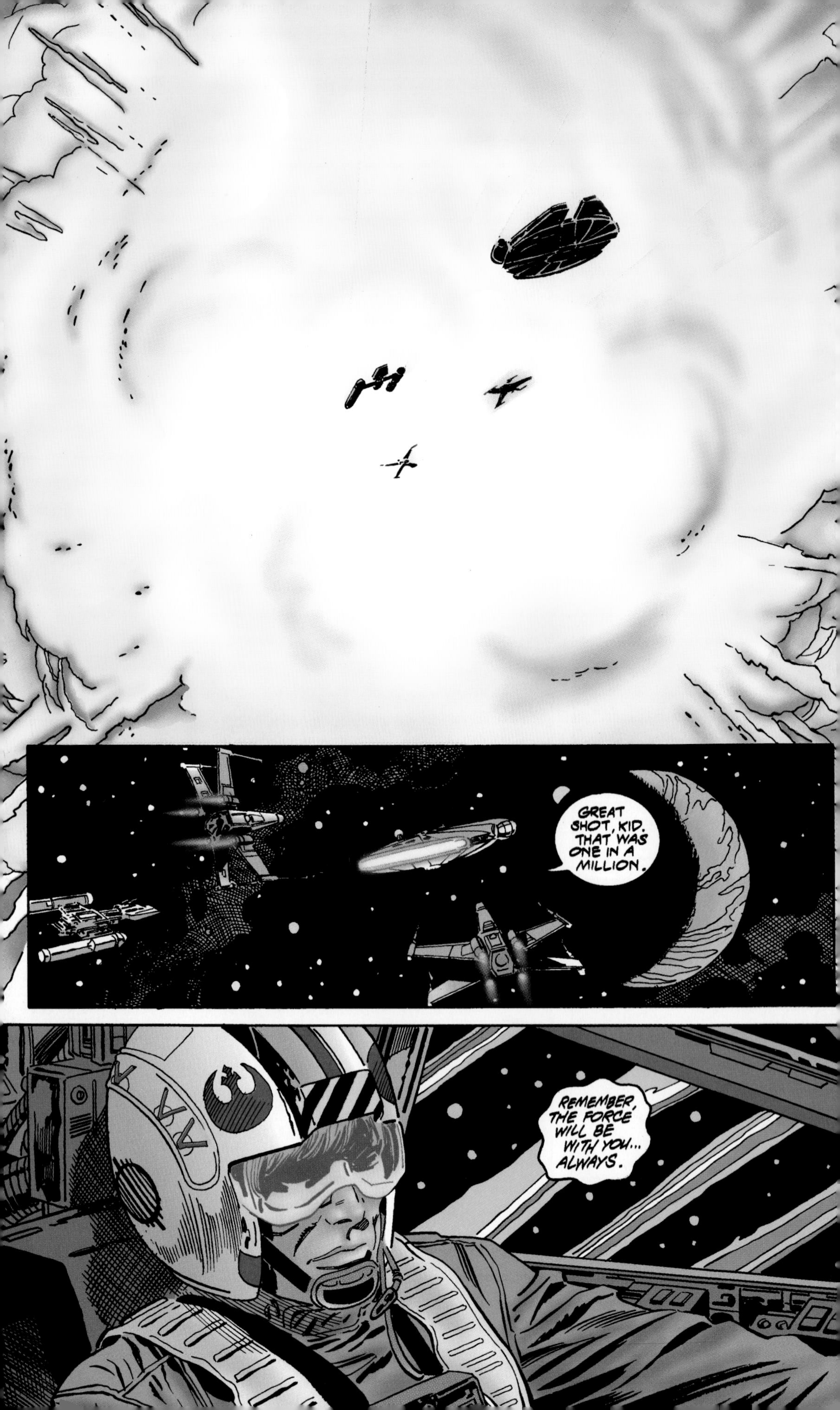
GREAT SHOT, KID. THAT WAS ONE IN A MILLION.
REMEMBER, THE FORCE WILL BE WITH YOU... ALWAYS.

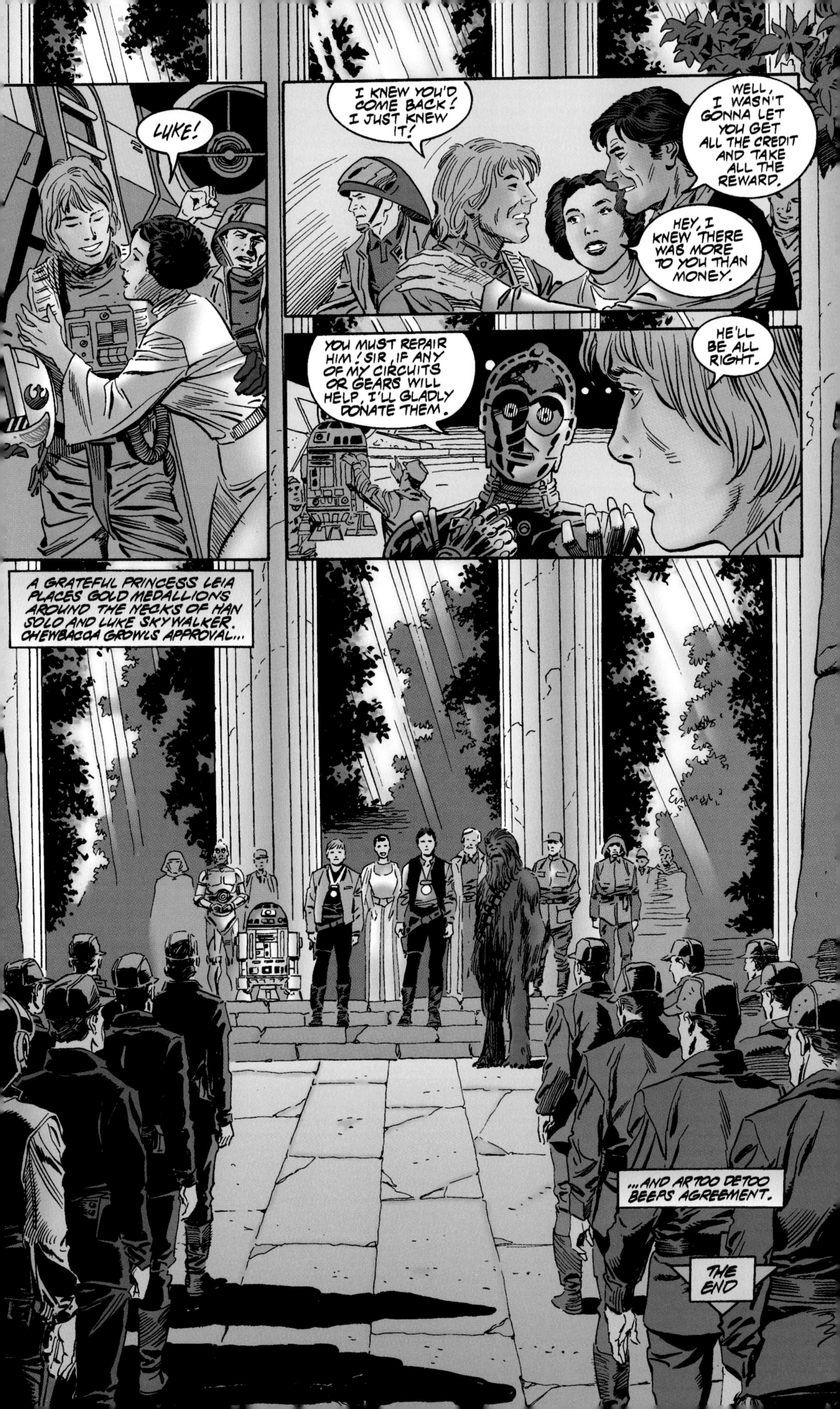
LUKE!
I KNEW YOU'D COME BACK! I JUST KNEW IT!
WELL, I WASN'T GONNA LET YOU GET ALL THE CREDIT AND TAKE ALL THE REWARD.
HEY, I KNEW THERE WAS MORE TO YOU THAN MONEY.
YOU MUST REPAIR HIM! SIR, IF ANY OF MY CIRCUITS OR GEARS WILL HELP, I'LL GLADLY DONATE THEM.
HE'LL BE ALL RIGHT.
A GRATEFUL PRINCESS LEIA PLACES GOLD MEDALLIONS AROUND THE NECKS OF HAN SOLO AND LUKE SKYWALKER. CHEWBACCA GROWLS APPROVAL...
...AND ARTOO DETOO BEEPS AGREEMENT.
THE END

The creative team behind *A New Hope* The Special Edition

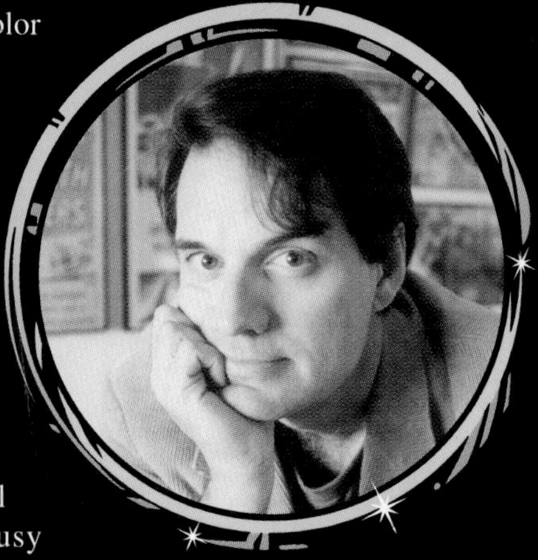

Bruce Jones was born behind a four-color press in Hackensack, New Jersey. Kidnapped at birth and raised by gypsies, the exact date of his birth is unknown, though dental records suggest it was sometime before the discovery of fluoride. His early career included a stint as a male nurse at a hospital for recovering alcoholics and brain-surgery patients, during which he coined the now oft-quoted phrase: "All things considered, I'd rather have a bottle in front of me, than a frontal lobotomy." Somehow, during his busy schedule of emptying drool cups, he found time to work on projects like *Amazing Stories*, *Creepy*, *Eerie*, *Vampirella*, and *Twisted Tales* to name a few. In recent months, Mr. Jones made headlines when witnesses reported him wrestled, by police, to the floor of the New York Stock Exchange, cursing vehemently and waving a pair of old sweat socks in the air. "I only wanted to exchange them for some argyles!" he was reported as screaming.

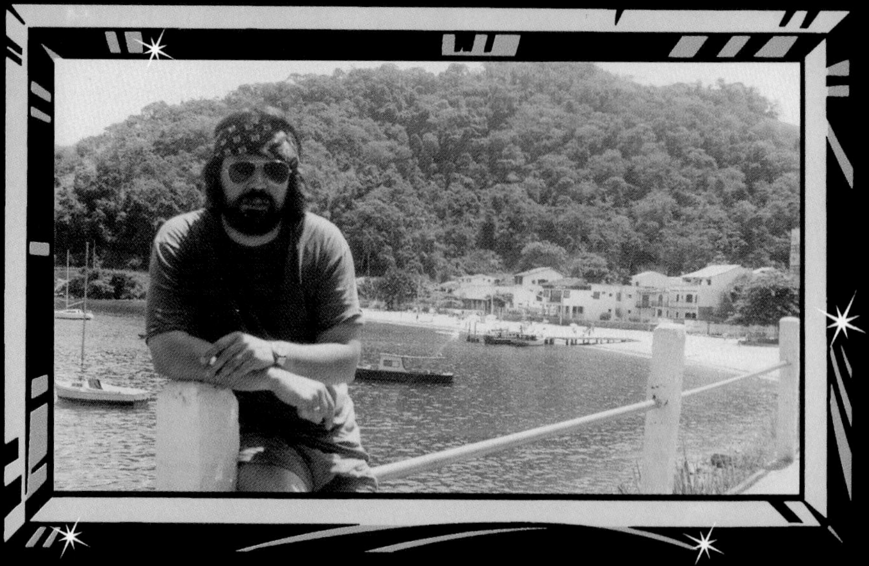

Although **Eduardo Barreto**'s work is new to the realm of *Star Wars*, he considers himself an "old workhorse" since he began his comics-publishing career 26 years ago at the age of 16. Barreto has worked for Marvel Comics, DC Comics, Archie Comics, Western Publishing, Tekno•Comix, and a host of European and South American companies and has illustrated a long list of characters including Superman, Batman, Indiana Jones, Aliens, Predator, and Mickey Spillane's Mike Danger. "I enjoy working in comics," says Barreto, "because there is a lot more creative freedom than there is in advertising or animation." He is thrilled to be working on *Star Wars* and is especially thrilled to be working with Al Williamson. Barreto lives in Montevideo, Uruguay with his wife and three children.

Al Williamson has been drawing comics for "110 years," and, he says, "if they want me to quit, they'll have to shoot me." Williamson's love for drawing comics is evidenced in his illustrations of some of comics' most famous characters. He assisted Burne Hogarth on the "Tarzan" strips, drew *Flash Gordon* for King Features and recently for Marvel Comics, contributed to the *Superman* mythos for DC Comics, and illustrated *Science Fiction* comics for EC. It was Williamson's depiction of Flash that caught the fancy of George Lucas who commissioned Al to do the (now) classic-strip adaptations of *Star Wars*. Williamson worked with writer Archie Goodwin and sometimes used his own son and daughter — Victor and Valerie — as models. Williamson and his lovely wife Corina make their home in Pennsylvania.

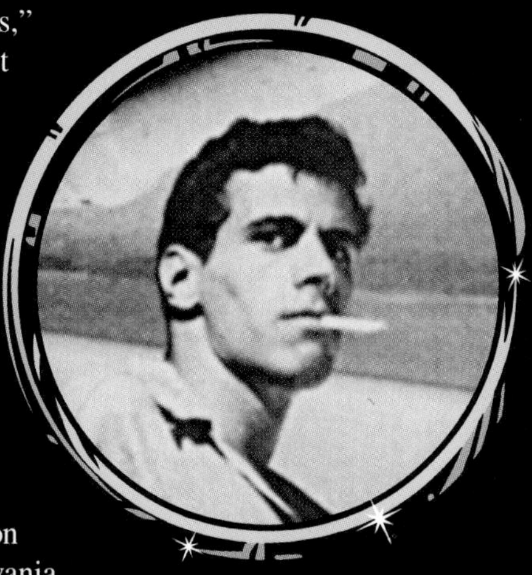

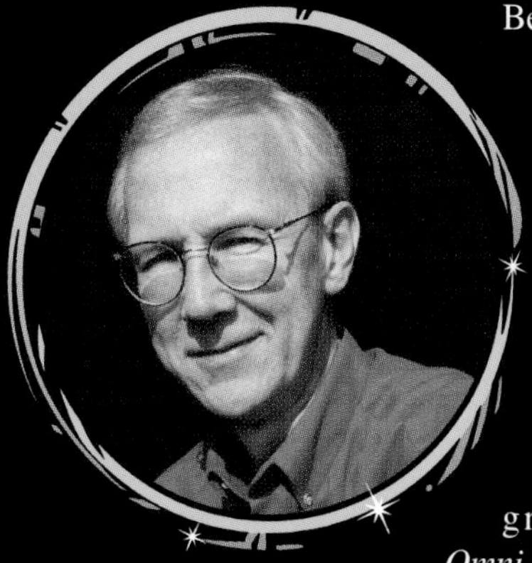

Best known for their collective work on the original movie poster for *Star Wars*, **Tim** and **Greg Hildebrandt** have enjoyed careers together (as the Brothers Hildebrandt) and separately. They won the Golden Eagle Award for their film *Project Hope* and are the award-winning illustrators of such well-known properties as *Star Wars*, *The Lord of the Rings*, *The Sword of Shanarra*, *Barbarella*, *The Clash of the Titans*, and *The Secret of N.I.M.H.* Individually, Greg's illustrations have graced magazines *Omni* and *Heavy Metal* and over a dozen children's fairy-tale classics. His cover for a *Spectre* comic won DC's Cover of the Month Award. Tim has painted art calendars for *Dungeons and Dragons*, *Realms of Wonder*, and *The Dragonriders of Pern*. He's also painted covers for numerous science-fiction and fantasy magazines and books.

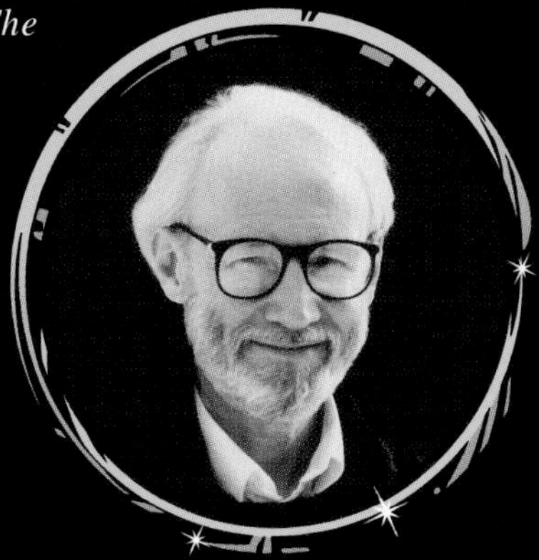

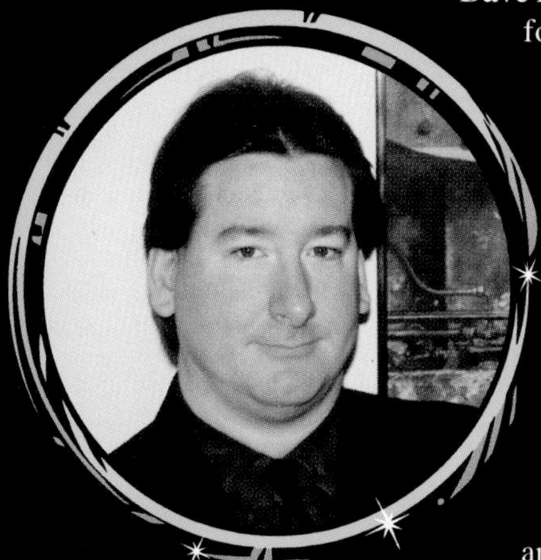

Dave Dorman is an Eisner award-winning illustrator best known for his photo-realistic renderings of action and fantasy subjects on such titles as *Batman* for DC Comics; the *Indiana Jones* and *Star Wars* series for Dark Horse; and *Aliens: Tribes*, an illustrated novel also for Dark Horse. His mass-market book covers include the best-selling series *Young Jedi Knights*, *Aliens*, *Lone Wolf*, *Surfing Samurai Robots*, and many others. Dorman has also done trading cards for Skybox, Topps, and Fleer; toy design for Hasbro Toys; motion-picture pre-production art; and motion-based ride conceptual art. Dorman's captivating cover art from the *A New Hope* comic-book series is featured on the following pages. If you look closely, you will see that the covers are actually four separate quadrants of a single painting.

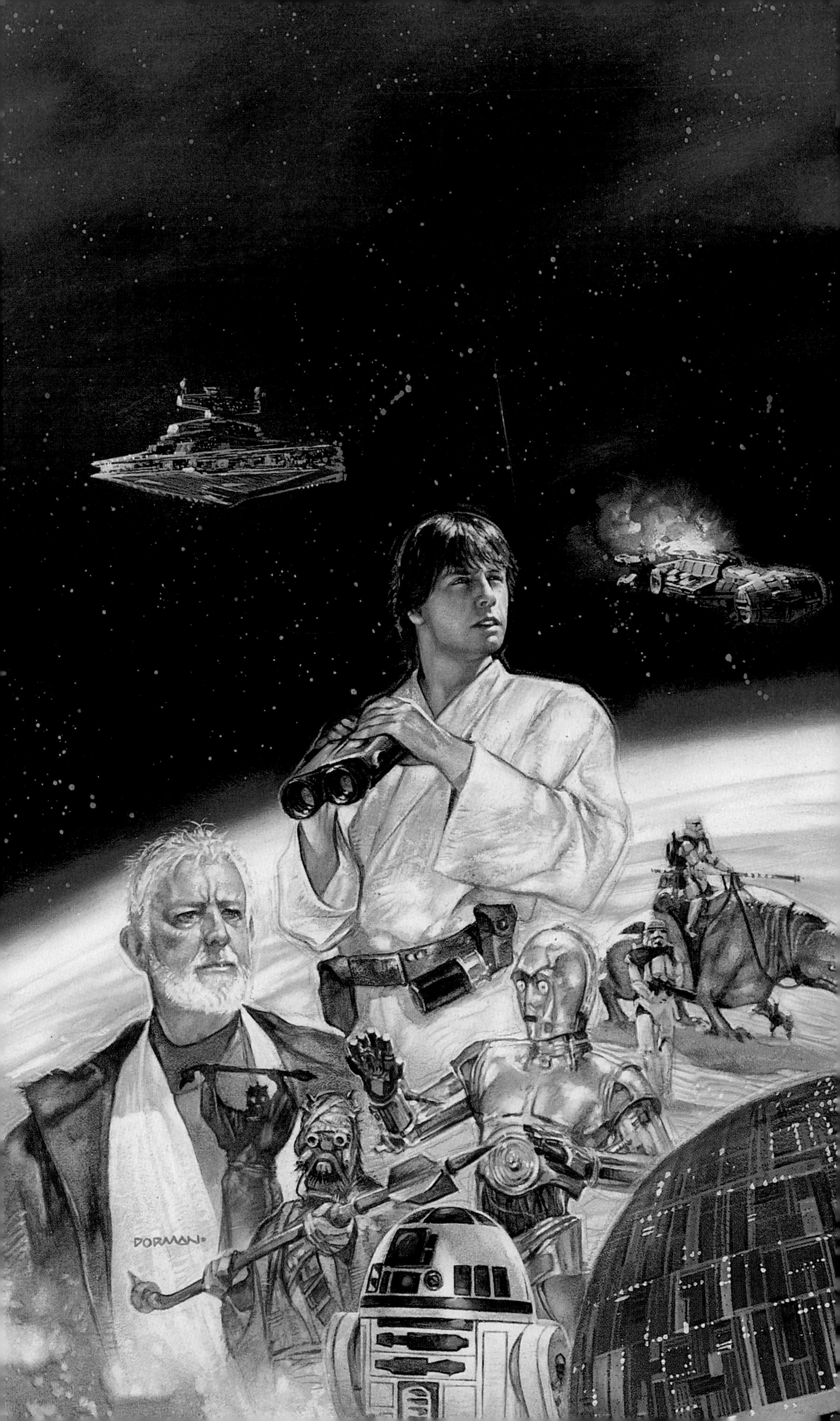
DORMAN

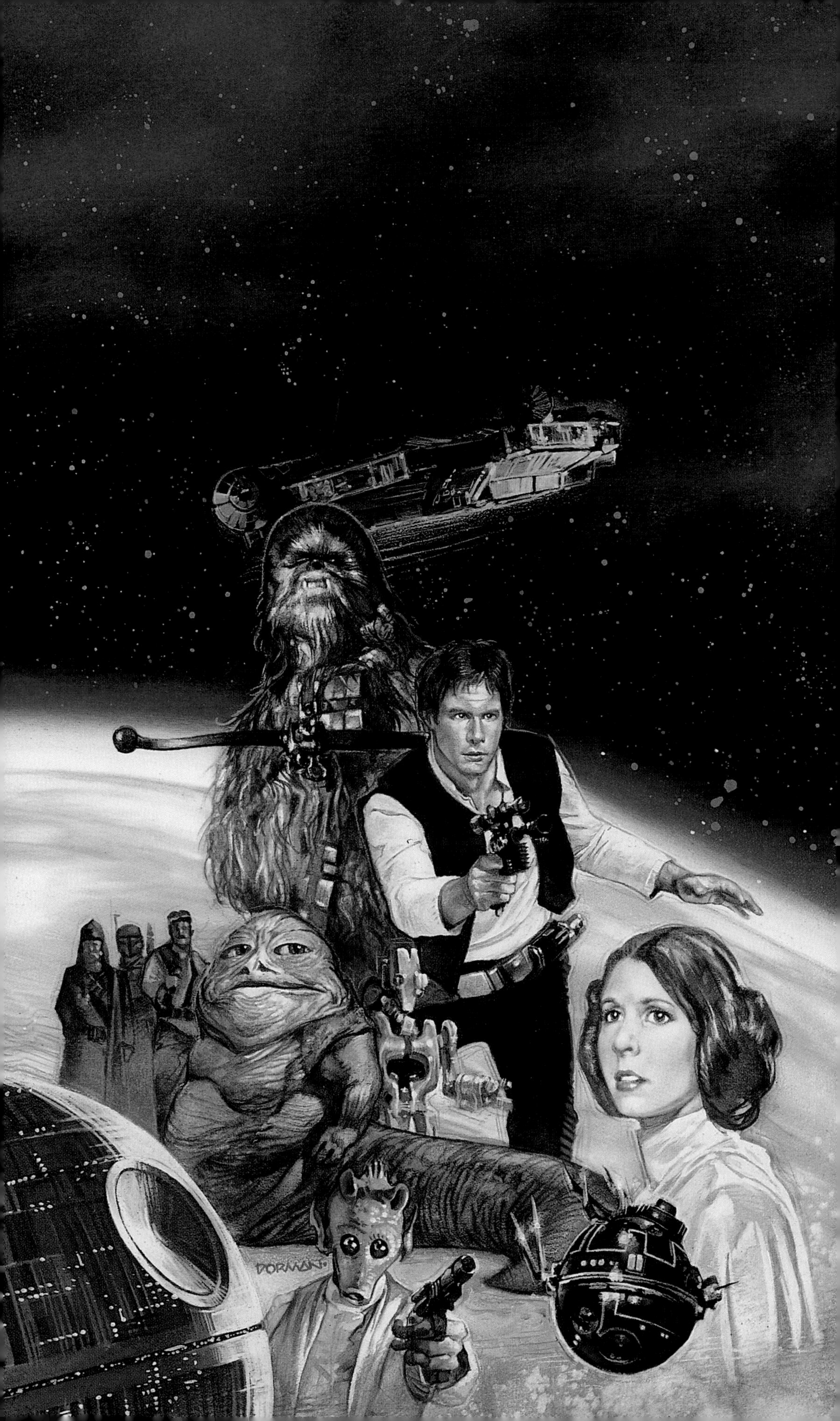
DORMAN

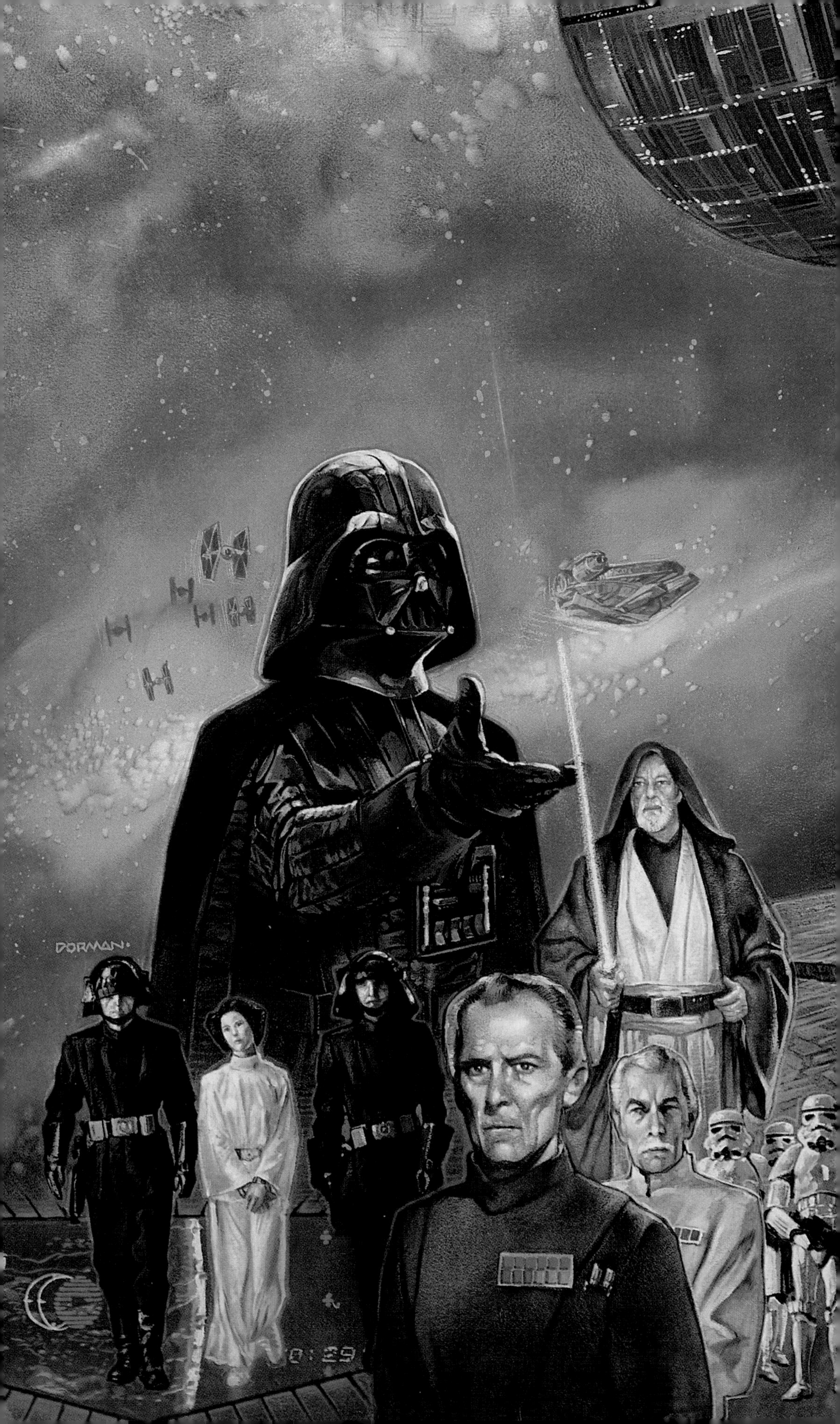
DORMAN

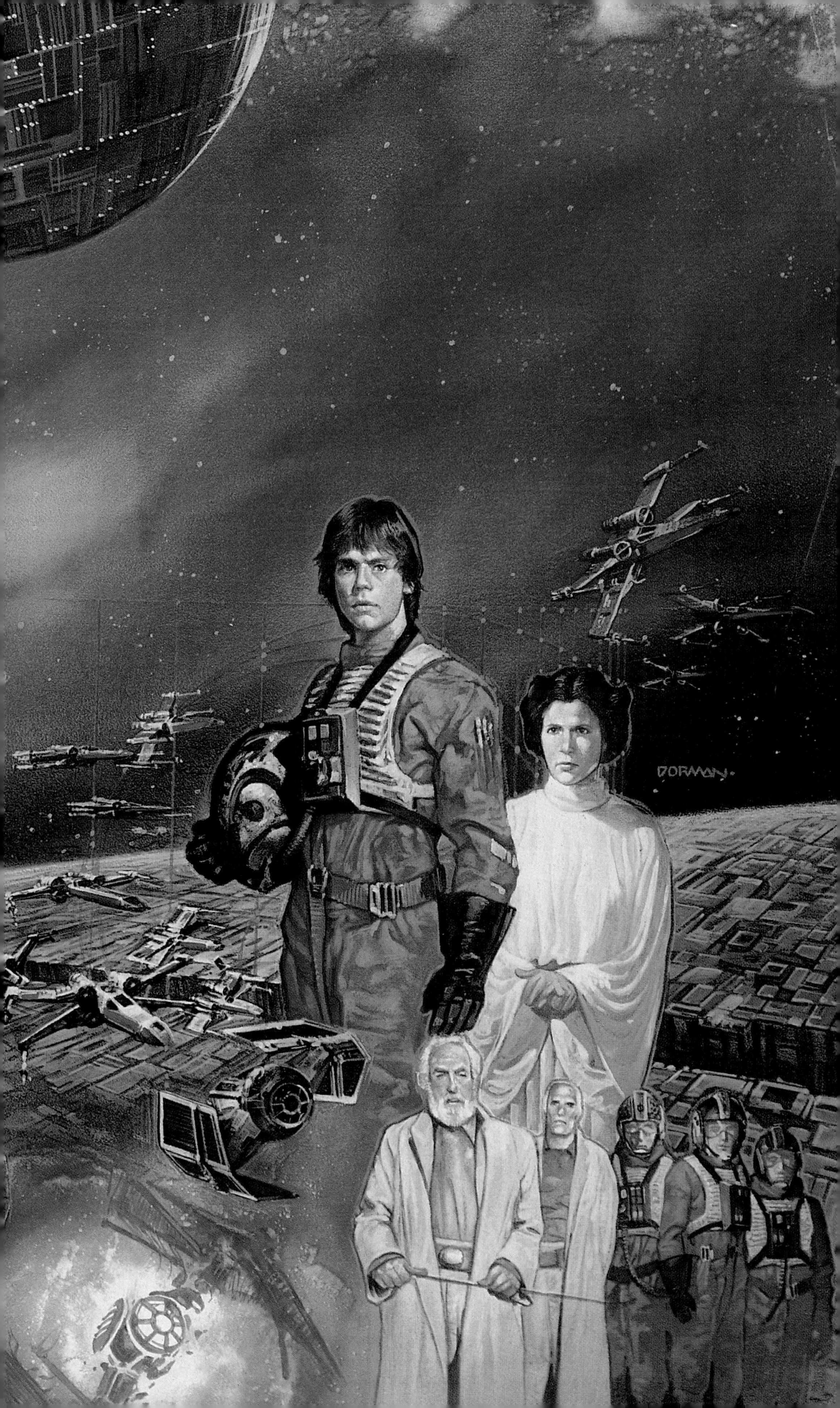
DORMAN

STAR WARS TRADE PAPERBACKS AVAILABLE FROM DARK HORSE

CLASSIC STAR WARS

Based on the classic newspaper strips . . .

VOLUME ONE: IN DEADLY PURSUIT
Goodwin • Williamson
192-page color paperback
ISBN: 1-56971-109-7 $16.95

VOLUME TWO: THE REBEL STORM
Goodwin • Williamson
208-page color paperback
ISBN: 1-56971-106-2 $16.95

VOLUME THREE: ESCAPE TO HOTH
Goodwin • Williamson
192-page color paperback
ISBN: 1-56971-093-7 $16.95

VOLUME FOUR: THE EARLY ADVENTURES
Manning • Hoberg
240-page color paperback
ISBN: 1-56971-178-x $19.95

Based on the movie trilogy . . .

A NEW HOPE
Thomas • Chaykin
104-page color paperback
ISBN: 1-56971-086-4 $9.95

THE EMPIRE STRIKES BACK
Goodwin • Williamson
104-page color paperback
ISBN: 1-56971-088-0 $9.95

RETURN OF THE JEDI
Goodwin • Williamson
104-page color paperback
ISBN: 1-56971-087-2 $9.95

THE SPECIAL EDITIONS

Celebrating the big-screen return . . .

A NEW HOPE
Jones • Barreto • Williamson
104-page color paperback
ISBN: 1-56971-213-1 $9.95

THE EMPIRE STRIKES BACK
Goodwin • Williamson
104-page color paperback
ISBN: 1-56971-234-4 $9.95

RETURN OF THE JEDI
Goodwin • Williamson
104-page color paperback
ISBN: 1-56971-235-2 $9.95

DARK EMPIRE

DARK EMPIRE
Veitch • Kennedy
184-page color paperback
ISBN: 1-56971-073-2 $17.95

DARK EMPIRE II
Veitch • Kennedy
168-page color paperback
ISBN: 1-56971-119-4 $17.95

DARK FORCES

SOLDIER FOR THE EMPIRE
Dietz • Williams
128-page color hardcover
ISBN: 1-56971-155-0 $24.95

DROIDS

THE KALARBA ADVENTURES
Thorsland • Windham • Gibson
200-page color paperback
ISBN: 1-56971-064-3 $17.95

REBELLION
Windham • Gibson
112-page color paperback
ISBN: 1-56971-224-7 $14.95

HEIR TO THE EMPIRE
Baron • Vatine • Blanchard
160-page color paperback
ISBN: 1-56971-202-6 $19.95

SHADOWS OF THE EMPIRE
Wagner • Plunkett • Russell
160-page color paperback
ISBN: 1-56971-183-6 $17.95

SPLINTER OF THE MIND'S EYE
Austin • Sprouse
112-page color paperback
ISBN: 1-56971-223-9 $14.95

TALES OF THE JEDI

DARK LORDS OF THE SITH
Veitch • Anderson • Gossett
160-page color paperback
ISBN: 1-56971-095-3 $17.95

KNIGHTS OF THE OLD REPUBLIC
Veitch • Gossett
136-page color paperback
ISBN: 1-56971-020-1 $14.95

THE SITH WAR
Anderson • Carrasco
152-page color paperback
ISBN: 1-56971-173-9 $17.95

Available from your local comics retailer!

Order directly from Dark Horse Comics by enclosing title, order number, and price of each book requested. Send your name, address, and check, money order, or Visa/MasterCard payment to:
Dark Horse Comics, Inc. Department BL 10956 SE Main Street Milwaukie, OR 97222

Or order by phone at **1-800-862-0052** *9:00 AM - 5:00 PM PST.*
Available in U.S. and Canada only. U.S. funds only.
For Visa/MasterCard purchases, please enclose card number and expiration date.
For shipping and handling, include $4.00 on orders of 1 to 4 items, $6.00 for 5 or more items.
No CODs, please. All sales final. Item(s) subject to availability. Please allow 4-6 weeks for delivery.